H. M. S.
COVENTRY

ANTI-AIRCRAFT CRUISER

A Narrative

by

GEORGE SIMS

George Sims
March 1972
No. 10.

ACKNOWLEDGEMENT

This book was inspired during a parade of Sea Cadets following the dedication of the memorial to H.M.S. "Coventry" at Coventry Cathedral, October 1965. My thanks to Eric Skelly, Frank Risdon, Alastair Durno, and many others, for additional material and their assistance in making this book possible.

G.S.

Original photographs are reproduced by kind permission of the following.

Charles Woolf M.P.S., R. Williamson, "Coventry Evening Telegraph", "The Daily Telegraph and Morning Post" and "The Times".

0950229008

940·531 862 38253 SIMS

940 545942 Sim
D480563
m54267

101 128 204

Published by
H.M.S. Coventry Old Hands
Lichfield House, Soho, London.
Printed by
Cook Hammond & Kell Ltd. London.
1972

W-A

CONTENTS

CONTENTS (contd.)

ILLUSTRATIONS

ILLUSTRATIONS (continued).

FOREWORD

Death and destruction are the inevitable result of war, but for those who take part in human struggles born of fear and greed, there emerges from time to time a strong bond of fellowship and deep friendship.

H.M.S. COVENTRY in the Second World War was the scene both of death and her final destruction and also of the seeds of a fellowship which has grown into the Old Hands association one of whom, George Sims, has seen fit to write a story of the ship.

This simple laconic story with its humour and its occasional cynicism about those who ordered the ship's destiny will be a wonderful reminder to all of us who served in her of a time we would not wish to repeat but from which we have gained an indefinable bond.

The younger generation are unlikely to experience the same conditions if they are involved in a war in future years. But they may like to turn the pages idly and see how it was done in a war of which they have read in the history books but which, as time passes, takes on an impersonal and political colour.

This book tells of a ship and the people who manned her. That the ship was lost in action was sad, but there were others to take her place. I am very honoured to be asked to write a foreword to a book which tells of the people who manned her and which will stand as a happy memory for those who remain and a memorial for those who died serving in her.

Admiralty House,
Portsmouth
10th October 1971

ADMIRAL SIR HORACE R. LAW, KCB, OBE, DSC, ADC

The Commander-in-Chief, Naval Home Command

Born 23rd June 1911 in Dublin. Related to Nelson through Nelson's niece, Charlotte Nelson, Duchess of Bronte, who was Admiral Law's great great grandmother.

Entered Royal Navy in September 1929 from Sherborne School, joining HMS Erebus at Devonport.

Served as Midshipman on the East Indies Station under Captain, now Admiral of the Fleet, Lord Fraser and obtained five first class certificates during Sub-Lieutenant's Courses.

Qualified in gunnery in 1937 and did an advanced Gunnery Course in 1939.

On the outbreak of war joined HMS Cairo (anti-aircraft cruiser) and after that ship was damaged in the Norwegian campaign, for which he received Mention in Despatches, joined HMS Coventry, also an anti-aircraft cruiser. Served in the Coventry for 18 months mostly in the Eastern Mediterranean under Admiral Cunningham—took part in the Greek and Crete campaigns for which he was awarded the DSC.

After a year doing anti-aircraft experimental work he joined HMS Nigeria in the United States where she was being repaired and subsequently saw service in her in the Eastern Fleet.

At the end of the war he had command of gunnery training ship Modeste and was promoted to Commander in 1946. After service in the Admiralty he was appointed Fleet Gunnery Officer Far East Fleet in 1949 and took part in the Korean War for which he was awarded the OBE.

After being second in command of the aircraft carrier Triumph, he was promoted to Captain in 1952 and was the first Captain of HMS Duchess. On completion of 18 months in command of the Duchess, he served for two years as Chief of Staff, Plymouth, under Admiral Sir Alexander Madden. He was next appointed Director of the Royal Naval Tactical School, Woolwich in 1956.

Was in command of HMS Centaur from August 1958 to August 1960. The ship was on a General Service Commission and served East of Suez from April 1959 to April 1960.

He was then appointed in command of the Britannia Royal Naval College, Dartmouth where he served from August 1960 to December 1961. It was during this appointment that he was promoted to Rear Admiral on 7th July 1961.

He served as Flag Officer, Sea Training at Portland from December 1961 to May 1963 and as Flag Officer, Submarines from May 1963 to May 1965.

He was made a CB in the Birthday Honours 1963 and was promoted to Vice Admiral on 5th June 1965. He was made a KCB in the New Year Honours List 1967.

Admiral Law's last appointment was Controller of the Navy from July 1965 to January 1970.

He took up his present appointment as Commander-in-Chief, Naval Home Command and Flag Officer Portsmouth Area on 16th March 1970.

Married in 1941, Heather Coryton. They have two sons and two daughters, and their home since 1945 has been at Petersfield in Hampshire.

In April, 1970 Admiral Law was appointed First and Principal Naval Aide-de-Camp to Her Majesty The Queen.

INTRODUCTION BY ERIC SKELLY

The rain swirled from a mass of dark clouds as I stood on Crewe Station during a cold February day of 1959. Travellers waiting resignedly on No. 6 Platform woke to the amplifier hum to hear that as a result of engine failure there could be delays of up to two hours with northbound trains. Slowly, here and there, shivering individuals turned from contemplating the surrounding monument to the industry and invention of their forbears and made for the buffet.

The door of the buffet opened, and a shaft of light fell on the features of a tall fair man. At once a voice called "Hey! Is your name Skelly?"

I looked warily toward the stranger, who was of heavy build and appeared to be a contemporary. Reluctantly I answered "Yes". "Well", continued the voice, "My name is Risdon".

Thereupon broke reciprocal smiles of recognition, and at once we began a series of enquiries about personalities in the ships company of H.M.S. "Coventry", the Anti-Aircraft Cruiser in which we had both served twenty years past. The exchange of talk became more and more animated, to be interrupted by the announcement that a Liverpool train would arrive shortly. The result was a hurried handshaking, and mutual promises of "I'll look you up", which in the way of things demanded too much trouble for fulfilment. Anyway, the pressure of modern life left little leisure to reflect on those years of conflict that were ushered in by a light hearted chorus about "Hanging washing on the Siegfried Line", dragged on through several years of yearning lyrics about "The last all-clear", and might have ended in numbed silence had not the Eighth Army purloined "Lili Marlene".

The second meeting between Frank Risdon and myself was truly remarkable. I boarded the train at Euston, found a corner seat, dumped my cases on the rack and proceeded to the dining car for some breakfast. It was crowded as usual, and the steward seeing me approach asked, "One sir?" and I nodded in the affirmative. He led me to the only vacant seat available and I was truly delighted to find that my opposite number was Frank Risdon. Again our paths had crossed—and within such a short time! Who knows, in the light of subsequent events, it would appear that some unknown force had deliberately set us upon a collision course.

The journey north was pleasantly spent in reminiscing; I cannot recall now who actually suggested a meeting, it was spontaneous, but we agreed to contact as many of our old shipmates that we were still in touch with, arrange a rendezvous and see who we could muster after such a long time, for more than twenty years had elapsed since we were all together on the "Coventry".

The Mitre, a pub in Chancery Lane, was to be the meeting point, and the date, Saturday 18th March 1961. This first meeting brought a dozen "old ships" to the Mitre. It was a good 'run ashore' and before departing to our respective home ports we agreed to meet again later that year. The date this time was the 16th September 1961 and the Mitre again our port of call. To our intense satisfaction and great glee our numbers had now swelled to twenty one! Among those present were Johnny Kirk, Frank Risdon, Alan Boon, Les Delmer, Ginger Russell, Claude Nice, Eddy Edwards, Winnie Wingrove, Slinger Woods, Ginger Kirby, Stan Fisher and Cliff Rolinson; regrettably names of all those attending were not taken and no nominal roll exists.

I must digress here to bring into the story an idea that I had had in my mind for some time. My business journeys took me often to the City of Coventry and I had seen the new Cathedral emerging from the ruins of the old. Each visit saw growth in it's development and I began to think that, as so many of us had served in H.M.S. "Coventry" and had been able to meet again, perhaps we could have a whip round and make a contribution to the Rebuilding Fund Appeal. During the evening I mentioned this idea to the assembled company and it was well received. As we had now been able to contact almost twice the number of our original meeting we decided to hold another reunion, but to let a year elapse so that we all could do as much as possible to contact yet more of our old shipmates. We agreed that it should be in the following September and as far as possible to hold it as near to the date that the old ship was lost in 1942. Saturday 15th September 1962 was the date decided upon. A small committee was formed, Frank, Johnny, Ginger Russell and myself and we parted company that evening at the Mitre with the promise of all efforts directed to making the next meeting a bumper one.

As the year progressed so our membership began to rise. From a notice in the "Daily Telegraph" to the agony column of the "News of the World", new members began to write in. Johnny Kirk had found our old Royal Marine Captain—now the Reverend Peyton Jones—and he kindly loaned me the next of kin nominal roll from "Coventry" and I was able to contact yet more of the old ship's company. On my next visit to the City of Coventry I made enquiries at the Cathedral Appeals Office and explained what I had in mind. Captain Thurston of the Appeals Committee was most helpful and furnished me with the address of Mr. N. Renison, a retired bank manager who was Hon. Treasurer of the Coventry Savings Committee during the war. After the loss of the ship an appeal was launched by this committee to replace H.M.S. "Coventry" and the astonishing amount of over £2,000,000 was collected!

Johnny Kirk had again been in touch with the Reverend Peyton Jones and sent on to me an extract from his letter in which "P. J." had written "I often thought that those we lost in "Coventry" should somehow be remembered in the new Cathedral and to this end when I was in Coventry last year on a mission, I presented to the Provost one of the ship's quarterdeck lifebelts, which was used when we abandoned ship". The knowledge that this lifebelt was in the City of Coventry, seemed to me to be the ideal form for the basis of a memorial to our lost shipmates–the one remaining physical link with the old ship that could possibly be "laid up" in the new Cathedral. I wrote to the Provost and was delighted to receive a reply from him indicating that I should talk over our thoughts and proposition of a memorial with the Reverend Edward Reade, one of the Cathedral staff.

To my great delight I found the Rev. Reade most sympathetic to our idea and it was also I felt, most fortuitous for "our cause", in that he himself was ex R.N! He had a most distinguished career in the Navy, in destroyers. We discussed many ideas and I gathered that the lifebelt was not considered to be quite the ideal form of memorial that would "fit in" the new cathedral. Frank Risdon volunteered to draw up a design and at the same time he had been in communication with Sir Basil Spence, the architect of the new cathedral. His reply was disappointing and suggested that the names of the subscribers to our appeal should be recorded in the Founders Book. We felt that it was not our names that should be recorded but those of our lost shipmates.

An appeal letter was sent out to all of our then known members, a bank account opened and slowly the money began to arrive. "P. J's" comment that, "I should imagine we should be able to raise £25 between us" was way out from the eventual cost of the plaque!

To our intense dismay the original design of Frank's was turned down; it would appear that all our efforts were frustrated. However another design was prepared by Frank and after some considerable time, we were informed by the Reverend Reade that this one had now been approved. Our next task was to launch another appeal for money as the estimate for this new design was much more than we had anticipated in the early stages. We were not too dispirited for time was on our side and our membership was growing steadily. Eventually three appeals had to be made to raise the necessary money and it took three years to finalize all the details. That it was made possible can only be attributed to the generosity of the members of the ship's company; nearly £400 pounds was donated by them, and by them alone, for no help was sought outside of the ex members of the ship's company. Our arrangements for the next meeting were going ahead. Permission had been obtained from the Commanding Officer of H.M.S. President, Head-quarters of the London Division R.N.R., for us to muster in the canteen of H.M.S. "Chrysanthemum" which was moored alongside the Thames Embankment. The gathering of old crew members began to gather momentum and in June of 1962 we contacted and had the names and addresses of 48. The next reunion date was arranged for Saturday 15th September, 1962 and this was in reality the first proper reunion. We were able to muster the remarkable number of 54 on this occasion, a notable achievement considering that 20 years had elapsed since many had met or seen each other. And it was most enjoyable to have with us that evening three of our old Captains, Captain Gilmour, Captain W. P. Carne and Captain Dendy ("Coventry's" last skipper). This reunion was a great success and eventually broke up with a firm vow to repeat the occasion next year.

During the ensuing year our negotiations with the Cathedral progressed. Frank's second design for the Plaque, now approved, consisted of a simple brass plate with the wording, H.M.S. "COVENTRY" Sunk off Tobruk 1942. This has been placed here by the survivors in memory of their shipmates killed in action." Underneath on a separate marble base were recorded all the names of those who were lost. Meanwhile the amount of money in answer to the appeal was slowly mounting and in March 1963 totalled £125. Plans for the next reunion were also being prepared; the same rendezvous as the previous year H.M.S. "Chrysanthemum" and the date set was for September 14th 1963. A suggestion from the ex-Captains Coxwain Ernie Prior that we should try and get a "Coventry" tie was well received and to everyone's great satisfaction it was found that Jack Crowther ex R.D.F. rating, was now happily settled into civilian life in the 'rag trade' and was able to produce for us a most handsomely designed tie, which included the ship's crest motif. The numbers attending this reunion were slightly down on the previous year, 50 names were recorded but the party made up in spirit what it lacked in numbers.

Now that the design for the Plaque had been approved and estimates obtained, on checking the amount in the 'kitty', it was seen that more money would be needed to cover the cost. A further appeal was launched and this brought up the total to £258, a most gallant effort considering the membership was only in the region of 120. Progress was being made and it was time to be thinking of a date for the installation ceremony—who would unveil it? Frank had been able to contact yet another of "Coventry's" old ship's company, at one time the Gunnery Officer, now Admiral Sir Horace Law who willingly accepted our invitation to unveil the plaque.

Meantime our efforts to contact old members of the ship's company was extended to trying to find the families of those whose names appeared on the Plaque. Through the good offices of Johnny Kirk, the Daily Telegraph columnist 'Peterborough' inserted a paragraph announcing the event. This most welcome piece of publicity enabled us to contact many more and one in particular. This was a letter from C. E. A. Humble, who wrote to say that he had commissioned "Coventry" in 1917 when she was launched from Swan Hunters yard on Tyneside! He wrote "I joined "Coventry" in August 1917 when she was Ship No. 1037, at Swan Hunters and left her in September 1920. I have many happy memories of the ship and am sure she was the finest I served in. I am nearly 80 now and often think of our perambulations in all the German Ports during 1918. Then to Stettin from where we brought about 600 or more P.O.W's home for Xmas arriving at the mouth of the Humber on Xmas Eve 1918. We used the large silk white ensign presented by the ladies of Coventry. The soldiers came up the jetty and we shone two 36" search-lights on the ensign at the mainmast and the cheers of the men were tremendous as they had no idea who was to bring them home. I am a Tynesider by birth and that is not the only reason I am very proud of the "Coventry", she was a real happy ship and a good one" All who had the good fortune to serve in "Coventry" will echo the remarks made by one who first commissioned her.

We were also very glad to have been able to find the family of Petty Officer A. E. Sephton, V.C. The service for the unveiling had now been established for Saturday October 23rd 1965. The event was well attended and reported in the local Coventry Evening News.

The installation of the Memorial Plaque in Coventry Cathedral has been one of the most important features of H.M.S. "Coventry" Old Hands Association. From the early thought of Reverend Peyton Jones in his letter to Johnny Kirk and to my own thoughts of collecting a donation to help rebuild the Cathedral, a lot of hard work and tremendous effort have been put into an ideal. Now the Plaque is there for all time, but this is not the end of the story. The account for the plaque came to £384 and on totting up our appeal fund we found we were still short of the required amount. This meant another appeal and like all good matelots each and all delved deeper into their respective ditty boxes and finally enough was forthcoming to settle the account.

Extract from "The Coventry Evening Telegraph" 25th October, 1965.

"The unveiling of a plaque in Coventry Cathedral to the memory of the 67 members of the crew of H.M.S. "Coventry" who died in the Second World War, became a remarkable "naval occasion" on Saturday. The Third Sea Lord, Vice-Admiral H. R. Law, who was once gunnery officer aboard the cruiser, which Coventry "adopted", drew back a White Ensign to reveal the words "H.M.S. Coventry, Sunk off Tobruk 14th September, 1942. This has been placed here by the survivors in memory of their shipmates killed in action". The plaque, which is of polished brass, is in the Cathedral's Navy Room, and beneath it are the 67 names on brass plates set into a Roll of Honour of translucent marble.

Three former captains of H.M.S. "Coventry", 70 men who once served in her, plus friends and relatives, made up a "muster" of about 230 people from various parts of the country.

Before the unveiling, all attended Evensong, at which the closing hymn was "Eternal Father, strong to save". One of the lessons was read by the Rev. D. L. Peyton Jones, who was commanding officer of the Royal Marines' detachment aboard the cruiser at the time she was sunk by German dive bombers.

The Precentor, Canon J. W. Poole, conducted the service, and other clergy taking part included the Rev. E. P. Reade, Vicar of Binley, who was formerly a commander in the Royal Navy.

A guard of honour, with piping party and bugler, was provided by Coventry Sea Cadet Corps, for Admiral Law as he ascended St. Michael's Steps from Priory Street.

The Lord Mayor and Lady Mayoress of Coventry, Alderman and Mrs. W. Parfitt, were also present.

In the Navy Room, the Provost of Coventry, the Very. Rev. H. C. N. Williams, told Admiral Law that acknowledgement of the debt owed to H.M.S. Coventry was overdue.

He said that the placing of memorials in the Cathedral had been deliberately avoided, and there was none. The war dead of H.M.S. Coventry were the only people to be thus honoured.

The memorial would be treasured and he hoped that friends and relatives of those who lost their lives would feel free to come again and show it to others.

Two women then laid a wreath at the memorial and the Provost recited Binyon's famous lines . . . . 'They shall grow not old", and said a prayer.

Four sisters from Wolverhampton, the eldest of them, Mrs. E. Bull, wearing the Victoria Cross awarded posthumously to their brother, Petty Officer A. E. Sephton, attended the unveiling. Petty Officer Sephton was killed aboard H.M.S. Coventry in an action off Crete on May 18, 1941, when he was directing anti-aircraft fire against enemy bombers attacking a hospital ship. His was the first V.C. awarded in the Mediterranean.

The Third Sea Lord, who like the other ex-shipmates, is a member of the Old Hands' Association of H.M.S. Coventry, joined the company afterwards at a "get-together" at the Craven Arms Hotel. Wartime acquaintanceships were renewed as men met who had not come face to face for 25 years. Two local survivors present were A. Warner of 33, Luscombe Road, Walsgrave, who was an Able Seaman, and Mr. William Weir of 1, Howard Road, Nuneaton, an ex-Royal Marine.

The association now has 154 members. It was formed several years after a chance meeting on Crewe station by Mr. E. M. Skelly, a publisher's representative of Stratford-on-Avon, and Mr. Frank Risdon, a London architect.

The 1965 reunion, when old "Coventry" ships company from all corners of the British Isles, after going separate paths for more than twenty years, met on the steps of the new Coventry Cathedral, was followed next morning by a church parade of Sea Cadets at which Captain Carne presented awards for proficiency. In this atmosphere George Sims realised the need for a chronicle, and next day started to write it. Once the project was made known, contributions from other participants either flowed in, or were gathered in conversation at subsequent reunions. We trust that the result will bring you a true picture of those forgotten days.

Once every year, on or near the 14th September, a gathering of their shipmates with families and friends come here to remember them.

In a changing and forgetful world, a memorial tablet speaks only to a small number that will never forget; but whoever is curious about those who made the memorial may find the history of the ship and the men who manned her enlightening.

CHAPTER ONE

THE HISTORY OF H.M.S. COVENTRY

The first "Coventry" was added to the "States Navy" when armed trading ships fought side by side with men of war, and the artillery duel had largely superseded boarding parties for deciding the issue of a sea battle. How she was acquired is related by Mr. Sylvester Richmond, Surgeon of the "Constant Warwick", (Captain Voysey), of thirty-one guns and one hundred and fifty men, who adds "we had at this time war with the Spaniards, who infested our coast much with small pickaroons, from four to thirty guns".

On the 17th February, 1658, "Constant Warwick" and the "Adventure" frigate sailed from Plymouth, and after weathering a heavy storm put into St. Marys, Scilly, for a few days. Out from here, about forty leagues from the Lizard, and with a north wind blowing, a ship was sighted to the north, bearing down on them.

As soon as the stranger sighted the English ships he put on more sail and sped towards them. They "put out Flushing colours to deceive them, and hung a board of timber and a grinding stone to the stern, to make our ship seem a merchant ship by her dull sailing". All guns were hauled in, and the gilt carving that denoted a warship was covered up. At 4 o'clock, the Spaniard, for such he was, came close enough to discover the trick and promptly made off. "Adventure" chased him from windward and "Constant Warwick" from the lee. In two hours, "Adventure" was close, and darkness was coming on. Moonlight enabled "Adventure" to keep the quarry in sight. "Constant Warwick" could not see either ship, but judged their position from the phosphorescent glow they raised in the sea.

At midnight, the wind increased, whereupon the quarry suddenly went about, and poured a broadside into "Adventure", breaking the tops of the fore and mizzen masts, and damaging the rigging. "Adventure" had some men killed, and many hurt by this sudden attack, and was forced to heave to for repairs, but she continually fired guns to direct "Constant Warwick".

The Spaniard, thinking "Constant Warwick" a merchantman in convoy came to take her, but on coming close realised his mistake and sailed on.

Now "Constant Warwick" increased sail, came up with the pickaroon, and finding she could outsail it, decided to wait for daylight before trying conclusions. By then "Adventure" was repaired, and "Constant Warwick" waited for the frigate to have intelligence of the enemy, but "Adventure" could not sail fast enough for the chase.

In full light, "Constant Warwick" hoisted the States Colours, the pickaroon meanwhile flying with all speed. "Constant Warwick's" captain came up to the pickaroon and hailed her Commander, who immediately ran up Spanish Colours. "Thereupon our gunners cheered and opened fire". We brought more of our guns to windward, and when ready came up under his lee quarter and fired, and so back astern again. "He, not able to open his lee ports, could bring but few guns on us". The battle lasted five hours, and the Spaniards used constant volleys of "small shot", which, owing to the rough seas, were poorly aimed. "By now, "Adventure" being repaired in his masts, came up too, upon which he yielded. We had only two men wounded; Richard Cross, shot a little above the ankle with small shot, and Venice Hide, his leg broken by the overturning of a great gun. The ship was a Biscayer of San Sebastian, mounted with twenty-eight guns, one hundred and eighty men, was called the "St. Michael" and the Captain named Domingo". She was afterwards refitted and put into the States service, and named "Coventry".

There would seem to be a logical connection in "Constant Warwick's" prize being named "Coventry", because Coventry dyers in the fifteenth century were famous for making a special blue dye, which gave a lasting non fading colour to the cloth and thread to which it was applied. And from the reputation of this product, a proverb had arisen "True as Coventry Blue".

Thus there appeared in the Navy List in 1658, the year that Oliver Cromwell died, "Coventry", a vessel of 191 tons, twenty-four guns, (Captain Nicholas Parker.) The Commonwealth maintained a strong Navy to meet pressure from the Netherlands in the matter of trade, and Charles II at the Restoration continued the policy.

After so much information of the beginning of the first "Coventry", we have none of her subsequent employment until the operation that resulted in her end. A war with the Dutch started in 1665 and a Dutch Fleet led by De Ruyter attacked Barbados, but was beaten off. The next year, the French joined the war as allies of the Dutch, and the French of St. Christopher (a neighbouring West Indian Island, now called St. Kitts) conquered the English portion with savage fighting.

Lord Willoughby, Governor of Barbados, sailed to the rescue with Frigates "Coventry" and "Hope", and several merchantmen, carrying one thousand soldiers. Off Martinico this squadron took two prizes, and Captain Hill of "Coventry", with four merchantmen, was sent to surprise six richly laden French ships at Todos los Santos. One of these had been taken, and another fired by her own crew, when a hurricane started. "Coventry" was blown ashore, and the French subsequently took prisoner four hundred and fifty men, including Captain William Hill. Lord Willoughby and the "Hope" with four merchantmen were nevermore heard of. The Rear Admiral's ship, with three others reached Montserrat a mere wreck, not having a mast standing.

Captain Hill was sent to France, but finally returned to England to face a court martial for the loss of his ship. He was acquitted "having defended his ship and prevented the enemy from taking possession of her several days, after she had been stranded on their coast".

"Coventry II" was built at Fisher Harding's yard in Deptford in the reign of William and Mary. The Navy List of 1694 shows her as 670 tons, forty-eight guns, (Captain George Mesteer). The complement was two hundred and twenty-six men. By now, naval gunners used mortars to throw explosive bombs into the strong points of enemy harbours, and under the supervision of one, Benbow, some of these engines of war were fitted in "Coventry". The Lieutenant's logs show that the bulkheads were strengthened for "close fighting", and that the press gang was used to make up her crew. For the next five years she was employed in Channel or Mediterranean convoys to and from Smyrna, even as far as Gallipoli. There were frequent occasions when armed parties in the ship's boats captured enemy craft.

In June 1701, "Coventry" transported five Companies of the King's Guards to Helvoetsluys, whence they marched to Breda. This was in connection with an English treaty obligation to send troops to Holland if that territory were menaced by an enemy. Louis XIV's troops had, in fact, just, occupied Belgium.

The next month saw them convoying the Royal Yacht in company of the Squadron of Admiral Munden. In these years Spain was the sick man of Europe, and European nations were lining up for what would be "the war of the Spanish Succession".

In 1702 "Coventry" accompanied outward and return convoys for Virginia. In the same year England, opposed by a coalition led by Louis XIV of France, was contending with the French and Spanish Fleets. Sir George Rookes Squadron, which included "Coventry", attacked Spanish treasure ships, which, convoyed from the West Indies by French men-of-war, had reached Vigo Harbour. The entire treasure was taken and fifteen French warships sunk. "Coventry" stayed some days in Vigo under command of Sir Clowdisley Shovel, and on October 23rd suffered damage from shore guns which killed three men and wounded seven. The next day French ships driven ashore were burnt.

Sir George Rookes action effectively checked the maritime ambition of Louis XIV.

On the 29th March, 1704, however, "Coventry" with a convoy sixty leagues east and by north of Scilly was cut out by two French 54 gun ships, and taken by Captain Duguay Trouin's ship "Jason". Five years later, H.M.S. "Portland" recaptured her in the West Indies, but she was not restored to the Navy List.

"Coventry III" was built at H. Adam's yard Beaulieu, and put in the Navy List 1757 as 586 tons, twenty-eight guns, (Captain Carr Scrope). The complement was two hundred men. This was during the reign of George II, and a period of naval expansion for competing with the French in North America and India.

In 1757, there being not enough ships to blockade all French ports, a squadron under Admirals Hawke and Mordaunt was sent to raid Rochefort, on the Biscay Coast. "Coventry" was part of that expedition. Despite the fact that on March 14th of that year, Admiral Byng, following Court Martial had been shot "Pour encourager les autres", the (Rochefort) Expedition Commanders would not come to a decision about landing their troops, and so "a great chance was thrown away" (James Wolfe).

On December 25th of that year, "Coventry", stationed in the Channel, took the French privateer "Dragon" of Bayonne. The "Dragon" had twenty-four guns, and two hundred and eighty men.

In 1759, the French prepared to invade England, and the population had not been so alarmed since the year of the Spanish Armada. But the Channel Blockade held; also General Wolfe's troops in a smooth combined operation captured Quebec, and in so doing gained Canada. After this the French and British Fleets sought each other out for a decisive engagement. "Coventry" was in the squadron of Sir Edward Hawke, who, hearing that a French Fleet under Vice Admiral de Conflans had left Brest to attack the British squadron of Commodore Duff, left Torbay on November 14th. Six day's later, Hawke's fleet was in the Bay of Biscay with the frigates "Coventry" and "Maidstone", scouting ahead on either bow of the flagship, when "Maidstone" sighted the enemy ships off Belle Isle. A heavy gale compelled de Conflans to shelter in Quiberon Bay, where, moreover, he would have a better defensive position. Hawke's ships, unusual for that period of history, had spent the winter at sea, so were, despite navigational hazards, able to follow in close and start an action. Rough seas and the coming of darkness shortened the action, but "Formidable" struck to "Resolution", "Thesee", and "Superbe" foundered, "Heros" and "Soleil Royal" ran ashore, later to be set on fire. Next year, "Coventry" employed on the blockade of Brest, made several captures of enemy craft.

Then came four years on the North American station, much of the time in New York Harbour. Here the log book indicates a very satisfactory scale of provisioning.

In 1775, when the war with the American Colonists was raging, "Coventry" was sent to join the East Indies squadron of Commodore Edward Hughes. In 1778, France declared war on Britain, starting operations in the East whilst Britain's forces were heavily engaged in America. Thus, on the 10th August, 1778, the East Indies Squadron of Sir E. Vernon, including "Coventry", fought a French squadron under Commodore Tronjoly. Aboard "Coventry" one man was killed and the Master and twenty-one men were wounded. On the 25th of that month, the French "Sartine" (32 guns), which had been detached from its squadron, was taken by "Coventry" and "Seahorse". The Frenchman had declined to fight.

In 1779, "Coventry" joined the squadron of Sir Edward Hughes on the Coromandel coast of India. On November 29th she was engaged with the small fleet of Hyder Ali, Sultan of Mysore. Hyder Ali had unsuccessfully attacked the East India Company's installations at Madras, and was now trying his luck. by sea. The French King had sent a squadron of ships commanded by Admiral Suffren to assist Hyder Ali.

On the 12th May, 1781, Sir Edward Hughes's squadron, moored in Tillicherri Roads, was attacked by fire ships. The boats of H.M.S. "Coventry" towed them clear. Next year, on August 12th, "Coventry", proceeding from Bombay to join the squadron off Ceylon, fell in with the French "Bellone" of 32 guns (Captain de Piervert). The ships closed to fight a fierce action for more than two hours. During the fight, the French Captain was killed, and the second and third officers of "Bellone" quarrelled over command, which practically paralysed the French ship. On sighting the main French squadron, "Coventry" beat a retreat, having fifteen men killed and twenty-nine wounded.

On the 12th January, 1783, "Coventry", now commanded by Captain William Wolseley, cruising in the Bay of Bengal, sailed into the midst of what was taken to be a fleet of British merchantment, but was, in fact, a squadron of French warships who promptly took her.

Later that year, French manned and added to the squadron of Admiral de Suffren, she took part off Cuddalore in the fifth and last of the indecisive actions between the squadrons of Admirals Hughes and de Suffren.

"Coventry IV" was built at Swan Hunters yard, Wallsend on Tyne in 1917, (4,290 tons) with five 6" guns, and a top speed of 29 knots. She joined the Harwich Force in which she stayed until the end of the war. Her function was to ward off attacks from Zeppelins and aircraft. From 1920-1924 she was with the Atlantic Fleet, and from 1925-1935, with the Mediterranean Fleet.

In 1927, "Coventry", with suitable "make-up" played the part of "Scharnhorst" in the British film "The Battles of Coronel and Falkland Islands". On August 1st, 1935 she was transferred to reserve. By April 15th, 1937 she had been re-armed with ten 4" guns, and recommissioned for the Mediterranean.

CHAPTER TWO

THE SATURDAY NIGHT SAILORS

H.M.S. "Coventry", a light cruiser of 4,290 tons and a maximum speed of 29 knots, carried six inch guns for fighting the Kaiser's navy when launched in 1917. By 1938, with sister ships, "Cairo", "Calcutta", "Carlisle", "Curacoa" and "Curlew", she had been re-armed to meet the much debated threat of air attack at sea, and was ready to fend off Hitler's aircraft with a battery of ten four inch guns in high angle mountings. The barrels were of 1917 vintage, but had been installed with a modern fire control system; and the provision of two director positions allowed for the independent engagement of two separate targets at any one time.

Air tactical theorists believed that dive bombing attacks were most likely to sink ships, so "Coventry" carried an eight barrelled pom-pom forward of the bridge. The eight barrels together could spit 720 shells a minute, and journalists always referred to these guns as "Chicago Pianos", thus giving a comforting suggestion of something really modern.

Before 1938, the London Division R.N.V.R. encouraged chiefly the training of signalmen. Those volunteers who insisted on choosing the gunnery branch were now and then drilled on the 6" practice loader, having suitably attired themselves for the drill. The six inch gun was the largest hand loaded gun used by the Royal Navy and its projectile weighed one hundred pounds. After business hours, superior looking young men from city offices would solemnly walk over the gangway and board "President" to don a gold braided uniform, and emerge from the ward room as naval officers, with a slightly rolling deck beneath their feet.

Not only were these young men trained in the specialist job of firing anti-aircraft guns but all the intricate facets of seamanship were assimilated within the hulk of this fine old ship. Not only on board, but in the quiet streets around the Temple and Kings Bench Walk, squads with rifles marched and countermarched, learning the routine of field training with small arms. "Saturday Night Sailors" as they were called took their job seriously, and, in particular, concentrated on mastering the gun drill.

After a friendly but formal introduction of the officer to the waiting gun loader crew, its members would at the word of command start the frenzied routine of lifting one hundred pound projectiles, and placing them in the breech to be rammed home by a comrade. Another would close the breech, and after the simulated firing the breech would be opened and cooled with the water soaked ram, and loading repeated. The tub of water for the ram evoked "wooden walls" traditions, a more palatable stimulant for the imagination than Jutland, the last fleet gun battle.

The main object, apart from avoiding serious injury to the participants from their own clumsiness, was to reach the regular service rate of loading. Often the drill was perfect, and rapid, deserving restrained praise. But no officer was ever guilty of sacrilegiously affirming that the regular service performance had been equalled.

All volunteers were required to do fourteen days sea training yearly, but could freely choose when they did it. After the 1938 crisis, however, the Admiralty showed great interest in gunners. Two four inch guns in high angle mountings were fitted on the quarter deck, complete with a director position, and a fire control room was installed below decks. No longer was it a question of gunner enthusiasts forming parties for six inch loader drill. Every gunner was allocated to a fifty man unit and asked to do sea training with that unit at a fixed time if possible. The units mustered at regular weekly intervals for drill. Attendance was good and the drill earnestly performed. Each gun had a crew of ten men, of which six were engaged in feeding ammunition. It seemed an innocuous activity on those warm summer evenings, as the wash of passing tugs with their strings of lighters put a slight roll on "President", and onlookers gazed idly from the Embankment parapet.

One evening, the R.A.F. had kindly sent an attacking aircraft to "President", and a unit was closed up with its' director diligently searching the eastern sky for its target. Just then the pin-striped and bowler-hatted figure of Lieutenant Commander McDougall alighted from a bus, and, running toward the parapet whilst gesticulating energetically skywards with an umbrella, roared "This way director, get round on it". He, of course, had observed the aircraft approaching from the west.

The training periods duly announced had subsequently been brought forward by a few weeks, and my unit found itself waiting at the quayside of Portsmouth Dockyard in mid-August. The silhouette of "Coventry" with its spreading air defence platform crowning the main mast was quickly spotted, as were two launches speeding towards us. For many months previous, every organ of public information had constantly spoken about changes that might occur in "an emergency", but few reservists realised the true relation of this euphemism to the novel training cruise just beginning, in which, wonder of wonders, they would actually be allowed to shoot. The launches came and I helped to stow the one provided for carrying bags and hammocks. One of the crew said to me in a conspiratorial tone "Yesterday two hundred men from barracks were sent overland to Gibraltar".

"Coventry" put to sea as soon as we were aboard and that evening reservists became acquainted with their training ship and shipmates, whilst relaxing in the recreation space and having a drink from the "goffer" bar. Gunnery practice started next morning, supervised by Warrant Officer Taylor. Reservists were closed up at the guns, given the minimum introduction, and had fired the first practice round before they quite knew what had happened. Having proved their ability to operate the guns, they were soon ordered to fire "barrage". The crack of the propellant explosive had been shock enough to the unaccustomed ear, but the rapid repetition of the sound as we strained to reach a creditable rate of fire seemed to lessen the impact.

After three days of this we anchored at Plymouth in sight of the Hoe. We had arrived in the forenoon of a glorious sunny day and "make and mend" was piped, with shore leave for most of the ship's company. The first liberty boat left crammed with an eager lively crowd, the "tiddly" regulars smiling inwardly at the "slop room" turnout of the reservists. An hour later another crowd of faultlessly dressed ratings waited impatiently for the second boat. The bosun's mate sounded his whistle; but the anticpated "Liberty men fall in" did not fall from his lips. Instead a doleful voice intoned "All leave cancelled". Frustrated liberty men, and hitherto indifferent men on deck, now keenly scanned the shore where everything was proceeding normally, and speculation began.

The length of leave for those ashore depended on the venue of their leisure activities. Several had settled in their cinema seats when the entertainment stopped and a notice on the screen recalled all "Coventry"men. By evening the ship's broadcasting system was churning out popular music non-stop, but there was no evidence of gaiety among the ship's company. And when three flying boats roared across the water and slowly rose skywards, the comment "They're off to bomb Germany" brought no repartee.

Darkness covered Plymouth Sound and a boat leaving the Hoe at 22.00 picked up the last of the liberty men. "Pipe down" had brought silence, soon to be broken for a short time when the cable party was mustered on the fo'c'sle preparatory to "Coventry" putting out to the Channel.

Next morning's breakfast was a silent meal and, at its close, reservists were piped to muster on the upper deck. Here, over the swish and wash of the waves, they heard that they were now mobilised in the Royal Navy, but would be given forty-eight hours leave on reaching Portsmouth. It was further stated that any man whose livelihood derived from a one-man business, or who had made arrangements for an imminent marriage might claim a delay in his mobilisation. The holiday atmosphere was now gone and the mobilised men returning to Portsmouth were mostly changed from the lighthearted reservists anticipating the fun of a little gunnery practice.

Going up the Solent, listless eyes and brooding faces were much in evidence. On the surface, an outgoing submarine went by and A. B. Middleton called out "Cheer up boys". We might have been on that one".

Once berthed at Portsmouth we were quickly ashore, provided with rail warrants, and made for the station. My brother and I went to a Somerset farm where my mother and sister were on holiday, and during the smooth ride through countless green fields we forgot the alarming nature of our own interrupted training and speculated on a possible trip abroad. After the greetings, we told our news and my mother wilted, like a flower struck by a gale. Next day we all arrived in London. The newspapers of passengers in the suburban train showed headlines about a Ribbentrop-Molotov pact, and the people themselves seemed like conspirators awaiting some portentous but doubtful event. One smiling and confident middle aged man kept the compartment agog while he regaled his admiring lady friend with reminiscences of his commissioned service in the Royal Navy during 1914 to 1918. "And did you", she trilled "actually meet Ginger Boyle". And as he replied, with a well embroidered affirmative, it occurred to me that he spoke of an admiral referred to on the lower deck as the "Horrible Earl of Cork", but known in more fashionable circles as the Earl of Cork and Orrery.

The forty-eight hours was up, and in the early morning most of the unit met again on the concourse of Waterloo Station before boarding the Portsmouth train. Wives and parents were in varying degrees of cheerfulness, and most maintained the demeanour that this was something of a spree; but the wife of Able Seaman Sullivan wept unrestrainedly because, she said she might never see her husband again. This must have been a little embarrassing for Spike Sullivan, a restaurant cook with close cropped hair and bullet head, who was a pugilist of repute; and possibly the toughest looking man in the unit. Arriving at Portsmouth we left the station, mixed with an irregular column of Territorials; all were burdened with full kit, and ready with facetious remarks about their likely destination.

Crossing the dockyard by avenues redolent of naval tradition and discipline, we walked the gangplank that led to "Coventry": and those who had dallied were reminded by the Duty Petty Officer that a strict naval discipline now applied to former reservists.

There had been changes in the complement of regulars. Chief Petty Officer Foster, the bosun, Petty Officers Davenport and Sephton, range taker and director layer respectively, with the seaman branch Petty Officers were still there, but most of the regular personnel not in key positions had been replaced by fleet reservists, even pensioners, one or two of whom were over sixty years old; and some who had been at Jutland. These men were soon indistinguishable from the regular seamen they had replaced, and brought a tradition that harked back to the time when the last sailing vessels had been with the Fleet. In time, one of them became noted for a spine chilling account of his experience at Jutland. Another, Able Seaman Munnery, whose face was permanently marked by privation and seemed like a museum specimen of harsher days, was not so articulate; but it eventually became common knowledge that he was sole survivor of a boat load of seven men left from a destroyer sunk in the North Sea during 1914–1918.

Once returned to "Coventry", the R.N.V.R.'s were mustered on the dockside, packed into a lorry and sent to barracks to draw full kit. By the lofty iron gate stood a group of oddly clothed and critical urchins who greeted us with cries of "Wheel 'em in". Our new kit included white shorts and pith helmet, but the obvious speculation was checked by knowing types who insisted that this was simply part of the standard full kit.

CHAPTER THREE

OUTWARD BOUND

Coventry stayed in Portsmouth for a few days loading stores and ammunition, and the crew were subjected to medical inspection and several inocculations. One or two of the more observant personnel were impressed with the unusual colour of the projectiles, a bright mustard colour that shrieked high explosive, to distinguish them from the practice ammunition used hitherto. And when some of those same projectiles were fused, an action which in peace routine was for safety reasons delayed to within minutes of actual firing, they felt a momentary uneasiness; soon dispelled however by the unheeding spirits of the lads rejoicing in the novelty of being sailors.

Many reservists had been mobilised in the "crisis" a year before, to witness the convivial reunion of old hands of Jellicoe's navy. A large number of these veterans of what had subsequently been dramatised and publicised as the first and last world war had preserved the uniform of the period; outstanding for its unflattering pancake cap. Even now the naval rating's uniform was not calculated to give him ideas above his station. The second call crisis reservists took a sober view. The first timers just enjoyed the excitement, and hoped that they would put a considerable distance of salt water between them and the office, shop, or factory before the panic died down again. All, however, were pleased when "Coventry" moved out into the Solent, then proceeded to the Channel. We occasionally glimpsed the receding town and its beaches, but before long were enveloped in a light mist; so two lookouts were immediately placed in the eye of the fo'c'sle. The sunshine was gone, the air chill, and few knew where we were bound. Occasionally to right or left we made out the silhouettes of the light cruisers "Danae" and "Dauntless" which accompanied us. One of the green sailors asked a question about where we were going, and an ingenious individual whose ear had caught a word or two blown from the mouth of a bridge signalman replied, "Because the air-defence platform makes "Coventry" specially suitable for the work, we have been ordered to find and shadow "Deutschland". A heroic assignment indeed for an old light cruiser with ten four inch H.A. guns served by reservists and pensioners.

In a few hours we were through the mist and ploughing on in clear daylight. Our attention was henceforward very much engaged by a programme of drills and evolutions, (as such occasions as "prepare to tow ship" had been christened by Admirals long forgotten), devised by Captain Onslow, aided and abetted by the gunnery staff.

Thus engaged we entered what initiates called "The Bay" to experience its boisterous seas and heavy swell; but steadily "Coventry" ploughed its furrow through the vast waste of green and grey, with the white flash of the bow wave in front, and a boiling wake behind. Beneath the grey skies fluttered the scarlet flash of its windswept ensign. Here "Danae" and "Dauntless" left us, setting course for the West Indies whence they would patrol the South Atlantic. The next day we found ourselves cruising through mist in quieter waters, and suddenly a sunlit cliff was visible over a distant horizon. "Gib" said the professional sailors, while reservists gazed at what they had in literature learned to call "The Rock". The well informed were quick to point out those areas which had been engineered for water catchment.

Coming closer we noticed white houses thickly clustered around the bay, and marvelled that the many powerful guns there sited were completely out of view. The regulars provided endless amusing chaff about rock apes and the unprintable erotic demonstrations they had witnessed at one time and another at an "exhibish" in Tangier, Gib's African neighbour. Gazing with interest at the variety of grey warships in the harbour, we speculated on shore leave at the famous port; but this was promptly stopped when we secured to the mole and stokers came on deck to carry out orders for a rapid intake of fuel and water. Within two hours we were speeding through the fabulous Mediterranean on an easterly course. We had reached the area where the more comfortably off "little men" had only recently been invited, by travel agents, to enjoy holiday cruises on ocean liners.

"Coventry" forged through the sunwarmed sea of ultramarine, sweeping dazzling white hills of water on either bow to fall away and flatten as they reached the wake. The dolphins came swimming alongside; shooting into the air to curve into graceful dives. Within hours the apprentice matelots had experienced all the more gaudy thrills of sea adventure books, even the sight of flying fish; indeed one such fish became stranded on the fo'c'sle.

The sunshine and warmth of the central sea dismissed all cares. A canvas swimming pool was rigged, and during their successive periods of leisure small groups of the ship's company swam and splashed in noisy skylarking. Hot days on a blue sea under endless clear blue sky were a fresh experience for most reservists. A few were uncomfortably sunburnt, and Able Seaman Lusty was prostrate for a whole day in the sick bay where the sick bay staff hastened his recovery from heat stroke. One evening it was explained to us that "darken ship" would be piped, and must be thoroughly performed, because during the night we should pass near Mussolini's airbase at Pantellaria. "Coventry's" engines were coaxed to their utmost at the same time. Early next day a rocky prominence broke the horizon starboard and this was our first sight of Gozo. We left it behind to shortly encounter more land, Malta! Volunteers were fascinated at the appearance of this island; the second of the chain of defence stations enshrined in the sagas of British sea power and empire.

Approaching the Grand Harbour of Valletta and with hope of shore leave in mind, we first remarked the unaccustomed lines of the daisas weaving about the harbour, then gave concentrated attention to the ancient palaces, domes and spires, not to mention the water front places of entertainment. Boy Ramsey, who had often stepped ashore there, remarked sententiously "There she is! A land of yells, bells and smells!"

"Coventry" made fast to a buoy with a wire hawser, and the stokers appeared on deck for their rapid fuel and water routine. The dress of the day was by now white ducks. One bumboatman was just able to get aboard and open his case of cotton clothing. A.B. Sullivan drove a hard bargain for a vest, and the Maltese was openly sulking because his anticipated further sales did not materialise. Meanwhile, dealing through a porthole, A.B. Lusty had acquired a petrol lighter at an attractive price. Then all hands were summoned to the quarter deck, there to haul in wire hawsers generously coated with foul blue mud. While we daubed our spotless white suits, Lt. McKean in a dazzling outfit that would have done credit to a Covent Garden performance of Madame Butterfly, stood clear on a bollard, all smiles, as he chanted in a cheerful kindly voice "Stamp it down". Who or what nobody bothered to enquire.

Out of harbour we carried on east in sunshine and blue water; and volunteers were beginning to get the hang of dhobying, an art in which they were then noticeably inferior to the regular seamen. On Sunday afternoon the hitherto blue water showed signs of a greenish tinge and there was an occasional patch of floating debris. A blur on the horizon promised land. "Alex" was the comment of the regulars, whilst the erstwhile Saturday night sailors craned their necks for some notable feature of approaching Alexandria. As we entered the harbour, protected from the sea by a barrier of huge concrete blocks, the initiates pointed out the sandstone stump of the Pharos, first known lighthouse, and one of the seven wonders of the ancient world. In time we should learn to known the grand modern dwellings by the eastern harbour, and the fly-infested squalor of Mex that lay behind the coal wharf on the opposite side. We should see King Farouk's palace, Ras-el-Tin, and the headquarters of the yacht club, whence the wealthy cosmopolitan society of Alexandria might, from deck chairs, observe every activity of the ships and boats in the harbour. But now, our attention was almost exclusively given to the groups of pale grey-painted warships of various sizes scattered about the harbour. Passing close to a destroyer, we noticed a few men in tropical rig of shorts and shirts, very much at ease on the fo'c'sle. An amplifier slung from a stanchion was relaying B.B.C. news to them, and we could overhear. We heard, albeit with an echo, the diffident but dignified diction of Mr. Chamberlain, saying that war against Germany had been declared. "Coventry's" main concern just then was to moor ship and pipe hands to tea. During the meal, reflection was more evident than comment. After tea both watches were mustered with rig of the day overalls, a most unusual order for the serene naval Sunday.

A large lighter came alongside and for a few hours we were all occupied in transferring high explosive projectiles from lighter to ship, and the remaining practice ammunition from ship to lighter. This rapid provision of killer projectiles, especially the armour-piercing kind, brought home the announcement we had heard. It was well into the night when work stopped; and hammocks once slung, sleep came quickly.

Next morning gunnery practice was ordered, and repeated so frequently that the novelty of shooting soon wore off.

Our daily firing practices were geared up and the results certainly looked good. The normal drill was to fire at a canvas sleeve or "drogue" towed by an old Swordfish aircraft, which was a realistic exercise in that the sights of all the instruments were trained on the aircraft but the guns were "thrown off" a certain number of degrees to coincide with the length of tow. The black shell burst would appear round the drogue in neat little patterns of six dots and it was very gratifying to see the pattern close in. The throw off was rather important and had to be very carefully set.

Few of us thought in terms of aircraft differing very much from the old "Swordfish" that towed the drogue. But in addition to gunnery there were exercises in aircraft recognition and spotting, and the air defence lookouts were given photographs of enemy aircraft and lectured on their names, type and performance. The comparative performance of the "Swordfish" was not stressed. Last, but not least, arrangements were made for a submarine to simulate an attack, and to come as near "Coventry" as possible. As many men as could be spared were stationed on the upper deck to learn recognition of the periscope breaking surface.

On return to harbour came the long-awaited shore leave. How pleasant it was to cross the sunlit water in either "Coventry's" launch or one of the lateen rigged feluccas which plied for hire. The feluccas were manned by sturdy and dignified Mohammedans who cleaned their boats each morning and started the day by bowing in prayer.

We would issue from No. 50 Gate in the stone wall surrounding the harbour on to the shining cobbles and sand-blown squalor of Mex, and take the lane by the timber yard to join the main road into town. When the single decker tandem tram arrived, liberty men filled it; some travelling first class with passengers in European dress, others with artisan Egyptians and Arabs wearing galibiehs in the less luxurious second class car. The windows of the second class car had no glass, and this led to a surprising experience for one of Coventry's E.R.A.'s, who lolled against the window ledge dreamily smoking his pipe. At a dreary looking spot where a pair of emaciated arab women in black clothing offered none too fresh grapes for sale, the tram halted. Just as it started off again, a small brown hand appeared through the window, and wrenched the pipe from between the smoker's teeth. A moment later a little figure in a galibieh was seen running to a nearby alley with his booty. It would never be recovered, but it is only fair to say that the mortality rate of these smart young thieves was very high. The tramcar coming down in the opposite direction often closed at surprising speed with fatal results.

Nearer town the tram crossed a bridge over the Mahmoudieh canal, and on the canal were sailing craft with lines that were probably familiar to Moses. These brought bales of cotton, and we would see those same bales carried over the bridge on carts drawn by two mules, noticeable by their prominent ears. We regularly passed a large painted hoarding, albeit ancient, that bore representations of dentures and the legend "Amercan Dantes". There was no sign of a surgery, and we guessed that this enterprising American dentist had left town years ago.

The town proper began on entering the Rue des Soeurs, in tradition renowned for its brothels. From the tram windows one was aware of a decayed quarter where the most prominent features were some scattered butchers shops displaying lumpy strings of little sausages, and small pale chunks of meat thickly covered in flies.

Mohammed Ali Square was the terminus, and here life began to be hygenic and elegant. From the tram, smartly dressed seamen and marines debouched to various places of entertainment and refreshment. The square itself had many bars and restaurants, with cane chairs and tables on a gay "terasse". One could find a bar in the smart French Avenue Fuad Premier, or drink expresso coffee at the Brazilian coffee shop in the Boulevard Saad Zaghloul.

Before being let loose ashore we had been warned against eating anything offered there, owing to poor standards of hygiene. However, on arrival in the fashionable Avenue Faud Premier, with its elegant French shops and spotless drinking places with white coated waiters, we were soon beguiled into refreshing ourselves. There were dishes of salted nuts and marvellous savouries provided free between delicious glasses of iced beer. We had a wonderful evening and returned to the ship well pleased.

Next morning I awoke with a severe pain in the stomach, and quickly imagined that I had contracted some hideous oriental disease; so reproached myself for the folly of ignoring official advice. On the mess deck I met a companion of the previous evening who instead of a cheery greeting, said solemnly "How's your guts mate?". Enquiry revealed that a third man was also suffering. With each of us somewhat solaced by reflecting that he was not the only one, we went to the sick bay. The M.O. listened to us with astonishing sympathy considering that we had ignored his advice, and asked us what we had eaten. When we mentioned prawns he said sententiously "Ah, prawns!, come this way". Opening a cupboard, he produced a large bottle of muddy looking medicine and poured each of us a glass and said "Come for more at midday if you haven't settled down by then". At this moment Lt. McKean came in and said "Let's have a glass of something to cork me up Doc, I've got a gunnery practice on". We too were engaged in gunnery practice which, with the M.O's medicine, worked a complete cure. Afterwards we were prepared to starve ashore but the food was too tempting. By avoiding shellfish, however, we kept out of trouble.

On an afternoon run, the more enterprising might go to nearby Ramleh terminus and take a tram to the extensive Nouzah Gardens which included the rose garden planted in honour of King Edward VIII; the bathing beaches of Stanley Bay and Sidi Bishr, or the roller skating rinks at Cleopatra and Sporting Club. Here the polyglot European lasses of Alexandria danced a very showy tango to new and exciting melodies.

Getting back to the ship was more interesting than leaving it, and now and then somebody returned worse for wear. The Fleet liberty boats all left from a well-lit quay at No. 14 Gate and the money changer's stall was always busy. One "Coventry" youth, an ex-Grimsby trawler man, here tried to sell a gold ring bought from a furtive dock side pedlar who had explained that he was selling property stolen by his brother. The derisive merriment of the money changers moved the duped "fence" to rush back in vain search of the alleyways. Few sailors walked back and the transport was either bus, taxi, or gharry, a horse drawn vehicle of Victorian vintage. Those missing the return boat were sometimes recognised by a friend in charge of another ship's boat who arranged to include "Coventry" on the run back. If there was any money left a felucca would take them home. By now we were paid in Egyptian piastres. They were always called "Ackers" and this word probably originated from the greek coin of ten drachmae "Deka Drachmae", the printing looking something like "Aeka".

There was great excitement when mail arrived from home, which was distributed immediately preceding "hands to dinner". The subsequent meal was eaten and cleared, ("Eat it and beat it!" was the cry of the mess cooks), more quickly than most, and there was a period of brooding silence as family greetings and news were devoured. In the leisure of the following dog watches we read the ample newspapers with endless items extolling the strength of the Maginot Line, and with various snippets reminding readers that a war was in progress, not to mention an occasional reference to "our sure shield". The recent rumours about the silent and inglorious disappearance of the aircraft carrier "Courageous" were not printed.

Sunday church services continued unchanged, except for the more frequent use of a prayer imploring deliverance of mariners from the violence of the enemy, sentiments with which we concurred unanimously. After service, it was the custom of Captain Onslow to speak to the ship's company on subjects they were bound to be pondering. Of the war, he said "I don't believe that it will last very long, but don't be taken in by the newspaper stories of Germany collapsing in a matter of weeks. The Government has decided to work on the assumption that the war may last three years. Everyone knows it won't last as long as that of course!"

Censoring the mail gave our officers a fairly accurate picture of how reservists were settling down to regular service, and the Captain took note of it in an "after church" address. Quite early on he had said "I don't suppose that you are used to sitting like a row of hens on perches when you go to the toilet! but these are shipboard conditions that cannot be altered! This was in fact no novelty to R.N.V.R's who had frequently rehearsed this function during drill sessions aboard "President". But with the passing of weeks, disenchantment with the role of "Jolly Jack" had clearly set in for some, hastened here and there by disturbing news from home. After one mail delivery, A.B. Pyramus had disconsolately announced that his girl friend had made pointed remarks indicating a cooling off. He was jocularly re-assured that "All the girls will be running after these bright militiamen now".

Thus the Captain had perforce to confide in a sabbath address "Some of you are beginning to find things a bit difficult and put the blame on ships routine. We are doing our best to help you to settle down, but it does'nt help anyone to hear remarks about a hell ship! (very pained expression here), and even if you think it really is a hell ship, for heavens sake don't write to the people at home about it, and make them miserable too!"

The majority of reservists readily accustomed themselves to novel living conditions. It was the conscript "H.O.s" later on in the war that would intone with quite the wrong emphasis the phrase frequently used by messdeck petty officers as they tried to encourage pride in clean and tidy surroundings "This mess is your home".

"Home" was in fact a stout wide board hinged to the ships side at one end, and supported at the other by steel rods hanging from the deck head. The seats (mess stools) were also supported at the ships side, but held up amidships by folding iron legs that now and then folded unexpectedly with comical effect for the men sitting opposite. The leading seaman, and those longest in the mess normally had the coveted hammock spaces over this domestic altar.

At the midships end on a square of "Corticine", (never call it lino), stood the gleaming "Tingear". The tea urn, (don't use Bluebell on the strainer), with the large rectangular box containing tea and "Pussers" sugar, of which one tablespoonful had the equivalent sweetening power of a teaspoonful of Tate and Lyles, the dishing up kettle, two baking tins, and two "Fannies" or boiling cans of the type perversely called dixies by the Boy Scouts.

At the ships-side end was an iron rack with plates and cups of ware, a tin of condensed milk, and as often as not, a bottle of "Alley Slopers" sauce. Beneath this a drawer with knives and forks, and the tin opener. Also bolted to the ships-side were racks holding black painted cylindrical tin cap boxes, also the rectangular wooden ditty boxes reckoned to contain family photographs and all that the seaman held dear. Amidships were banks of steel lockers having about four cubic feet capacity in which all kit must be stowed. Any item of kit found loafing or "sculling" about was confiscated by the mess deck petty officer and put in the "scran-bag", redeemable for a limited period on payment of a bar of soap. From this custom arose a picturesque phrase "Dressed like a scran bag".

Many R.N.V.R.s, encouraged perhaps by Captain Onslows exhortation prior to the first winter of war to "Bring back with you the warmest civilian overcoat you've got", also used suitcases to carry their kit—a procedure, indeed a privilege, reserved for petty officers and equal rates. Some months after the first hectic days of mobilisation a certain over zealous R.N.R. officer hinted that these unauthorised containers might be thrown over the side if not otherwise removed. They were, for a few weeks, but gradually re-assembled.

Some of the Victorian methods used by the R.N. to combat V.D. seemed an anachronism in the eyes of the better informed personnel of 1939. Indeed, it had not been found necessary to reserve a marked part of the heads for "CDA's", or to establish the special mess for V.D. subjects which, in mess deck jargon, was called "Rose Cottage". Nevertheless, a handful "caught the boat up", and their leave was stopped during the period of medical treatment. The crude hilarity of wooden ship days still lived in most of the fleet reservists and one of these, seeing an erstwhile CDA youth going ashore, shouted with a grin "What's on Augustus?—Going ashore to try out your new 'un?"

Naval catering generally did not encourage gluttony. Breakfast was usually a slice of bread and margarine and a cup of tea. In the early days some of the regulars were startled by "Corn flake merchants" who were accused of using more than their share of condensed milk. Occasionally a rating would buy a threepenny tin of fish paste from the N.A.A.F.I., and with some effort manage to broach it with the mess tin opener; and indeed there was nothing against having boiled eggs or kippers if the spirit was willing. The "Coventry" system was "Canteen messing" (i.e.) provisions were drawn from the ships stores, and or bought from the N.A.A.F.I., meals prepared by the "Cooks of the mess", and taken to the galley for cooking. One cook, bringing his dish late to the galley was admonished by the cook "I can't cook that" to which he rejoined "Never mind, flare it up like you do the rest of the stuff". At meal time this dish was found to be burnt and inedible. There was a subsequent enquiry at the Court of the First Lieutenant, who, on learning of the witty repartee pointed out that there could be no complaint against the cook who had done as he was bid.

By rota, two ratings were appointed cooks of the mess each day. Their duties were to fetch the issue, prepare and fetch the meals, serve the meals and wash the dishes The most onerous part of their duties however was to scrub and scour the mess for First Lieutenant's Rounds on Mondays to Fridays, and Captain's rounds on Saturdays.

After breakfast the cooks went to draw the meat issue which was sometimes suitable for "Straightbake", although now and then a miserable section of ribs known as a "Mouthorgan" was issued. Leading Seaman Turner of No. 7 mess frequently remarked that the Marine butcher was always cutting up a peculiar variety of animal that had no legs, and after the mess cooks had returned with a "mouthorgan" three days running he had a private chat with the butcher which resulted in a "straightbake" being issued in exchange. The more enthusiastic cooks would put up a "duff", and some even managed custard.

Some leading seamen were excellent caterers, and I well remember dining from a large leg of pork on a Sunday when we were berthed in Alexandria Harbour. For some reason a gang of Arab labourers came aboard, made a bee line for the mess decks and competed in offers to empty the "Gash" (waste) bucket. Our bearded son of the prophet was rewarded with the remains of the pork. Ensconcing himself on the deck among the lockers he enjoyed the meal of his lifetime, baring the joint to the bone. The expression on his face was beatific—he had indeed glimpsed paradise.

A stock Naval platitude was "Bullstalk baffles brains", but the germ of wisdom in that succinct text was developed by very few; and many of those that used it with great effect when on the swings lost their grip when on the roundabouts. Years of conditioning both in the Service, and in civilian surroundings, gave a magic power to gold braid, brass buttons, and an official bellow. A green officer careless with this magic could reduce a considerable labour force to a state of mental paralysis, albeit concealed by automatic and ineffective motions, while the few that knew what had to be done carried out the task and cursed the stupidity of their fellows. A notable example occurred when "Coventry" made fast to "Rodney" at Scapa. Half a dozen "Coventry" hands "supervised" by an officer and petty officer, and assisted by a leading seaman, passed wire hawsers to the battle ship, and in a few minutes had secured them on "Coventry's" bollards. Aboard "Rodney" however, some thirty seamen, panicked by the barking of an individual resplendent in new uniform, performed a comic ballet lasting twenty five minutes before the work was completed. Even Lt. Commander Robb R.N.R., with his professional prejudice against R.N. methods had to compliment his working party.

Cleanliness is a fetish of the Service which ensures health and comfortable living, and the altar of personal cleanliness was the bathroom; a separate one provided, of course, for higher rates and other segregated classes. The seamens bathroom was not an area of gleaming porcelain baths with glittering taps, but a twelve foot square space within steel bulkheads. One of them was the ships side, and admitted light through three portholes. Naturally, everything was painted white. The deck was tiled, and there were rows of enamel basins mounted in tip up racks. These were served by cold water taps, but hot water could be brought in a bucket from a nearby hot water tank. The lords of hot water were the stokers who turned on the steam at regular intervals. There was always a rush at dinner time to fill the mess kettles for washing up, especially if the meat was mutton.

The multitude washed and shaved here at reveille, and immediately preceding the departure of liberty boats. Anyone wanting a bath waited until the bathroom was less crowded. Then he would fill an enamel bowl with hot water, strip naked, and apply soap suds universally, completing the process by tipping the bowl of water over his head.

'Dhobying" or washing clothes also centred here, but the usual custom was to take one's bucket of hot water to a convivial rendezvous and work in a social atmosphere. Drying was the main difficulty. The authorities were grudging the provision of suitable spaces, and if unexpected shore leave was piped a new dried clean shirt could vanish. Many ratings used the services of dhoby firms, operated either by stokers, or the friends of stokers having the privilege of using warm spaces near the boiler room. Except for the periods of First Lieutenants' or Captains' rounds there was never a time when a tablet of soap, maybe new, maybe thinned almost to non existence could not be found in the bathroom. Thus, it was always possible to go in and wash your hands without trouble. All men with cleaning duties were termed "sweepers", and the position of bathroom sweeper with its dhoby advantages was a coveted one, often traded for a stint of free dhobying.

Apart from the periods of night action stations, the sailor was not troubled by sleepless nights, indeed, in most cases he was inclined to take a nap whenever a suitable occasion occurred. Almost sacred to the grog drinker was the period for getting his head down "after dinner" on the fo'c'sle when the weather was kind, on the mess stool when it was not. Certain classes, like signalmen, were permanent watchkeepers with "four on—four off" in times of full activity, and occasional longer "off" periods. But the majority of seamen were watchkeepers only at sea in dangerous areas where the guns were constantly manned.

But excepting such times, there were always during the dark hours several occupied hammocks swinging on the seamans mess deck. The darkness was relieved here and there by the dull blue glow of the "police" lamps, and heedless of the pitch and roll of the ship, recumbent men with relaxed features slumbered peacefully. Very rarely one heard snoring, but it was not unusual for a sleeping man to utter a string of slurred words, not one of them distinct or intelligible. This hushed and shadowy surrounding gave a cloak and dagger atmosphere to the activities of those men from middle watch guns crews who came to "doctor" the Kye". "Kye" was the crude cocoa that was issued at mid watch to maintain stamina. The process was to take the "fanny" of "Kye" from the galley to the mess deck, proceed to a food rack of a mess other than that to which one belonged, and add generous doses of tinned milk and sugar. On the bridge a signalman would serve the officers with a more delicate brew derived from the familiar tins of Rowntree or Bournville. Some officers however were fanatically devoted to "Kye", which according to mess deck myth they were "not entitled" to drink. In naval lore, "Kye" was invested with fantastic properties, of which the most remarkable instance was that of a "Kye" drinking Chief Petty Officers wife in Malta; she conceived, and bore a child just a month before he returned from a two year commission.

Leave, or being set at "Liberty" for a few hours always began with an inspection by the Officer of the Watch. In U.K. the dress was usually blue flannels with white cap in summer, blue in winter. The turn out was always excellent, but in the beginning, the R.N.V.R's, although regarded with some tolerance by the inspecting officers, were according to the regulars, "dressed like scranbags". There were some grounds for this in the Mediterranean where the regulars sported cotton cloth, blue edged "Number sixes", and the reservists had only canvas suits. In home waters regulars all had cloth greatcoats, but reservists were issued only with oilskins. At Chatham, most reservists acquired greatcoats, but once back from Norway they were never worn again. Liberty men making for "shore" through a naval dockyard ran the gauntlet of scrutiny and report by the officers of any ship they passed. On return, if transport by launch was involved, every appearance of complete sobriety was enforced, and anyone singing was promptly silenced.

Quarrels were rare on board, but once in a while hasty words between junior ratings led to the challenge "All right then, hop up on the fo'c'sle" whereupon the aggrieved parties would scramble up the messdeck ladders with an excited throng at their heels. This was the prelude to a stand up fight between country lad "Dutch Holland" and a superior talking young rating from Kensington. "Dutch" promptly aimed a savage blow, and his adversary equally promptly took avoiding action which caused him to slip on the iron deck. Falling awkwardly, be broke one of his fingers so the fight was stopped. The sequel was his transfer to the hospital ship in Alexandria Harbour where he was detained for a month. This, and one or two other contests were the exception rather than the rule, as most grudges were fanned by the intoxicating atmosphere of the sailors haunts ashore and reached culmination in violence on the jetties whilst waiting for the last liberty boat back to the ship. At "hands fall in" next morning a number of faces were seen to be "filled in" (this is a sailors descriptive of a swollen face where the eyesockets are on an even contour with the remainder of the face), but apart from these occasional flurries every man aboard lived remarkably peacefully with his shipmates considering the close proximity of over four hundred men within such a confined space.

Sailing in the harbour was also very popular, and of course football. Whatever the climate or terrain, whenever a sailor could get ashore, he would organise a football match. The first pitches we played on had shallow trenches traversing them, but as our team improved we gradually ascended the scale until we finally played matches in Alexandria Stadium, a magnificent affair. Transport was always a problem as Alexandria has surely the longest dockyard in the world. The lavish service transport that was laid on later in the war was unknown at this time, the usual conveyance being only the rattling old tramcars. These were the more exciting events of life aboard, but much of the time was occupied in living out the somewhat monotonous daily routine when there was little prospect of interference by the enemy.

The peace time "constitutional" of scrub decks before breakfast was not practicable with camouflage paint on the decks, and was replaced by a drill to ensure better efficiency at the guns. After breakfast the bosun's mate would pipe "Both watches of the hands to muster on the upper deck" whereupon everybody would stand in lines facing inboard, and grouped according to "part of ship". Petty Officers checked that all were present and in the rig of the day, unless a rating was in one of those coveted positions which allowed the wearing of overalls.

Divisional Officers and their juniors grouped amidships, even more correctly attired. In general, the juniors concentrated on radiating confidence and cheerfulness, while their elders put on expressions of sober judgement. At a discreet distance, warily watching every detail stood the Chief Petty Officer Bosun, or "Buffer", and "in the wings" as it were, the two Gunnery Instructors, conspicuous by their smart turnout and alert bearing; although these men smiled now and then, it was of fleeting duration.

As soon as the First Lieutenant reached his place, the "Buffer" called the hands to attention, and reported their presence to him. This officer would as readily reply "Stand them at ease", and the action be taken. After a short conference between the First Lieutenant and the Divisional Officers, orders would be transmitted through the "Buffer" for various special parties to "Fall in amidships", and then proceed to work.

There were "sweepers" appointed for every conceivable space below decks, and even for the guns. If in harbour, there would be various boats crews, and the cleaners of whalers, and usually "side party", "gunners party", even "double-bottom" party to be called out. The man never mentioned in any of these musters was an important official known as the "Captain of the Heads", who was responsible for the seamens latrines.

Once the specialists had been set to work, the remainder would be detailed to work "part of ship" (the divisions were Fo'c'sle, Fore-top, Main-top and Quarter deck). Petty Officers of tops would then devise tasks of sweeping, scrubbing, washing paint work, scouring guard rail wires with wire brushes, or painting those same wires with boiled linseed oil. If in doubt, he could detail hands either to remove paint with chipping hammers; or put it on with brushes. The main object of the exercise appeared to be to save idle hands from temptation by the devil.

21

At mid-morning came the pipe "stand easy" when some hands took the opportunity to smoke, and all repaired to the mess-deck for a cup of tea, and ten minutes of chatter. "Up-spirits" piped at eleven o'clock brought many a smile of anticipation, and near midday "Clear up decks" was a prelude to "Hands to dinner".

After dinner "Both watches" was repeated, and work carried on, with the interruption of another "stand easy" until "Return stores" and subsequently "Hands to tea".

The dog watches, (from 4 P.M. to 8 P.M.), were generally periods of rest and recreation, except for those unfortunates liable to heed the pipes of "Men under punishment to muster". The last chore was initiated by a pipe calling on duty sweepers to clear up mess decks and flats for First Lieutenants' Rounds.

At nine o'clock "Jimmy", preceded by the Royal Marine bugler and attended by the Officer of the Day, Duty Petty Officer, and Master at Arms, or Regulating Petty Officer, made a tour of all mess decks and flats, ready to pounce on the slightest irregularity.

The days programme (daily orders) was always published on typewritten notices placed at strategic points, and every order initiated, was piped throughout the ship by a gang of "Bosun's mates".

In quite a short space of time this way of life had been assimilated by that considerable number of the ships company whose lives had until recently been programmed on more liberal lines. The younger element were in the main charmed by the novel surroundings and the Middle-East sunshine, but those with heavier responsibilities back home were not so easily contented. Doubtless the Captain had these in mind when later he commiserated with us at lying inactive in this lively fair weather anchorage. "I know", said he, "that you are all fed up with hanging around here, and would sooner be somewhere where you could have a smack at the enemy! But don't worry, your turn will come, and I believe that this war will largely be fought out here in the Middle East and in the Far East".

Yet, about a fortnight later, there was a slight commotion just before dawn, when special sea duty men and cable party were roused from their slumbers for duty. The hands came on deck to find "Coventry" cruising steadily westwards and there was quiet satisfaction. We renewed our brief acquaintance with Valetta and then reached Gibralter where the destroyers "Mohawk" and "Cossack" joined us. Next we noticed the rolling swell and growing chill of the Bay where the ship's amplifier gave us an accidental burst of "Lord Haw Haw", but he was switched off whilst closing his programme with a melodious rendering of "The Day Thou Gavest Lord is Ended". In the months that were to lengthen into years aboard "Coventry" that same amplifier would familiarise us with several ditties. Max Miller rendering "You Can't Go Away Like That", or "Winnie Gave a Whistle", and Leslie Sarony's ballad about "Sweet Fanny Adams". Older songs like "Any Old Iron", "With the End of My Old Cigar", and "I'm 'Enry the Eighth I am" were equally popular.

We were glad to be back in blue serge when Portland greeted us on a misty autumn morning, and we immediately noticed the long lines of neutral merchantmen detained for cargo clearance. Once anchored, Leading Seaman Heliwell took the mail ashore by the first boat. Half an hour later we saw him coming up the after gangway and heard him confide to the Corporal of Marines in an unsteady voice, "Royal Oak's gone!" This news had a noticeable effect on the older fleet reservists and pensioners, and during the afternoon cruise to Portsmouth the upper deck was crammed with men off watch ostensibly taking the air, but covertly alert to spot the peeping periscope. Conversation was sober, and all unnecessary noise was discouraged by some, who suspected that the enemy might hear it with a super scientific sound detector.

Darkness had fallen when we reached Portsmouth Harbour and the regulars commented on the phenomenon that for once the bright lights of the Queens Hotel were out. Immediately we were secured alongside a man came aboard selling milk from a churn. We were given a few days leave and found little change at home save more complete blast shields and sand bagging of all official buildings. A pronounced change was however noticed by one reservist, a volunteer from a distinguished profession. Once ashore he telephoned his wife who immediately hastened to join him. Celebrating their reunion with a well chosen meal in the most pleasant surroundings, the ensuing coversation, though lengthy, was checked by the thought of booking a hotel while the ship remained at Portsmouth. The nicest hotel was unfortunately fully booked when they enquired, so they tried another and were vexed to find it full too. At the third hotel a similar result, and by now they were tired of groping about the blacked-out and unfamiliar streets. On a dawning suspicion his wife made the next enquiry while her husband waited out of sight, and succeeded in booking in at the hotel. Her husband joined her in triumph to be told by an embarrassed receptionist that she must obey an "Officers Only" ruling. The returned hero contained his feelings and the pair were directed to a hostel befitting his ratings uniform, where they were very kindly received and well accommodated. Doubtless he smiled later, as did the rating at Invergordon in 1937 who related to me how a notice in Plymouth Park reading "Dogs and Naval Ratings not admitted" was removed at the remonstrance of an Admiral.

CHAPTER FOUR

ACTION STATIONS

The weekend leave was over all too quickly and we prepared to be off again, this time to the mouth of the Humber where the great coastal convoys from the north and south passed each other. So far the interest displayed by the German Air Force in our shipping had been very slight but a large attack on a convoy had been made in the North Sea and it was obvious that there were going to be more. Equally obvious was the likelihood that the attacks would be made where the concentration of ships was largest and the mouth of the Humber was one of these areas.

During the days of blacked-out Portsmouth the pensioners in "Coventry" were delighted to be replaced by fleet reservists, and with this slightly more vigorous complement we made our second departure from Pompey. (Why Portsmouth is known to naval ratings as "Pompey" is no more clear than why Plymouth is always called "Guz"). There were purposeful lookouts for air and surface, and no facetious remarks about the "Deutschland". Our course was north east and at dusk we entered a port where several merchantmen were docked, and were surprised to see women in dungarees working aboard. This was Immingham and we were anchored in the broad estuary of the Humber.

Next morning bright sunshine was soon driving the mist from the estuary surface. It was October 21st, Trafalgar day, but there were no official celebrations and nobody remarked on the anniversary. Men on the upper deck keenly watched the movement of river craft.

At mid-morning, a sense of excitement permeated the ship's company as the rumour spread that a convoy off the coast was being attacked by enemy aircraft, and there was speculation about "Coventry" proceeding to assist. Now was a chance to show that our four inch guns could "shoot them down like pheasants". There were orders summoning special sea duty men to their stations, the anchor was raised and secured, and "Coventry" moved forward at increasing speed. Beyond the wide mouth of the estuary rolled the sea, and just then "Sticks" Hancock, the seaman bugler, a dour leather faced man, sounded "action stations" with the panache of a concert artist.

The guns were quickly manned by ratings each complete with shrapnel helmet, anti-flash hood and gloves, and gas mask. All guns were very soon reported ready and we briefly surveyed the scene. Through a slight mist we could make out the lines of merchantmen to seaward with destroyers patrolling the flanks. There were one or two R.A.F. aircraft carrying out the same function at low altitude. The lapping of water and the whisper of a light breeze was all we could hear, and guns' crews relaxed from the tension started by the action bugle. On No. 1 gun, two men asked permission to visit the "heads" and Sub-Lt. Rogers, R.N.V.R., first time in action as officer of quarters, was in a momentary quandary. But the businesslike voice of First Lt. Junor passing on a round of inspection called "Let them hurry to it now"! I don't suppose anybody will want to miss the fun". The continued silence might have verged on anti-climax, until words calmly and clearly enunciated in a pleading tone of conviction by Lt. Briggs, the gunnery officer, drifted to our ears from the bridge above. "I'm sure it's one of theirs, sir"; and at that, the chatter of a Lewis gun aft fell on our ears. Then the boom of a tremendous explosion.

"All guns load, load, load" yelled the communication numbers. Ammunition supply men leapt to place their 56 lb. projectiles on the brass rollers of the fusing machine, whence they were snatched by another hand and punched into the semi-automatic breech by a third. As the steel breech block displaced the fist of the rammer, who took care to stand clear, the firing buzzer sounded, and the massive barrel whipped back so fast as to be invisible to the eye, while the 30 lb. projectile screamed skyward. Recuperated rapidly by two cylinders of compressed air, the gun breech opened to eject the brass casing of the spent propellant, and the next fused projectile was promptly rammed home. After several salvos loaded by sweating gunners had been loosed, the cease fire order came.

The fo'c'sle gunners glanced about them for evidence of a shattered foe, and glanced in vain, but the men on the after guns had seen a great salt water geyser spurting from where the bomb fell in "Coventry's" wake and realised what the enemy had intended for them. Some of the more aware ratings had heard the whine of aircraft motors and observed that the first enemy to attack "Coventry" had been a Dornier "Flying Pencil".

After the alarm and excitement of the attack, guns crews had settled down to a waiting role on the almost silent sea, when an order was received to keep a good look out and report any unusual surface object or disturbance to the bridge. A crew member on No. 1 gun was quick to notice what he thought to be a periscope on the starboard bow and urged a rapid report to the bridge. There an Aldis Lamp blinked, and a patrolling aircraft instantly changed course towards the suspected area of sea. The aircraft was seen to signal a destroyer which raced to the spot. Soon after "Coventry" shuddered several times as the shock waves of the depth charges hammered her. There was no surface manifestation of a successful attack but we trusted that "Coventry's" contribution had been effective in at least discouraging an ambitious U-boat captain from aggression.

At this stage the omission of dinner produced a ravenous hunger that even the excitement of a game of life and death could not hold off. Supplies of corned beef sandwiches brought to the guns by the galley staff were rapidly distributed and devoured, the odd sandwiches being allocated by lot. Eating brought relaxation and stimulated good humour; but soon fresh excitement came in the shape of a black sphere bobbing on the waves about a quarter of a mile from the ship. A floating mine was the guess of everyone. Several marksmen were issued with rifles and the ship slowed, but there were no hits. When the captain asked W.O. Simmons how much longer he wanted, the W.O. respectfully insinuated that were the captain in his position he would appreciate the difficulty of giving an answer. Meanwhile the marines opened fire from the quarter deck with a bren gun. Several clinks were heard but the sphere continued its tantalising dance. Thereupon the captain, wary of the possibility that U boats lurked, increased speed and resumed position.

At dusk we sighted Flamborough Head and several drifters, a poetic ending to the first day in action. For some time now the convoy had proceeded without alarm and in gathering darkness "Coventry" parted from the merchantmen, then relaxed to cruising stations and set course for Immingham.

On the mess deck the events of the day were recounted with cheerful satisfaction, and Able Seaman Norcott, loudly claimed to have averted disaster by opening fire with his Lewis gun while the bridge was debating whether or not the approaching bomber had hostile intent. Next evening the watch ashore explored blacked out Grimsby and returned with reports of unlimited prospects. They had heard that enemy aircraft had indeed been shot down, (doubtless by the guns of H.M.S. "Coventry"), and that some of the enemy, badly injured, lay in the local hospital.

A fault had developed in "Coventry's" steering gear, and repair at Immingham was possible. This entailed the blessings of five days home leave to each watch and of course several runs ashore in Grimsby. At home uniforms and sand bags kept the population aware of military preparedness, and now and then an old soldierly type would broach conversation about what it was like "out there".

But Immingham realised that it was no phony war, though exposed to nothing worse than red warnings. Whilst docked, "Coventry" sounded action stations and vainly looked about for something to shoot at. However, the destroyer "Jersey" berthed near us, was undergoing repair of damage inflicted by a torpedo which killed seven of the crew. The torpedo trainer, on watch in a cabin mounted on the torpedo tubes, went over the side and plunged to the depths with them, when "Jersey" was hit. And our sister flakship "Calcutta", on the other side of the dock, was suddenly ordered to put to sea during a moonless middle watch. The duty part of the watch from "Coventry" loosed the hawsers in silence, stumbling there and back over the sleepers of the freight truck rails.

For the shore goers there were varied attractions in Grimsby after the tram ride from Immingham dock. The darkness of the close packed vehicle was relieved by the glow of small dark blue electric lights which seemed to hypnotise all passengers to silence. Some went to the British Legion Club where dominoes was the vogue, others to various public houses. The local theatre had a good variety bill which included Elsie Carlisle singing "We're going to hang out the washing on the Siegfried Line". And of course there were cinemas. Those inclined to tell sensational tales made veiled references to a mysterious establishment termed "Betty Bloods". In the local newspaper there were reports of concern for the morals of both maidens and men in these early days of belligerency and blackout. In fact we were so riotously feted that the local Womens Institutes became quite alarmed and petitioned the Lady Mayoress to start a campaign to protect the innocent young sailors from the dangers of night life in Grimsby. Bless them, they meant well, but I am afraid this campaign was a great source of amusement on board, their zeal would have been far better directed in protecting the young maidens in the area. For months afterwards letters would arrive with a Grimsby postmark addressed to such fictitious characters as "Jack . . . ." believed to be a Stoker, H.M.S. "Coventry".

These worried people would have been delighted to know that when leave occurred in daylight a good many of the men from "Coventry" resorted to the bracing beaches of Skegness. There they met ratings from a training establishment occupying the site of an erstwhile holiday camp. The only remaining vestige of its gay trappings was the welcoming notice "Our true intent is all for your delight".

CHAPTER FIVE

MAINTAINING THE NORTHERN BLOCKADE

The men with dates ashore got a rude shock when in the chill of a November dawn, "Coventry" slipped downstream and was plunging on a choppy sea by full light. All around us were herring drifters tossing like corks, but the seamen manning them went about their business with the nonchalance of ordinary mortals on terra firma. The daylight run north was a stern test of newly acquired sea legs, but the wintry gale and dark clouds proved to be allies for us against the Luftwaffe, however zealous the pilots may have been to follow the Fuhrer's directives.

During the middle watch "Coventry" had entered the Pentland Firth, and by turns leapt, shuddered, and plunged in tremendous seas that threatened to overturn her. The cruising station gun's crews, most unlikely to be called into action at night on such a sea, were, under the direction of Sergeant Coombs, ordered to check all sea doors. To most of us it was a novel experience to cross the mess decks in darkness below a ceiling of swinging hammocks, on an improved version of the Brooklyn Cakewalk that we had tried at fair grounds in years past. Dried peas, broken crockery, rolling pins, with smashed jars of pickles and spilt rice and raisins, shuttled with the roll of the ship. The duty watch was remarkably cheerful, just in from the fresh air; in contrast to some of the men between decks who were beginning to turn green. None was more cheerful and encouraging in the work than Sergeant Coombs whose destiny, sad to relate, later took him to the ill fated battleship "Hood".

By morning light the seas were no calmer and few really enjoyed their breakfast. Chief Petty Officer Foster, the Buffer, on directions from a spruce looking First Lt. Junor, sporting a white silk scarf, mustered the hands and put them to clearing up the mess deck. Many of the reservists were struggling against the miseries of seasickness, and he did what he could to cheer them up by assuring them that he had been far worse when he started in a destroyer. The chief was a believer in reassurance. He had arranged for thick matting to be lashed to the guard rails by the guns as protection against bomb splinters; and whenever the topic of sustaining damage from the enemy was mentioned, he would say "You'll never find this ship sinking under you! Her designer copied the build of the German "Blucher" that wouldn't sink after half the fleet had blazed away at her for hours". On deck, the guns crews, when not occupied with "exercise action" ordered from the bridge, surveyed the raging sea and watched furious waves battering a series of turf capped skerries of varying sizes. Such were the effects of seasickness that some wished they were standing on the firm skerries.

These matters were trifling however in contrast to the problems to be dealt with by the Captain. Both "sea" boats had been damaged during the night, and just as the ship neared a dangerous rocky channel there was a report that the power steering apparatus had failed.

A party of seamen were quickly sent to man the huge iron wheel in the after tiller flat, and four hefty men strained on either side of the wheel. From a gangway above, the Chief Bosun's mate roared the orders transmitted from the bridge. "Port twenty",—minutes of hard labour as the wheelmen forced the heavy rudder against the pounding sea. Then "midships", and the frantic labour repeated. Some of the party began to imagine themselves back in the age of galley slaves, but the sense of danger permitted little reverie. On the bridge there was sudden tension. Rolling seas breaking over massive rocks were sighted dead ahead at less than a quarter of a mile away. Engines were instantly put astern. The ship was rolled and shaken by the opposing forces. For some minutes time stood still and it seemed that the rocks were closer. But disaster retreated, and the steering party, by continuous hard labour, directed "Coventry" on a safe course.

The storm eased as the morning wore on, and quite unexpectedly we entered the comparatively calm anchorage of Sullom Voe, an inlet to the mainland of the Shetland Islands. Under a sky of brilliant blue, flecked with the tail end clouds of the receding storm, we looked across an expanse of dark water to the stark landscape of crags of varied shapes, and green slopes without a single tree. On closer acquaintance we connected the treeless state with the constant hurricane winds that scoured the land, and noticed that the thatched roofs of cottages were secured by having at least two stout ropes across the ridge with a huge boulder hanging at either end. On the poor grass a few flocks of sheep grazed, and there was a collection of scattered grey stone houses, the homes of the hardy Shetland sheep farmers.

There were several ships in the Voe, noticeably the S.S. "Manila", a depot ship for the flying boats of the northern patrol, which ranged out over the lonely wastes of the Arctic Circle, patrolling the escape route beyond the minefields, the only hope for Hitler's raiders getting into the North Atlantic. It was our job to protect this ship and her brood of flying boats and we were not left in doubt for long of how important the Germans regarded the part she was playing in this vital sea strategy. The fleet oiler "War Diwan" and H.M.S. "Caradoc", a "C" class cruiser not converted to anti-aircraft armament were also in the bay. Aberdeen drifters were employed for runabout work and when one of them called "Friendly Girls" passed us, various witty comments were uttered.

We anchored in a central position, and a rapidly reviving ship's company having restored cleanliness and order was soon after piped to "stand easy". "Caradoc" was now under way and making for the exit, watched by the gun's crews that were on duty. The working parties meanwhile, chaffed over cups of tea at the mess tables. This was more like it—until the alarm rattlers filled all ears with a horrible metallic chuckle that had men to action stations in seconds.

A high flying Dornier was over the Voe, and soon the smoke puffs of our shells showed near it. The enemy maintained course in a dignified manner but went away, doubtless with a very clear picture to show the people at home. Once it was clear that no further danger threatened, routine was resumed. We reflected that here was the place mentioned in the newspapers, where our stupid enemy came regularly to jettison bombs on barren hills with now and then fatal results to the rabbits. Indeed some of us had seen and heard the Crazy Gang exposing these alleged cowardly flying men to ridicule as they sang "Run Rabbit Run".

The next morning was a pleasant one, and on routine duties we remarked on the clear water that allowed us to see small fish swimming close to the ship's side; but unexpectedly the alarm rattlers chattered and dispatched us immediately to action stations. After "all guns ready" there was a lull, and gunners looked vainly overhead and all around for the cause of alarm. In a building by the jetty a signal lamp blinked. Almost at once the director controlled gun laying and training clocks started to tick. All guns were trained on a gap in the hills backing the Voe. Silently we watched and waited. "Six of 'em!" rose a concerted yell, when two parallel rows, each of three approaching mono plane silhouettes filled the gap.

"Load, load, load", shouted the communication numbers. Projectiles waiting on the fuse machine were duly set and the fixed ammunition punched in the breech. The breeches almost instantly whipped back, and ejected the brass containers, then recuperated to be reloaded at once. Several salvos were loosed, but the aircraft came steadily on. "Barrage" was then ordered, and an advancing thicket of black smoke puffs and steel splinters was spread before the six approaching Heinkels. Thereupon, they turned away and made off.

Firing ceased, and everyone was exuberant, though here and there a man expressed disappointment that our attackers had departed calmly and unscathed. We found later however that morale in and around the Voe had risen high as a result of our demonstration which was far superior to the efforts of poorly armed "Caradoc". Unfortunately, the surprised six, cheated of their prey in the Voe switched their attention to Lerwick Harbour and destroyed two Sunderland flying boats moored there.

Extract from "The Shetland Times" 25th November 1940

Raiders' Visit

The German machines were Heinkel bombers, and they first appeared over the islands in the area where bombs were dropped on two occasions last week, apparently having as their objective naval and air craft. They met with heavy anti-aircraft fire, and, without dropping any bombs, made off in an easterly direction. Later, they were reported to be flying over Whalsay, and about five minutes after mid-day they flew over Lerwick, approaching from the north-east. Flying in formation the six planes flew exceptionally low over the town, at a height of about 150 feet, coming down almost as low as they could fly with safety, and the roar of their engines brought people out all over the town to watch with almost unbelievable surprise the squadron of enemy bombers passing closely overhead. Markings on the planes could be most easily seen, with crosses painted on the under-carriages, and some of the men in the planes could also be seen.

Attack On Flying Boat.

Flying southwards over the town, the planes banked at a low altitude, and turned westwards and then northwards where they made for the North Harbour. Breaking formation they swept over the harbour, where a flying boat was at mooring buoys, and opened machine-gun fire on the flying boat. They then circled the town again and came back over the North Harbour, and the planes dropped bombs which many people saw falling. Most of the bombs fell well clear of the flying boat, and another bomber

ADMIRAL SIR HORACE R. LAW, K.C.B., O.B.E., D.S.C., A.D.C.
The Commander in Chief Naval Home Command

Plate One

PETTY OFFICER A. E. SEPHTON, V.C.
Killed in Action 18th May, 1941.

H.M.S. "COVENTRY"

Plate Three

A.B. George Sims

Ldg. Seaman E. Skelly

A.B. F. Risdon

A.B. "Johnnie" Kirk

This Group Includes Petty Officers Goldring, Simmonds, Davenport (C.P.O.)
Sephton, Bracking, Cousens, Ryder, and Brown.

A.B. Skelly

A.B. Skelly   A.B. Connell   A.B. Ellis   Signalman Chambre   Ldg. Seaman Gardiner

Plate Five

Enemy Raid on Shetland 13th November 1939

First Bombs Aimed at "COVENTRY" in Shetland

Cartoon by A.E.L. Lews

A.B's Conner, Middleton, Halloway
(Front Row) P.O. Jenkinson, A.B's Lusty, Carr and Battersby

A.B's Levett, Delmer, Mott, Foster, Wingrove, H. Sims, Kirby
(Front Row) Sullivan, Woods, Weaver

A.B's Troughton, Nelson, Connell, Troughton, Skelly

Plate Seven

Ammunitioning Ship

Filling Ready Use Lockers

dropped what was thought to be a torpedo, which exploded in the sea some distance from the boat, throwing up a huge column of water. The next plane also dropped a torpedo which fell wide of the mark, and another column of water was seen.

Flying Boat Set On Fire

The bombers continued their attack on the flying boat, five planes dropping further bombs. One of the German planes dived over the flying boat and machine-gunned it, and the boat caught fire, flames and a huge column of smoke shooting up, which could be seen from most parts of the town.

Henceforth, "action stations" was routine from daylight to dark, but the enemy kept away. A prize of £1 was offered by the Captain for the first man reporting an enemy aircraft, and after several days A.B. Caspar an ever neatly dressed "Geordie" regular claimed the prize. His aircraft was obviously on reconnaissance, as it confined its activities to flying high on a course directly above and straight down the Voe. Several salvos were loosed, but treated with frigid disdain by the enemy. This pantomime was repeated on several occasions much to the annoyance of the gunnery staff. But one morning three Heinkels made a very brisk approach on more or less parallel courses, and dropped their bombs reasonably close, roaring off soon after. One of them, however strafed the fo'c'sle with his machine guns at the end of his dive. A loading number on No. 1 gun saw the hem of the trainer's duffel coat being nibbled away and realising the cause was bullets, fainted. Some time after the enemy had gone we learned that Able Seamen Harry Sims and Arthur Wingrove, the layer and trainer respectively of No. 1 gun had been fanned so close by the death dealing stream of bullets that their under vests were cut through and skins grazed.

The First Lieutenant organised football games between "Coventry" and "Manila", having found a suitable level stretch of peaty ground on a plateau half a mile from the jetty. One afternoon the game was interrupted by three roaring planes approaching low near the ground. The teams broke off playing, looking wildly for non existent cover and making for the nearest ditch. A shout of "they're Gladiators, play on" was a welcome relief. Sure enough they were the tough compact little biplanes that were to fight so gallantly in Malta and Norway, and they gave us a tremendous uplift seeing them bank steeply and turn away with roaring motors back to their base at Wick.

Shore leave was also given to a part of the watch during the afternoons and we would make the long run in to the jetty in the motor boat, often getting soaked if the sea was choppy. It was vigorously exhilarating striding over the hills, the greenness of the landscape, the windy sky, and the glint of the sea. We would sometimes come across a lonely cottage where a crofter and his family lived their simple life, raising sheep and weaving the famed Shetland Wool. They were shy but friendly folk, desperately poor but proud of their heritage.

The Captain's greatest fear seemed to be the onset of boredom in the ship's company. Football, walks ashore, and evening excursions to the cinema or canteen of "Manila", even with Alice Faye on the screen, were not in his opinion adequate. So he arranged for a bus to take parties of liberty men to the bright blue lights of Lerwick at intervals. As accommodation was strictly limited, on the single antiquated bus, the order of opportunity was chosen by lottery.

Local maidens, who mostly cherished an ambition to marry off the island, quickly introduced the lads to the pleasant cafes that had seen no tourists since Mr. Chamberlain's declaration. For the older hands, a beer bar had been specially opened for service men; because Shetlanders had voted the islands dry in the far off days when a little alcohol down the throats of the polyglot fisher crews thronging the town during the herring season meant hell let loose.

The bus left Sullom at dusk with neatly dressed and alert men. Several of the men joining the return bus from Lerwick were in varying states of conviviality. The road was narrow, and the route picturesque. Now across a peat heath, then through a rock gorge, sometimes along the shore of a voe, often perched on a precipice above the sea with foaming rocks far below. Usually the revellers sang limericks with great content to a scandalous chorus that began "Little Robin Redbreast". About the most refined lyric was "A policeman from Andover Junction" diffidently rendered by a young R.N.V.R. rating. Now and then harmony was incomplete. An argument would be continued by resorting to "filling in stations" and combat was joined while some continued to sing, and others cheered on the belligerents. The bus would begin to rock crazily on the dark and dangerous narrow road, with the motion adding to the fury of the contest and the total din.

On one occasion the bus jarred to a halt, and the driver, white faced, appeared through the snatched open door to yell "If you stupid bastards must fight, settle it outside now! We nearly toppled off the cliff back there". It was obvious that the driver would not continue the journey until some semblance of order was restored in the bus. Added to this crisis was the news that "Blackie" was missing from the bus, although he had definitely been at the embarkation point. "Blackie" was a Royal Naval Reservist stoker, a veteran of Jutland, who always looked as if he had just stepped out of a coal bunker in a Dreadnought. Short and square with small black eyes under bushes of black eyebrows with a fringe of greasy hair completely covering what little forehead he had. Grumblingly the contestants slumped away to their seats with a great show of reluctance. As the aisle cleared Blackie emerged into view. He had been lying in the gangway under the trampling feet during the whole of the battle and was obviously long past the stage where he was feeling no pain at all. So the two problems were resolved in one and the driver was able to proceed on his arduous and difficult journey.

Back aboard "Coventry" an enquiry followed, and on the reluctant testimony of those whose senior rating obliged them to give evidence, Jock Harkison was convicted,wrongly, according to some of those present. This led to his being drafted, and ultimately joining the "Hood".

One returning bus was remarkably well behaved. R.P.O. Scott happened to be aboard. On arrival at Sullom, however, there was a shrieking gale, and such wild seas that no boat could be sent to bring back the revellers. At the suggestion of the R.P.O., a signalman struggled against the wind, clutched a post on the jetty, and signalled with a pocket torch. He returned after fifteen minutes to report failure. "Give me that flaming torch" roared Scott, "I'll make those blind bats see something". He rushed into the blackness toward the jetty. A few minutes later he returned, minus cap and torch, soaked to the skin and his number one suit badly tattered and oozing with a thick smelly slime. Having fallen off the jetty, fortunately into shallow water, he had returned to curse the fates and anything else that came to his mind. The revellers listened with sympathy and respect before dozing fitfully. In chill discomfort they dragged out the hours of darkness keeping as respectful a distance from "Scotty" as the confines of the bus would permit. At morning light the seas were less wild, and a cheerful energetic crew brought in the motor boat for the marooned travellers.

Up to now, such infractions of discipline as had occurred in "Coventry" had been within the competence of the "Courts" presided over by the First Lieutenant or Captain, with the well known penalties of stoppage of leave, and pay, and penal tasks during normal hours of leisure.

But soon after the initiation of "Lerwick leave" two A.Bs who missed the return bus decided to stay in town until "Authority" caught up with them. Rumour had it that each had met a most accommodating hostess, and had charged such shipmates as they had met to "Tell the Captain we'll be back when our money's gone". Both men were in the regular service, and both were of the errant type known as "skates" in the mess-deck vernacular. In due course they returned to the ship, and were questioned by the first Lieutenant.

For an offence of this gravity, the Captain was obliged to submit the evidence and recommended penalty for Admiralty scrutiny, and in due course a "Warrant" authorising punishment arrived. Thereupon the following ceremony ensued.

The whole ships company were mustered, and in the presence of the offenders, the First Lieutenant read out the "Articles of War" as applicable to the offence. This certainly made an impression, as for most offences the punishment was "Death, or such other punishment as may be hereinafter mentioned".

Thereupon, the circumstances of the offence were related followed by the statement " . . . . I, Bruce Balfour Junor, did personally and publicly investigate the matter, calling the Officer of the Watch who stated . . . ., and the accused who stated . . . ., and he calling no-one on his behalf, I did adjudge him guilty". The facts of the case, with all the evidence, having been thus related to the whole ships company the Admiralty sentence was promulgated, and the ships company dismissed.

In this case, the two offenders besides losing several weeks pay, and all prospect of leave for some months, were discharged from the ship to serve a period in cells. Justice was clearly seen to be done. On an occasion about a year later when a much younger "Coventry" A.B. was due for "Cells", a friend who was older, and moreover had experienced this punishment himself, confided to the departing victim "Go in wearing a thick jersey under your shirt, and if "he" says anything about it, tell him you've got a cold or something. Because I can tell you that if you don't, it's so cold at night you won't get any sleep". Such was the camaraderie of Naval "criminals", and quite a number of Masters at Arms seemed to treat men sentenced to severe punishment with a degree of kindness that seemed incompatible with their official duties. Most Petty Officers in detention barracks, however, were of a different character.

To many of the ship's company the scenery of the Shetland Isles lacked appeal. One morning however there was a spectacle of unusual interest. Anti aircraft guns manned by the Army were ultimately to defend the Voe and a long line of ant like men were seen making organised progress up a slope to a prospective gun position. For a start they were lightly laden, but as the morning wore on it was obvious that considerable exertion was now being coaxed from them to complete their tough assignment. The advantages of being a naval gunner were now appreciated by men who had not realised that there were any alternatives.

The Shetland day began to get very short and this made visits by the Luftwaffe so difficult that they seemed to have forgotten us. There was time to anticipate Christmas pretty well as usual. Not completely of course, as the rumour of the savage sinking of the "Rawalpindi" by the Scharnhorst made us realise that the Shetland Norway patrol was in the teeth of the war. On one occasion a boatload of Scandinavians from a torpedoed merchantman came rowing into the Voe as nonchalantly as if they had been paying a social call. The news of a Russian attack on Finland made small impression, and the "Graf Spee" victory was not fully appreciated. It was a great boost to morale when full details were known. About the middle of December, wonderful food parcels arrived from home, and in addition the Lerwick butcher provided excellent pork and poultry. I never enquired about the reception given by his mess mates to an inebriated stoker who hugged a leg of pork all the way from Lerwick, and dropped it over the side as he transferred his weight somewhat unsteadily from the launch to the after gangway.

The number of days to Christmas grew smaller and it became evident that we should spend Xmas aboard the "Coventry". A concert was organised, and when the mail arrived with the parcels from home we were all set for Xmas that was the next best thing to Xmas at home. On Xmas Eve we were invited by the R.A.F. to a cinema show and sing song on the "Manila". This was a great success as the R.A.F. mess was not dry as on board H.M. Ships, beer was not only obtainable but plentiful.

On Christmas day we were at action stations earlier than usual. The Captain explained, by recounting a Christmas morning during 1914-1918, when aircraft from his ship were launched for an attack on Wilhelmshaven. During the morning the destroyers "Icarus" and "Inglefield" entered the Voe. Their Christmas celebration was to be a few hours in harbour, and the opportunity to visit the draughty tin shed on the jetty where the Naafi sold beer. An empty sack started a journey round "Coventry's" mess decks, and when full of assorted delicacies for the festive table, plus a supply of freshly baked bread, was presented to the destroyers.

At dusk the guns crews were thinking only of the coming festivities, when "Coventry" received a disconcerting signal from "Inglefield". It requested "Coventry" to send a boat for the body of a rating who, having over indulged in neat rum, laid on his back in drunken sleep and was asphyxiated by his own vomit. The Captain decided to avoid the complete ruin of the festive occasion by sending the body ashore, and enjoining the motor boat's crew to keep silence.

For them, the journey from "Inglefield" to the jetty with their lifeless burden was an eerie experience, as the boat swam steadily through drifting banks of mist across the dark and silent water. The shrouded corpse was manhandled to the end of the jetty where the Post Office stood nearby. The Gunnery Officer, who was in charge of the party knocked loudly on the door of the house. To the startled Post Mistress he explained his errand, hopeful that she might relieve him of the corpse. She was understandably shocked, and suggested the church. Again the party took up its burden, and slipping and sliding on stony paths, or stumbling in unnoticed puddles, were thankful to reach the church. The Minister was roused and notwithstanding the macabre apparition from the Voe immediately agreed that the body should rest in the church overnight.

On board "Coventry", the guns crews left their guns when complete darkness had covered the Voe. They had time to clean into "number ones", ready to start the traditional festivities. The mess deck was gaily decorated with a mixture of naval signal flags and coloured bunting, plus the holly, tinsel, and cotton wool snow, dear to the civilian. Blown up rubber condoms served as balloons. The mess tables were laid with customary Christmas extras and with all treasured family photographs on view. The Captain and officers, unusually relaxed and cheerful, visited every mess and enquired the health of the ratings and their families. This ceremony was not prolonged, and the mess cooks were to receive the "ready" signal from the galley at its conclusion. The long awaited signal came and the festive meal lasted much longer than the routine ship board meal. The officers had very kindly arranged for every rating to be presented with a bottle of beer. Those who subsequently ventured on the upper deck encountered a snow storm, and by morning a white pall covered everything on and around the black waters of the Voe.

At the routine action stations next day in Christmas card scenery, there was a distinctly charitable atmosphere.

The next special event was an inquest concerning the death of the "Inglefield" rating, attended by the Captains of most of the ships in the Voe. Next day, a funeral party in charge of Petty Officer Layhe attended the service in the church. From there they carried the coffin three quarters of a mile across snow covered fields to the hillside cemetery. The words of committal were spoken, the farewell shots fired, and with the grave diggers bare headed standing by, the coffin was lowered. Ceremony over, Petty Officer Layhe marched his party promptly to the beer canteen, and stimulated lively conversation until our boat breasted the jetty.

The snow lay several days on those parts of "Coventry's" upper works away from the guns but was eventually cleared in a general snow ball battle involving all hands—Officers and ratings!

On New Year's Eve, Lerwick leave was at a premium, and even so an attempt was made to bribe the driver to stage a breakdown. He refused, saying that there had been one breakdown on Christmas Eve and the coincidence would be too strong. The lucky ones enjoyed fabulous hospitality and reluctantly left the homes of feasting, singing, and dancing, to catch the return bus.

Next morning routine started, and there was the inevitable talk of New Year resolutions; but it was sternly interrupted when the rattlers chattered. The ship's company, vaguely realising that here was an attack before the customary opening hours, found the enemy close upon them, and shooting started as soon as the guns were ready. This enterprising Dornier did not attack from seaward, but approached from the inshore end of the Voe, to be welcomed by successive clusters of black smoke bursts and steel fragments. (It was said that the shells were travelling so slowly at the height of the plane that the pilot might see them coming. However war time pilots have never confirmed this).

Flying high, and on a steady course, the Dornier came from astern, and the gunnery staff were anxious to get a convincing hit. Petty Officer Goldring, Quarters Officer of No. 4 and 5 guns, which were situated on the raised iron deck in the ship's waist, was intoning the essentials of good shooting as if at a special parade on Whale Island, and improving the effect with a honeyed voice that radiated encouragement. Then the enemy's nose dipped and Goldring ejaculated "Blimey, he's going to dive bomb us". Just before this, many guns had made successive reports that they were not bearing. This skilful attack could now be met only by the multiple point-five Vickers machine guns aft.

The four inch guns crews stood idly gaping as the silent grey attacker dived, watching his projecting machine guns, and waiting for the Vickers to beat them to it. The Vickers spat a short burst and Chief Petty Officer Davenport saw the tracers stream into the fuselage. Then two barrel like objects, apparently chained together, left the aircraft and hurtled towards us. In my ears sounded the confident voices of Gunnery Officer Lecturers with their convincing argument about the near impossibility of a bomb hitting a moving ship. Fortunately I did not reflect that anchored "Coventry's" movements were restricted to short slow swings in alternate directions. Spellbound I watched the falling objects, slowly nearing us, and was just conscious of the odd crouching postures assumed by idle gunners to use any possible cover. The Chief Ordnance Artificer, oil can in hand, stalked as rapidly forward as his dignified status allowed. With relief I saw the falling objects splash into the Voe a few yards from the ship's side. I was about to rejoice when "Coventry" was flung violently upwards. The deck seemed to rise and hit me in the face. Next there was a nauseating drop which tumbled me on deck. After this a deluge of salt water.

The Dornier checked its dive in time and circled the Voe a few feet above the waves. "Coventry's" gunners tried to follow it with four inch shells, and every other ship in the Voe spat a stream of fire to back up the hail from "Coventry's" forward mounted pom pom. A bright flash was seen near the Dornier's cockpit, and this was variously interpreted as fire, signal lamp, or the flash of a machine gun. But the enemy was gradually able to gain height and fly seaward.

Later that day we heard how the men below decks, thrown against the bulwarks as the ship reared up, were plunged into utter blackness when the electric supply failed; then heard the gurgling of water in every direction.

One imaginative signalman, who was on duty at the post office telephone kiosk at the time, asserted that waiting customers ducked under the counter as pom pom shells burst on the paving outside. The depot ship men had followed the contest with commendable keenness, and were that same evening able to sell us a good snapshot of "Coventry's" near miss.

Daring Attack on Warship

According to eye-witnesses from the district, an attack was made on a warship of H.M. Navy, which was one of two which were in a Shetland voe at the time. It was a little after 10.15 that people in the district first heard the sound of enemy aircraft. The two planes were seen flying very high. Soon afterwards they encountered sharp bursts of anti-aircraft fire, and then there was a period of quiet as the aeroplanes circled out of range. About 10.45 they returned to the attack, and one of the bombers made a daring and desperate attempt to bomb one of the warships. At first, onlookers saw one of the machines flying fairly high and drawing the anti-aircraft fire upon it. They next saw the other machine circle round at a lower level until it was between the sun and the warship. From a height of a few thousand feet it power-dived upon the warship. Swooping almost to the masthead, it discharged two heavy bombs, both of which fell into the water. From the shore a huge mass of water and smoke was seen to rise around the warship, temporarily obscuring it from view. The aeroplane flattened out and went away in a north-easterly direction, and for a few moments disappeared over the hill. Then it turned and flew up the voe in a southerly direction, flying very low once it had passed the warship on which its attack had been made. The warship opened a terrific barrage upon the plane, which appeared to be in trouble and was seen to wobble.

Driven Off By Fighters

British fighters made their appearance shortly afterwards. People in the North Mainland and the Island of Yell saw a dog-fight between a British fighter and one of the bombers, and another bomber was seen flying away further south with a fighter in hot pursuit.

Sheep Killed and Telegraph Wires Cut.

Shells from the anti-aircraft guns fell over a wide area. One dropped in Yell and pieces of shrapnel were found miles from the scene of firing. Some shells passed very close to houses, and a piece of shrapnel went through the roof of a shop in the North Mainland. As a result of the gunfire on the plane as it was flying low, five or six shell holes were made at the places where unexploded shells had hit the gound. Another anti-aircraft burst killed three sheep which were grazing on a hill. Telegraph wires were severed either by a shell or by splinters. The wires were cut half-way between two poles, and, as they were taut with the frost, they would easily snap.

Everybody's wits were sharpened by this event, and there was a rush to the guns some days later when aircraft engines droned overhead. But it was a false alarm. A week later, however, three Heinkels arrived and began their attack without ado, all from the same direction. The guns gave them a hot reception and bombs were hastily released from a moderate height to fall wide.

The next event took the form of a "flu" epidemic which rapidly filled the sickbay and necessitated an annexe in the recreation space. But by now the army guns were ready. On February 15th, therefore, the medical officer made a quick round of his domain and declared almost everybody fit for duty.

Shortly after "Coventry" raised anchor and headed for the sea, after first clearing tangled cables from mountains of empty tin cans on the sea bed with frozen fingers which seemed to fuse to the cold steel of the wires. Passing the skerries we took a good look at the crags and rock cliffs of the hospitable island and quite a few hoped for a return. "Coventry" thrashed along at top speed through the wintry seas without incident, until the freezing climate of the Humber estuary gripped us. Here we had reached an area heavily sown with magnetic, acoustic, and other ingenious types of mine; so the order "clear the lower deck" was given, to increase survival chances should "Coventry" be unlucky. Going slowly through a swept channel we noticed several mast tops just clearing the surface and even more melancholy was the sight of an Italian merchantman sunk by the stern, bows skyward like a cathedral spire above the mist banks on a cold grey sea.

There was excitement next afternoon when it became clear that we were approaching Chatham, though the evidence of sunken shipping sobered us. After the Shetlands, the dockyard seemed like bedlam. Once secured, leave was piped, and Londoners made a bee line for the railway station. Many stopped en route to buy service greatcoats. In the Shetlands we had been kept warm by our civilian overcoats brought aboard earlier on the advice of Captain Onslow.

At home we were welcomed, and in the case of my own home, had the benefit of a special delivery of coal because the coalman was so pleased about the navy taking Altmark in a recourse to ancient boarding tactics. In "Coventry" guns had served us well; not for us to consider the great expense of ammunition, and that the enemy aircraft were at the limit of their range.

Sung to the Tune of "Big Hearted Arthur"

"Men dressed as seamen they call us
Otherwise sons of the sea
Working from morning till evening
Cleaning the old "Coventry"
All of our guns are well plastered with brass
But Quarters Clean Guns is a bit of a farce
Except when the Gunner's Mate happens to pass
Men dressed as seamen they call us
Otherwise sons of the sea.

Jerry once used to call on us
But now he is as shy as can be
At six of his planes we once fired with zest
The locals all think that our shooting's the best
But if we are good gunners then God help the rest.

Two Dorniers called in on New Year's Day
To assist us in making whoopee
With four inch we slaughtered the sheep on the shores
The point fives were silent from some unknown cause
And half the ships company needed clean drawers."

A.B. George Sims.

CHAPTER SIX

REFIT AT CHATHAM

It was pleasant to be in dock at Chatham with the prospect of a lengthy refit. One of the items was to re-align engine room machinery unseated by the near miss at Sullom. Londoners shuttled to and from home, either by train or in the cars of the Volunteers, who always filled every seat with shipmates. There was an almost revolutionary portent in "men dressed as seamen" riding in cars over the carriageways which discipline decreed to be the proper place for ratings when walking. (The pavements were for officers only). The later trips were especially pleasant on those early spring days with budding trees and golden sunshine. Gas masks were carried as an essential part of uniform, and it was not wise to leave these unwatched when calling at the Royal Sailor's Rest in the morning for a cup of tea before going back aboard.

The provincials used their leisure roaming Chatham, with its narrow streets, and pride in its connection with the Royal Navy, Royal Engineers and Charles Dickens. Even the dockyards still preserved a ship-building slipway on which the wooden walls of byegone days had taken shape. The principal entertainment offered to the town's floating population was the old fashioned public house with its even older fashioned denizens.

Refit gave the opportunity to paint ships side in slow time, and with meticulous care. One group that kept together on neighbouring stages hailed from Wales and revelled in singing. Led by Able Seaman Logan they made the working days seem short with their melodious verses. A comic element was ever present and especially when the choir rendered a slightly amended version of that old ballad chorus "You take to the boats lads, you save yourselves". Singing was very much evident, too, in the shore bathrooms where dhobying took place in the evenings. It would not have disgraced a cathedral choir had ditties like "Home on the Range" and "Coming Round the Mountain" been less blatantly secular.

While the sailors home from sea frolicked in a pacific routine, they saw each day evidence that the Admiralty contemplated activities of a truly military nature. Every morning, the "Battalion", comprising seamen wearing webbing equipment, and with rifles at the slope issued from barracks, led by the Chatham Seamen's band. They proceeded to a large area of waste land to practice infantry manoeuvres. In the evening, again led by the band, they would return with a serious martial demeanour, unusual in matelots. One "Coventry" rating recognised a former shipmate in the ranks, and subsequently met him in the barrack canteen. He was told of a lecture to some of the "Battalion", informing them that they would in the near future be landing on an island where there might be some anti-British feeling!

The newspapers revealed only isolated facets of the war. Shipping losses quoted in thousands of tons to a public shy of arithmetic, and knowing little of ships, blurred realisation of the endless struggle by merchantmen, escorts, and mine sweepers against 'U' boat, mine and bomber.

One Sunday paper, however, carried an article that pointed beyond the Maginot Line. Leslie Hore Belisha likened the iron ore supply reaching Germany from Sweden to a pistol aimed at Britain's heart. The Finns had just signed a peace treaty with Russia, thus silencing the many advocates of British troops joining in that fray.

An event which made more of an impression aboard "Coventry", however, was the departure of Captain Onslow, First Lt. Junor and Gunnery Officer Lt. Briggs. The first replacement was Commander Norman as First Lieutenant. He had the habit of always carrying a telescope when on duty, and this in the dockyard. Shortly after he joined, a large quantity of stores arrived and with them a film unit to record the brisk way in which the "Silent Service" took stores aboard. Most shots showed ratings moving "at the double". Subsequently a propaganda film called "A Cruiser Prepares for War" included some of these shots.

Two of the after 4" guns which had somewhat restricted firing arcs were removed, and extensions made to both masts for carrying contraptions of rods that were said to be aerials. Next to the mizzen mast, a roomy iron cabin was fitted. These additions were vaguely referred to as "R.D.F."

On April 9th, 1940, the radio and newspapers went into convulsions about the Scandinavian Blitz. Frequent repetition of the words "All ships in the Skagerak will be sunk" pleased everybody. Captain Warburton—Lee's tragic victory at Narvik had made it clear that the navy was on top, and the loss of H.M.S. "Glowworm" was made bearable by harping on the human kindness of the Commander who had turned back to search for a man lost overboard. The story of Quisling checked enthusiasm by introducing a healthy uncertainty. One heard of acquaintances serving in the Norway ships who had been injured, and began to wonder whether the Luftwaffe at Trondheim, was a worse proposition than the Luftwaffe at Sullom. "Coventry" was meanwhile fitted with "degaussing" gear, which rendered magnetic mines innocuous. It was at this period that a bunch of ratings arrived on board to operate the "R.D.F." Prominent among them were A.B. Alastair Durno and A.B. Jack Crowther, straight from a training course at Skegness. Few of the ship's company were curious about the new installation, and the operators never discussed it.

Commander Norman unexpectedly restricted weekend leave to near compassionate cases. Then something got into the traditionally lethargic dockyard maties which transformed them to human dynamos. They cleared off the ship in a few days. Their last effort was to erect waist high fences of thick steel plates at the ship's side around gun positions.

There came a rumour that an Admiral was to take up residence in the Captain's cabin. Then Captain Gilmour joined the ship; and Lt. Commander Dreyer, famous in the "Graf Spee" action, came as gunnery officer. Rear Admiral Vivian ultimately arrived, and on the 29th April we left the dockyard for Sheerness to take on ammunition. The lyric of a popular song which asked "Who's the lucky boy who's going your way?" was now parodied as "Who's the lucky boy who's going to Norway?" The first "buzz" was Tromso where arctic night was then in season. Just as well thought some.

On the 2nd May, "Coventry" was leaving Sheerness under sombre grey clouds that were about to weep rain. We noticed an approaching warship and were intrigued to identify it as belonging to our own class. "Curacoa" was entering harbour. She should have looked like "Coventry" but the tripod main mast was gaunt and bare; all the lower works had been blasted away by a 500 lb bomb she had collected off the coast of Norway. Unlucky "Curacoa" was ultimately sliced in two by the "Queen Elizabeth" whilst in convoy. The crowded troopship struck the cruiser amidships with apalling loss of life. Many old comrades of H.M.S. "President" days, including the Gunnery Officer, Lieut. D. H. Bodger, died in this tragedy.

CHAPTER SEVEN

NORWAY

Proceeding north through the mine swept channel the Captain tested the hastily installed R.D.F. and it's newly trained operators. R.D.F. was an old name covering a new method for using a radio transmission to find and report the height and bearing of clouds for the needs of meteorology. Robert Watson Watt had realised the military potential and here was it's earliest application at sea. There were no technicians to service the apparatus, and operators with three months training began their trade as "Pointers" to the suddenly aggressive Luftwaffe. Both the Captain and operators were dismayed at the disappointing results of tests initiated when friendly aircraft were sighted.

On arrival at Rosyth glorious sunshine welcomed us, and we were cheered by shore leave. For many it was the first sight of the magnificent bridge as we passed under to anchor in the broad roads. Returning at dusk we were to hear from "Aurora" ratings tales of disaster concerning a landing in Norway made by the Territorial Regiment of Sherwood Foresters. The losses were of course attributed to over-ardent leadership. Hindsight would show that this confused rumour was better for our morale than an informed military critique would have been.

Some items in "Daily Orders" showed the lines on which the First Lieutenant was thinking:—Watertight Openings—a number of instances have occurred since leaving Chatham of watertight openings being improperly secured by ratings leaving the compartment. The watertight subdivision of the ship is vital. Secondary Lighting—Oil secondary lighting is to be kept burning at all times. This is the responsibility of the Lamp Trimmer, who is to go frequent rounds to attend to the filling and trimming of lamps.

On the 7th May there were gunnery and R.D.F. trials. R.D.F. was still poor, but before long the Gunnery Officer, Lt. Commander Dreyer, would be heard to say that R.D.F. gave a range plot that gunnery officers had hitherto only dreamed about. That evening we left Rosyth. Next morning at 10 a.m. we were riding in the familiar waters of Sullom Voe, and overhead was a snooper flying too high for type recognition. We left at noon. All next day we pursued a course north by east.

Consideration of unpleasant possibilities was initiated in "Daily Orders":—Six torches, for use by repair parties will be placed in each of the following positions . . . . Failure of electric power and oil secondary lighting may be expected after a near burst of a large bomb, and it is essential that an adequate supply of electric torches is immediately available to repair parties. And the next day's orders instructed all ratings to wear steel helmets when on duty, and to keep them handy at all times. Further, explanatory sketches showed the most effective methods of taking cover from either shell fragments or bomb splinters.

By now we were expecting the Luftwaffe at the end of every minute, and waited to check the performance of our new H.O. (Hostilities Only) gunners against the Shetland veterans they had replaced. We had not long to wait, for at mid morning R.D.F. reported aircraft, and shortly afterwards we saw approaching us a small convoy which was being heavily bombed. On our meeting the convoy another group of bombers tried to sink it. Though not under direct attack, our guns entered the quarrel and we saw that our new gunners were, if anything, more war-like than those they had replaced. The returning ships were "Penelope" and "Isis", both of these damaged and under tow at six knots, with "Calcutta", "Zulu", "Campbell", "Witch", and two merchantmen.

That evening we were joined by two British "J" Class destroyers and the French destroyer "Fougueux". Next day we sighted the fang like rocks of the southern tip of the Lofoten Islands made famous by Edgar Alan Poe in"The Maelstrom", and soon after a spouting whale. Towards midnight, moving in the eerie twilight of the arctic circle, the alarm rattlers made us leap to action stations. But soon after, we were delighted to recognise the approaching aircraft as Skuas from "Ark Royal". It might be a quiet number after all!

Then we approached Ofot Fjord over quiet black waters hemmed in by towering white hooded mountains. We passed a French destroyer and then one wearing the flag of Poland. Once accustomed to the weird arctic light, one might accept this scene as being suitable for a specially romantic Christmas card.

Nevertheless, Commander Norman promulgated "With constant changes from action to defence stations, the supply of meals becomes extremely complicated. If it so happens that you yourself don't get enough to eat, inform your O.O.Q., (Officer of the Quarters) and don't just have a howl about it.
Arriving in Ofot Fjord we noticed several moored ships well dispersed and with a forlorn appearance.

These were ammunition ships, manned only when a warship came alongside to replenish magazines. Our first duty was to guard H.M.S. "Eskimo", which had reached Skjel Fjord with its bows shorn right back to the bridge, after receiving a hit from two torpedoes in the second battle of Narvik. Rounding the narrow entrance from Rombaks Fjord we perceived "Eskimo" lying in the shelter of the sheer mountain side, where she had withstood several bombing attempts and machine gun strafings. At some distance on the opposite shore lay the wreck of the enemy destroyer "Hans Ludeman". "Coventry" anchored opposite "Eskimo", taking advantage of similar mountainside shelter. "Eskimo" was awaiting the arrival of H.M.S. "Vindictive", whose shipwrights would prepare her for the tow home.

Her aldis signal lamp blinked as soon as we arrived, and made known shortages of stores. There was an urgent need for clothing, as the kit lockers of the majority of the "Eskimo" ratings were in the fo'c'sle which now lay in the depths of Ofot Fjord. "Coventry" ratings were asked to give whatever kit they could spare. A whaler left "Eskimo" and when it reached us we were surprised to see it's bleary eyed crew. Some, ill clad, wore the oddest misfit garments. But they raised a grin on coming alongside, and once provided with food, cigarettes, and several items of warm clothing, gave a cheer as they set off for the insecure floating outpost which they were determined to sail to U.K.

When we left "Eskimo", on fjord patrol, we came on a motor fishing vessel which signalled and then approached us. Two R.A.F. officers subsequently boarded "Coventry" to explain that they were surveying the fjords to find aircraft runways. A survey party had left England in two flying boats which had been shot down, and the flying boats subsequently destroyed by incendiary bombs. But, the aircraft crews had salvaged the Browning machine guns and ammunition, and the whole party were now working from the fishing vessels they had acquired.

At the beginning of next morning's patrol, near the junction of two fjords, we had spotted the tall mast of "Resolution". Almost a symbol of security. Soon the weak rays of a pale sun, that had begun to appear before day routine began, gave a clear view of our surroundings. We were hemmed in by snow covered mountains, on a vast pond, where the sheer mountain walls dropped deep below water. But in places there were rocky shores on which roads ran. The mountain sides were wooded and had scattered houses, all under a thick snow blanket.

Just as it was beginning to seem incongruous to be at action stations, a shout of, "Alarm, enemy aircraft", jerked the shore gazers into reality. After two salvos came a new order, "Take cover". Guns crews thereupon lay prone on the deck, and blessed Chatham dockyard maties for the new steel fences. A harsh screaming filled our ears for several seconds, to be followed by a series of detonations suggesting a giant jumping cracker. Half a dozen tremendous white geysers stepped steadily to within a hundred yards of "Coventry's" stern. A comedian was quick to suggest that here was Hitler's secret weapon. A bomb, that if aimed wide of it's target, bounced across the sea in pursuit. This was the overture to our entertainment in "Bomb Alley", and thereafter we lived at the guns for five weeks, with never more than two hours between attacks. For soon the midnight sun banished the friendly gloom that used to come in place of night. At the start it seemed impossible that "Coventry" could survive for long.

Very soon after that first bombing attack with it's weird sound effects, a periscope was reported, and one had the impression that "Coventry" was trying to take to the air as she rapidly increased engine revolutions. The remedy, however, was to enter a mountain penned inlet guarded by anti-submarine nets, while the report of "U" boats was analysed by H.Q. We, at that time, were unaware that a Walrus flying boat had surprised and sunk a "U" boat in Narvik Fjord, and that from the documents found, Admiralty intelligence had become aware of the positions of all "U" boat squadrons operating in the Norwegian seas. After a couple of hours, a rather bored ship's company were severely shaken by the yell "Aircraft overhead". At once the gun barrels were raised to maximum elevation, while unutterable curses were heaped on the air defence lookouts and "R.D.F." Tension mounted as we craned our necks and saw slow gliding wings hovering far overhead. But tension relaxed to mirth when the seagull lazily moved it's wings to glide away. The First Lieutenant's orders subsequently admonished :— The periscope seen this morning comes as a good warning to the anti-submarine lookouts—don't imagine it's only the air we have against us. Any rating on the upper deck should report AT ONCE if he sees anything suspicious.

There must have been some warmth in the arctic sun because the snow began to melt and reveal the bright coloured paint of those scattered dwellings, the sombre green of the pine forests, and the bright green of the meadows visible ashore. Foaming cascades leapt down the mountains to plunge into the placid fjord. While the guns crews might occasionally survey this scenery, the air defence lookouts, ever watching a blue sky in which a selection of enemy aircraft were constantly on view, were the first to recognise a new phenomenon. The white vapour trails of high flying aircraft.

"R.D.F." (radar) was at a disadvantage in the mountain walled fjords, and the air defence lookouts had a heavy responsibility. As soon as an enemy approached to attack, the Gunnery Officer prepared to give him two or three salvos during his bombing run. The Navy had learned that no anti-aircraft ship could carry enough ammunition to plaster all comers when aircraft, in large and frequent waves, made attacks. Barrage, a technique that had dismayed the "Sullom Six", was now a thing of the past. Time after time guns crews were alerted as soon as an enemy aircraft was seen to turn towards "Coventry". Then shooting started, to continue while the bombing run lasted. The Navigating Officer watched the attacker, and when he called that bombs were released, the guns crews were ordered to take cover. The Navigator, having observed the course of the bombs, would order an alteration of helm to avoid them. On the order, "Take cover", gun's crews instantly flattened themselves on the iron deck, and almost burrowed under the coconut matting placed there to keep their feet from slipping. As the bombs screamed down, they hopefully pondered the chances of a miss. Increasing vibration of the deck indicated the spurt demanded from the engines, and the ship heeled violently on altering course. A roar of exploding bombs near the ship confirmed a miss, and the exulting gun's crews would leap up, eager to start shooting at the next attacker. At first the chances of surviving seemed negligible, but fatigue and custom soon dulled nervous reactions, which were replaced by mechanical defence reflexes devoid of emotion. Stokers were very conscious of the silencing of the guns at bomb release, when guns crews were taking cover. On the other hand they hated the drum rattle of the pom pom, which announced a dive bomber past the main defence. Lookouts were fascinated by the small dots that issued from the plane, seeming to hang motionless in the sky, until they plummeted in a wide arc, to grow monstrously in the final terrifying fraction of a second.

There was a sporting chance with a single attacker, but eventually six Heinkels attacked in concert. Holding close formation, they released their bombs in a pattern calculated to cover any conceivable avoiding action by "Coventry". Once bomb release had occurred "Coventry's" only chance was to maintain course and speed in the hope that the bombers aim and setting were misjudged. "Take cover" duly ordered, the gun's crews flattened themselves on the deck. The vibration and hum of the aircraft engines filled their ears. Next, came the thin wailing of the bomb sirens, quickly growing to a ghastly ear splitting crescendo. The earliest arrivals rattled and shook the ship, which seemed to be cruising on boiling water. The rest of the pattern prolonged, but did not much increase the effect. Hope sprouted at this point, and a second later it was all quiet. Lucky again! jump up and clear away cartridge cases before the next bastard has a go!

Hours later there came a lull when gun's crews, in turn of watch, could visit the bathroom and mess deck. We could relax and take stock. Then somebody noticed the black score cut in the ship's side on the starboard side of the fo'c'sle. Whistles feigning astonished incredulity covered many a heartfelt prayer of thanks.

The Daily Bulletin of Tuesday 14th May, 1940,
Contained a Dispatch from a Reuter Correspondent as follows:—

"This morning I saw from the foretop of our Flagship the Naval bombardment and capture of BJERVIK on HERJANG FJORD just north of NARVIK. Under the cover of our guns British and French troops landed and stormed the snow clad heights with dash and precision in face of machine gun and rifle fire. French tanks landed by the British Navy supported the attack from the right. Machine gun nests in the ruins of the town were systematically blotted out."

In these times many sailors fondly imagined that they might seem heroes to the inhabitants of the little towns by the fjords. This illusion was shattered by Able Seaman Pegg R.N.R. He had joined for the bounty in hard times, and now ruefully contrasted his naval pay with the enhanced wages earned by his comrades still in the merchant service. A.B. Pegg was an air defence lookout, and claimed that he had been able to turn his binoculars on the nearby town while guns were firing. "And", said he, "There they were, riding their flaming bicycles, carrying shopping bags as if we didn't exist!"

Daily Bulletin—Tuesday, 14th May, 1940.

The map shows the Narvik area where Coventry has been patrolling today. Start at Bogen and work round places of interest.

Bogen. This is where we went yesterday after leaving "Vindictive" and party, and where we returned last night.

Herjangs. The four planes which passed over us and were fired at by us this morning eventually dropped their bombs on Herjangs and Bjerkvik.

Bjerkvik. This is where the big landing of French troops took place a short while ago. These troops have since done jolly well.

Rombaks. This is where the second battle of Narvik took place. The "Narrows" marked with a cross are where the "Eskimo" had her bow blown off by the torpedoes of a German destroyer, who had beached herself as shown.

Narvik.   "S"   The long scar in the woods with stands on either side is the local "Ski Jump"

              "T"   Marks the railway tunnel in which the Germans have a 3 inch gun—they run it out and have a crack at someone and then pop back again. Very wise!!!!!

              In Narvik Harbour there are 18 sunken ships, the results of both the battles of Narvik.

              "Q"   Shows the rough position of one of the British howitzers which were bombarding this afternoon.

              The destroyers "Fame" and "Wren" were bombarding enemy positions this afternoon, the bursts, however, were not observed.

              "Aurora" bombarded Narvik last night as a parting gesture.

              Two 500 lb bombs were dropped on us today but landed about 250 yards away.

Mess Gear. Under the present scheme of action meals mess gear is almost certain to get muddled unless it is marked. Leading Hands of messes should see to this.

Supper. It is intended to break down to Defence Watches after the last flight of Heinkels this evening. This should be about 1900, Fritz permitting First Watchmen will go to supper at 1930 and will close up at 2030.

Clean Ship. As it appears that the ships company will be at Action Stations daily from early in the morning to, at the earliest 1900, repair parties of all descriptions will have to be called upon to keep the ship clean and tidy.

On the whole, quarters are being kept reasonably clean by action crews but there is still a lot of ratings who toss their fag ends and paper on the deck expecting a non-existant party of seamen to sweep it up for them. This, particularly, applies to guns crews. Clean up after you, even if it isn't your part of the ship!

Action Stations. It is very probable that the first "Alarm Aircraft" will come before the hands are called. There is no time to dress after the alarm and ratings must arrange their sleeping attire so that they can go to their quarters at once.

There are certain ratings who are members of repair parties, etc., who realising that their presence at their action stations is unlikely to be vital in the first few moments of the encounter, saunter slowly to their positions through narrow gangways.

The score of attacks was mounting, and in one single bomber engagement, Able Seaman Ballard on No. 5 gun was killed. There was no hit on the ship, but a steel splinter had found it's mark. Action orders demanded that he be at once carried from the gun, but even before the sick bay staff arrived, his fate was all too plain. At what must have been evening, the funeral was announced. All men off duty went, some straight from the bathroom, others still grimy; and all in assorted outfits of overalls, second best blue serge, or duffel coats, to the quarter deck. There, by the rails, sewed in his hammock, was the body of a shipmate who had chaffed his comrades and cheerfully acted on every command only a few hours before. The funeral service was read to the congregation of dulled exhausted men. The ever present menace of the enemy compelled brevity. The release was made, the corpse splashed and sank to the depths, and very soon after, perforce, the gunners were sent to work moving spent cartridge cases to a central stowage, ready for return to the next convenient ammunition ship.

The pattern of routine was beginning to make its' mark on the ship's company. The frequent bombing attacks, and lack of sleep, had created a trigger happy crew, jittery and jumpy at the slightest alarm. Long friendships that had endured the ups and downs of service life were in danger of being broken up by a careless word or action, a mess mate would turn with biting invective over a trivial incident. Lack of sleep did not help matters, and now with twenty four hours continuous daylight, the Germans gave us no let up at all. We were expending about three thousand rounds of ammunition per week, and the replenishment of ammunition was quite a problem. Only obtainable from the ammunition ship, it was virtually impossible to go alongside during normal waking hours on account of the persistent bombing attacks. We therefore ammunitioned during the middle watch, and even this was hazardous. On many occasions the captain slipped the wires and steamed away at full speed, leaving the far from happy boarding party to watch the attack on their defenceless ammo ship with its' hundreds of tons of T.N.T. from a somewhat uncomfortable seat.

Once alongside an ammunition ship everyone was acutely conscious of abnormal danger, and worked quickly to shorten the visit. The 15" gun charges and depth charges in the holds of these ships then took on an extra horrifying appearance that seemed to reduce our 4" fixed ammunition almost to the category of fireworks. By contrast with the apprehensive attitude of so many of the visitors, the men on the ammunition ships were calm and deliberate. Models at Tussauds could not have been steadier. Frequently gunners were detailed to assist in the ammunition ships or the magazines of "Coventry". In such circumstances they were very much aware of water lapping the ship's side far above them, and in the event of an alarm being passed for action stations, performed amazing acts of levitation to reach their guns, almost on the instant.

One of the first things the Admiralty had learned was how quickly a flak ship could empty it's magazines. Even with restricted shooting there was difficulty in keeping them full. After every attack on "Coventry", Mr. Smees, the Gunner, would visit every gun, notebook in hand, and with the affability of a village grocer booking orders, enquire of the Officer of Quarters how many rounds had been used. The most picturesque ammunition station was at a point known as the "Goldfish Bowl", properly called "Lavangs". Here, were several supply ships, and it was noticeable on board one, flying the French tricolour, how quickly they manned their single "mitrailleuse" as soon as "Coventry" arrived. Once "Coventry" had secured to the ammunition ship, another clockwork like function would occur. A motor cycle engine in the distance would roar into life, soon to fade into a quiet drumming, then silence. Meanwhile all hands available, including the most pacific designation of Chief Petty Officer, would be straining mind and muscle to shift rounds of 4" fixed ammunition as rapidly as possible into "Coventry's" magazines. After a few minutes the alarm rattlers would send everybody running to action stations, like suddenly electrified ants, and "Coventry", gun barrels rising, and securing wires awash, would be drawing away ready for the approaching Heinkels.

Sleep was now becoming an intense longing, as nobody had enjoyed more than an hour at a time in the last few weeks. A.B. Barnes and A.B. Risdon had a lucky break in this respect one night. They went alongside the ammunition ship, and these two seamen were detailed off by the Gunners Mate to go down No. 5 magazine amidships to man the hoist and stow away ammunition. They opened up the hatch covers and went below. It was warm and cosy in the magazine as they perched on the ammunition boxes waiting for the first load to come down. They seemed to be waiting a long time, and settled more comfortably on the boxes hoping to snatch a precious few minutes sleep. Within a few seconds they had both gone fast asleep and knew nothing more until awakened by the crashing of bombs and reverberating shudders in the ship from our own guns firing. Still half awake they stumbled to their feet and rushed to their gun, where the guns team was working at a furious pace to keep the gun firing with two men short. The action was short and sweet, and when a breather came we were able to discover what had happened. Apparently it had been decided not to use No. 5 magazine after all. The Gunners Mate had forgotten all about them, and they had been asleep for three and a half hours.

On one occasion the high level bombers were accompanied by two Stukas, which chose an unarmed store ship as prey. "Coventry" harried them with deterrent fire, but once their dive had started our shooting had to stop for fear of shell damage to the ship. We watched hypnotised as the deadly birds swooped on their quarry, released bombs, and flattened out at little more than funnel height. Miraculously the bombs missed.

Harstadt was the most unpleasant ammunition station. This was the army base for a projected attack on a small but determined force of German mountain troops with the survivors of sunken German destroyers which held Narvik for Hitler. Dither in the Allied Command was enabling their constant reinforcement and supply from the air. On one side of the fjord at Harstadt, were several allied ships beached, having been run ashore after sustaining crippling bomb damage.

At our first visit, a party from "Coventry" went ashore in a whaler to attempt de-fusing a German torpedo found there. Before they returned, the Luftwaffe began a heavy raid, so Captain Gilmour started "Coventry" moving and shooting. This was anathema to Rear Admiral Vivian, who considered it a point of honour to wait for the whaler. The wisdom of this procedure might be emphasised by a quote from the daily orders when commenting on an earlier air attack—"The nearest bomb dropped 50 yards away, which wasn't bad shooting from four miles up!

There was always a raid when we visited Harstadt, and one incident will give a measure of Navy morale.

H.M.S. "Vindictive", subjected to attack by several aircraft, was lost to view behind an exceptionally thick and lengthy curtain of bomb spray geysers. It was so thick, and lasted so long, that we began to despair of the ship's survival. Then the bow of "Vindictive" was seen slowly emerging. The spray raised by the bombs had hardly subsided, when a rating was seen doubling towards the quarter deck, paint pot in one hand, and a paint brush in the other, presumably to paint over the scratches. Fortunately, there was some limited air support for the ships in Bomb Alley, and those troops ashore whose commanders were trying to take Narvik without a frontal landing. Three of them sailed into six Dorniers that were dropping their routine bombs over the shipping in the fjord. We marvelled at their acrobatics, and aggressiveness, and complete disregard of our flak, but the Dorniers had the legs on them and drew away, not before, unfortunately, one of the Gladiators caught a burst from a rear gunner. The old stringbag went into a gentle spiral and black smoke trailed astern. Our hearts sickened at the unfairness of it all, but a shout went up as we saw the white blob of a parachute opening out in the blue sky and floating gently down. Apart from this incident, we had no help at all. Imagine the excitement in the mess deck, when the "buzz" went round that a squadron of Spitfires had arrived to give us support. That evening we saw them landing on the nearby runway, the graceful elliptical wings darkly silhouetted against the glow of the setting sun. Even the troops with the hopeless task of trying to hold back the German advance from the south, (this was not known to Harstadt lower orders), were not entirely lacking air support. Most of the aircraft flown in from fleet aircraft carriers were "Gladiators", but the Spitfires operating from Bardufoss airfield made more effective execution, and we once had the pleasure of seeing a large enemy aircraft plunge clean into the fjord while a pursuing Spitfire climbed, and turned into a "Victory Roll". The R.A.F. claimed that thirty six enemy aircraft were shot down; Harstadt anti-aircraft gunners claimed twenty three.

"Coventry" was given a forty hour respite from the fjord patrol, and, paradoxically, headed seawards to recuperate. Reviving energies were promptly harnessed by the Captain to scrubbing and cleaning, so much so, that there were hankerings to get back on patrol. Reporting back to Harstadt on the 17th May, we found an expedition in preparation. Irish Guards and South Wales Borderers were going to land at Bodo, to support another force of guardsmen who were trying to check the German advance from Southern Norway to relieve Narvik. The most prominent ship in our convoy was the cruiser "Effingham", with motor transport vehicles, and guns, and a vast assortment of stores stacked on the quarter deck. In the twilight the convoy, including the anti-aircraft cruiser "Cairo", and destroyers "Matabele", and "Echo", had glided out of momentarily silent Harstadt, making it's way though a maze of mountain girt waters. Meanwhile, the Polish liner "Chrobry", carrying the main force of Irish Guards for the Bodo landing, had been bombed and sunk off the southern end of the Lofoten Islands. The destroyer "Wolverine" had picked up six hundred and ninety-four survivors.

Our approach had avoided the attentions of the Luftwaffe, but anxiety was nevertheless considerable. At length we reached a rocky bay, quite deserted and sombre, under cloud cover. We were pleased to learn that this was our destination, and keenly interested when "Coventry" manoeuvred to let "Effingham" pass. She steamed ahead boldly, as in a Victorian tableau. It was inspiring to see the proud ship pass us, and we were looking forward to watching the landing, when to the horror of everyone, the "Effingham" suddenly heeled over, and swung in a narrow circle to port. A cloud of black smoke rose from her funnels like a death pall, coinciding with a grinding jar as "Coventry's" stern bumped on rock. Engineer Commander Pugh, not a young man, hurried to the quarter deck, and almost immediately shouted to the bridge through cupped hands, "We've got a hole aft". But already we had gone astern into deeper water, and quickly retreated to a safe depth.

What had happened to "Effingham?" She had struck an unchartered rock that had ripped her hull, flooding the boiler rooms and adjoining compartments so swiftly, that damage control was impossible, even had there been time. She began settling fast. It was a race against time to get the troops off safely. All available boats were put into service, and the destroyer "Echo" ran a ferry from "Effingham" to us. A former canteen manager of "Coventry" was among those rescued, and he was greeted with much chaff, and such remarks as "Cash box a total loss I suppose, Manager?"

Rumour promptly blamed the disaster on an alleged treacherous Norwegian pilot, who naturally had been shot forthwith. But the truth of the matter was more like a cautionary tale. A short cut had been taken with the proverbial lamentable results. "Echo" worked swiftly, and in a short time "Coventry's" mess decks were crammed with seven hundred and fifty South Wales Borderers, three hundred and one Guardsmen, one hundred and twenty R.A.M.C. details, and two hundred and ninety five of the "Effingham's" crew. Piles of kit littered those areas of the upper deck remote from guns. Most interesting were the boxes containing a selection of grenades, whose canny owners quickly removed them to safer storage.

Leaving stranded the slowly sinking ship, with it's vast quantity of stores and munitions for war at sea and on land, we turned back to Harstadt as the whole operation had now to be abandoned. Cloud cover helped us, but several unrelieved watches at action stations had brought a lethargic tendency. A huge low flying plane blundered beneath the clouds and roused us with the roar of it's engines. Quickly it returned through the clouds, having most likely been a troop or freight carrier. But fire control and gun's crews had been alerted, creating such alarm that the army officers issued from the ward room, and with a great show of making ready their side arms, proceeded to the mess decks. However, the convoy reached Harstadt safely and without firing a shot.

Next day many London R.N.V.R.'s aboard "Coventry" felt personal sadness at the news of the loss of H.M.S. "Curlew", a sister flak-ship, which like "Coventry" was largely manned by London volunteers. "Curlew" had been supporting "Ark-Royal", whose aircraft had provided some air cover for the Bodo operation. But on arrival at Lavangs for a spell as guardship, she had almost immediately succumbed to a bombing attack. "Coventry" received the last radio transmission from "Curlew", and soon after went to take her place. On the still, ice cold waters of the fjord, oil patches, and here and there lifebelts and caps, still drifted when we arrived.

H.M.S. Coventry

Daily Bulletin—Tuesday, 21st May

The activity of enemy aircraft yesterday evening rendered the production of a bulletin impossible.

We left Harstadt at 2017 for Skaanlandt, which is adjoining Lavangs, there to act as A.A. protection for the merchant ships at anchor.

Shortly after our arrival, a quantity of Heinkels variously estimated to number from six to sixty, made a series of very determined attacks both here and at Harstadt.

Here at Lavangs they dropped some twenty bombs—two of which fell unpleasantly close to our forecastle, port side, but no damage was suffered other than to the suits of No. 1 gun's crew which were drenched with sea water.

The pom-pom's claim to have bagged this very determined dive bomber is substantiated by observers on the bridge.

Many of the bombs were dropped around the merchant shipping, and some appeared to be aimed at the Pier at Skaanlandt. At Harstadt the bombing was more successful for the oil tanks ashore were set on fire.

Today, 21st May, started in earnest when an unobserved Dornier dropped some unexpected bombs about a hundreds yards from the ship. Luckily scrub decks had been nearly completed!! More bombs were dropped around the merchant ships, but without any success. As yet we do not know whether Harstadt has been bombed to-day.

At last, the expedition Commanders had been able to agree on attacking Narvik from the sea, (as advocated by the Earl of Cork and Orrery several weeks before, and subsequently favoured by the French General, Bethouart).

The small German force commanded by General Dietl, had originally been ill-provided with weapons and ammunition, thanks to the destruction of it's supply ships by the Royal Navy. We understood them to have only one 3" howitzer, which, mounted on a railway truck, was brought out of a tunnel, fired, and returned to cover. Since the action of Captain Warburton Lee, they had received considerable supplies and reinforcements by air, and when beset by allied troops, were well supported by Stukas. Our troops, on the other hand, had the assistance of the guns of the Navy wherever possible.

Extract from Daily Orders

On May 25th we were officially informed that so far, one hundred and eleven bombs had been dropped on us.

On the 27th May, in the strange daylight that hardly ever altered during the traverse of the sun, the cruisers "Southampton", "Cairo", "Coventry", and five destroyers, met in Ofot fjord, and took up positions close to the shore around Narvik. Never having seen any sign of life in the town, there seemed no enormity in what was about to begin. H.M.S. "Southampton's" 6" guns set a slow drumming rhythm to the bombardment, and the four inch artillery of the smaller ships, provided an irregular accompaniment. Soon, smoke arose in a column from the town, and accummulated to form a blanket just clear of the mountain tops. Early on, a line of splashes near the starboard side of "Coventry", indicated that a machine gunner was attempting to liquidate some of us. Our pom pom directed a prolonged burst at the point of origin of the bullets, and the splashes troubled us no more. Ashore, all we could make out were opposing streams of tracer bullets. General Dietl's men were stubbornly resisting the attack, largely mounted by the Norwegians, the French Foreign Legion, Polish Legion, and Chasseurs Alpins of General Bethouart. We were surprised at the absence of the Luftwaffe; this was, in fact, due to our having air cover from Hurricanes from Bardufoss. but fog covered this airfield before the attack on Narvik had succeeded. Our protectors were thus unable to get airborne, and the Luftwaffe arrived in force to give us, as it were, a taste of our own medicine. Bombardment ceased and all ships scooted around to avoid the droppings of high level bombers.

The Earl of Cork had to consider whether he was justified in exposing his ships to the full force of the Luftwaffe without any fighter protection. Thereupon General Bethouart decided that all he now needed was the artillery support of two destroyers. Consequently the Admiral ordered two destroyers, with "Coventry", ("Cairo" had been hit), to stay and finish the job.

During this period a squadron of six Junkers arrived, spotted "Coventry", and decided that she would be their target. Fortunately for "Coventry", the fog at Bardufoss had cleared a little earlier, and two flights of Gladiators were now airborne, and hastened to protect the bombarding ships. Flying high over "Coventry", the Gladiators spotted the faster and more heavily armed Luftwaffe hunters preparing to swoop on their prey. At this moment, the British Squadron Leader became aware of another Junkers on his tail, an enemy that he must lose if his own squadron was to be effective in preventing a bomb attack on "Coventry". Fortunately the slower Gladiators had an advantage over the Junkers,—a tighter turn.

Squadron Leader Hull banked in a sharp turn preparatory to attacking his enemy from the beam. The Junkers kept on course. Now Hull was on the Junkers tail, and hit him with a short burst of fire. The bomber jettisoned its load in an attempt to escape, but a moment later received the coup de grace from the Gladiator. In flames, the Junkers plunged into the fjord not far from "Coventry".

Within hours of this, the Allied forces entered Narvik, with Norwegian troops in the lead, at the invitation of General Bethouart.

Years later we should learn that orders had been received from London on the 25th May to evacuate the Narvik area. But this French General refused to leave our Norwegian allies before showing that he could beat the German troops there.

A few days after bombarding Narvik, we found ourselves riding quietly on the friendly swell of the open sea. Nearby were several large merchantmen, and destroyers hurrying hither and thither. We were acting as an intermediate station for soldiers embarking in the troopers (for such were the merchantmen). Now we made close acquaintance with the French Foreign Legion, Polish Legion, and Chasseurs Alpins. All these French trained troops carried loaves of bread strapped to their person, and most of them were provided with bottles of red wine. When the destroyers came alongside, and the soldiers approached the guardrail to tranship, we offered to take their rifles to facilitate the operation. But not a single French-trained soldier would let go of his rifle. One group of Chasseurs stayed aboard long enough for one of their number to entertain us with music from a guitar. With somewhat rusty French we began to talk, and very early in the proceedings the guitarist stated that all wars were arranged by Capitalists, and were really no concern of the working man.

It was generally realised that we were going home, because, it seemed, we had gained our object in capturing Narvik. Everyone was so pleased, and it is therefore of interest to sketch in retrospect the prominent features of the war situation at that time.

General Dietl and Co., had been driven out of the town rather than beaten, and the Wehrmacht was advancing inexorably from the south to their relief. Our South Norway Expeditionary Force which was hopelessly inadequate, had been worsted at Namsos and Andalsnes; and there the Royal Navy, without air cover, had found that ships could not carry enough guns or ammunition to beat the Luftwaffe. Our commanders in South Norway soon realised that there was no hope of holding Norway, and the Norwegian generals could see that their armies would be left in the lurch. In France, the Wehrmacht had circled round the Maginot Line, to chase our soldiers to the coast. The responsible judges of these ill-prepared offensives had hastily abandoned the Prime Minister who had carried on a leaflet war, and in panic rallied behind a hitherto unpopular warrior—Churchill!

Our "Worms Eye" view of the war had the Narvik success as a background, with the current activity of a victorious army embarking unhurriedly for transfer to home, or another front. One of the curiosities that drew some of our attention from the foreign soldeirs was the tanker "Oil Pioneer", which had a Chinese crew. The Chinese were markedly cheerful and industrious, and seemingly oblivious of the war. It was fortunate that we ourselves knew so little of what was going on. That we were leaving General Ruge, with his Norwegian army to get on as best they could with the invaders was not known to us. Also, that the modern and heavily armed German warships "Scharnhorst", "Gneisenau", and "Hipper", were on their way to shoot up the Naval Forces in the fjords, and were in our latitude within a distance of a hundred miles.

Embarkation completed, the convoy assembled and got under way. The destroyers carried out the familiar patrolling; there were keen lookouts on the upper deck and air defence platform, and the R.D.F. was sweeping steadily. The mountains of Norway began to recede, ultimately to drop below the horizon. The recently acquired habit of looking up suppressed any desire to look back.

After two days, battleships of the Home Fleet were sighted, and coincidentally, pursuing squadrons of Luftwaffe overhauled us. We dropped readily into the "barrage" routine, and were at the same time favourably impressed by the bunched ribbons of fire stretching from the capital ships to the noses of the enemy aircraft. On the horizon were seen brilliant flashes in the direction of the second group of our homeward bound convoy. Presumably they were under similar heavy air attack from the Luftwaffe, but no indication was given as strict radio silence was maintained.

Then came news of tragedy, H.M.S. "Glorious", bringing back the Hurricanes, Spitfires, and Gladiators with the pilots that had helped us in the fjords, also destroyers "Acasta", and "Ardent", with the tanker "Oil Pioneer", had been sunk by "Scharnhorst", and "Hipper". The opening salvoes had destroyed the radio equipment in the "Glorious", preventing the vital signal being sent to our own battleships just over the horizon. Little did we realise, that the firework display we had seen, was the funeral pyre of our comrades. Later we would learn that this fast and powerful enemy force had been prevented from hunting our own convoy by the self-sacrificing dash and courage of H.M.S. "Acasta", commanded by Lieutenant Commander Glasfurd.

Glasgow was our haven, and all-night leave was piped as soon as the ship was secured. Notwithstanding the sleepless weeks in the land of the midnight sun, and the bad news of our companion convoy, smartly dressed men quickly streamed over the gangway to haunt the pleasure dromes of the town until the small hours. Next morning we put to sea.

On Sunday the 16th June we lay off the Tyne, and next day proceeded up river to Wallsend, remarking that there was little evidence of gaiety as we passed Whitley Bay. The following day we docked at Wallsend slipway.

Once secured there, Admiral Vivian had the ship's company mustered, and addressed them with words of praise, going on to say that where all had done so well, he felt unable to single out anyone for decorations. In lieu of these, he said he had requested the Admiralty that the ship's company be given generous leave. A pandemonium of cheering broke out, and within five minutes a group of liberty men were in number ones, with cases packed, and waiting for the pipe.

The London train travelled nearly the whole length of England, carrying many London Volunteers who now considered themselves proven sea warriors with remarkable tales to tell. The early terrors and fore-bodings there had been at our introduction to bomb alley were utterly forgotten. In fact, our attention was now completely absorbed in looking at the strange people of other counties, and listening to their distinctive accents. It was a glorious sunny day, fields, trees, an occasional distant hill, and sometimes a river or stream, made a delightful landscape as the busy puffing engine raced home. There were frequent stops, where sometimes parties of smiling people crowded on. Many carried picnic baskets, while most had the luggage and paraphernalia indicating a lengthy holiday such as they had enjoyed for many years now. Few of them heeded the sailors, possibly resenting that this official load occupied space that could have added to their comfort.

There was no sign that they were perturbed about the news that the men sent to hang out the washing on the Siegfried Line were now doing their best to effect an orderly evacuation. They would never have credited General Gamelin with remarks in which they were linked to "chickens".

On reaching home, I heard opinions expressed that "Things were pretty bad". The invincibility of German tanks was taken for granted, but it was pointed out that it would be difficult—probably impossible—to land these by air.

Whatever the reverses to expeditionary forces, the reputation of the Royal Navy was untarnished. The legend of "Our sure shield" was unshaken—for the present.

"Coventry" had miraculously passed in and out of the fjords under cover of the guns. But for the fleet in general, guns had failed to beat the bomber.

Sung to the tune of "Thanks for the Memory"

We've travelled far and wide together
But have we travelled too fast
Through quiet seas and stormy weather
Since this war was forecast
Its all right up to now, so lets hope our luck
will last.

Thanks for the memory of washing tropic wear
Fresh water all too rare
Establishments in Sister Street where women aren't so fair
Oh thank you so much
Thanks for the memory of Grimsby in the dark
Girls out for a lark
The things I never learned at school but found out in the park
Oh thank you so much
Sweet were the loving words spoken
And many the principles broken
So even the Bishop awoke and we had to go to Sullom Voe
Then thanks for the memory of all aboard us queer
Lerwick leave and beer
The plane that called on New Years Day
And got his bombs so near
Oh thank you so much.

Oh thanks for the memory of Chatham and refit
In films we made a hit
They even filmed the telescope of Mr. Nickabit
Oh thank you so much
Thanks for the memory of that delightful hole
They called the Goldfish Bowl
The fellow on the motorbike was Nazi heart and soul
Oh thank you so much
Remember the panic of oiling, of action while dinners were spoiling
Getting ammo with everyone toiling
The midnight sun was not much fun
Then thanks for the memory of pongoes by the score
French, Polish, and some more
The night we spent in Glasgow and the time we had ashore
Oh thank you so much

Thanks for the memory of towns along the Tyne
Five days up the line
The times we've been to Jesmond Dene
By light of pale moonshine
Oh thank you so much
Thanks for the memory of Scapa and Lyness
Beer tickets and the rest
The trip we made to try and get the "Shark" out of a mess
Oh thank you so much

Remember the minelayers loaded
The number of duds that exploded
And evenings to pleasure devoted
When we sailed around to Plymouth Sound
Then thanks for the memory
What Devonport could show strolling on the Hoe
It was a shame but all the same, at last we had to go
Oh thank you so much.

A.B. George Sims

SUMMARY OF AIR ATTACKS, NARVIK AREA

Date	Time	No. A/C	Of Bombs	
Sat. 11th May	11.04	3	12	Off Narvik, convoying "Penelope". Bombs near her.
14th May	05.15	1	4	Escorting "Eskimo". Bombs near "Vindictive".
	07.21	1	2	Dropped starboard side, good distance.
	07.43	1	4	Starboard quarter. 1 mile away.
	10.20	1	2	Port beam. 3 cables from A/S Trawler.
	11.17	1	2	Near A/S trawler.
	12.26	6	No record	Around "Eskimo's" Convoy generally.
	16.35	1	2	Port side. One mile.
	17.16	1	2	Off Bogen. Large bombs, near "Aurora".
	17.54	1	2	Port side, 2-3 cables.
15th May	12.26	1	2	Starboard side, about 2 cables.
16th May	11.40	4	16	Near "Wren".
	12.25	1	4	Port quarter. 1½ cables
	13.41	1	2	2 small bombs, well astern.
	13.42	4	13	11 Starboard side, 2 Port. 2-3 cables.
	17.34 to 19.22	32	24	Continuous attacks. Oiler "Broomdale". Chief objective, but some near "Aurora", some near "Coventry".
	23.34	3	8	Mostly around "Broomdale".
17th May	01.28	1	2	Port quarter, about 2 cables.
20th May	18.13	3	6	All wide.
	18.16	1	2	Dive bomber (Seen to crash in flames).
	18.29	1	2	Dive bomber. Near Port bow.
	18.35	3	6	Dive bombers. Large bombs, astern.
	18.59	1	2	Starboard bow, fairly close, large bombs.
	19.03	1	2	Large bombs on army camp ashore.
	19.30	4	6	At Merchant vessel on Port Bow. 2 large, 4 small.
	19.39	1	1	On the beam. 2 cables.
	20.01	1	4	Near Merchant vessel ahead.
	20.05	1	2	Ahead, near.
	20.07	2	4	4 large, number of small bombs, mostly near merchant vessels.

Date	Time	No. A/C	Of Bombs	Remarks
21st May	10.03	1	3	Starboard quarter. 1½ cables.
	10.04	1	5	Port Beam. 2 cables. A/C unobserved
	10.57	2	7	Around Merchant vessels on Port Bow.
23rd May	12.40	4	11	Starboard bow. Nearest bombs 20 ft.
	12.50	3	10	Port Bow. 30-50 feet.
	12.52	1	1	Large bomb by dive bomber. Port bow, did not explode.
24th May	04.23	1	2	Dive bomber (at Harstadt).
	04.47	1	2	Near "Southampton".
	04.54	1	4	Near troopship.
	04.59 to 08.07	36	LN	Estimated over 100 bombs on shipping in Harstadt roads. Some fell on shore. Mostly around ships "Vindictive", "Coventry", "Southampton", "Cairo" and "Beagle" as well as Merchant vessels.
	19.32	1	2	Near "Delight", large bombs.
25th May	09.44	1	1	Astern, close.
	09.50	1	4	"Condor" type A/C dropped bombs near Narvik.
	12.32	4	LN	Bombing Lavang Fjord.
	12.37	1	4	Starboard beam. 1½ cables.
	13.17	1	4	Port Quarter. One cable.
	13.22	1	4	Starboard Quarter, one cable (A/C at 22,000 ft.)
26th May	14.50	1	8	Port Beam. 3 cables.
	15.46	1	2	Unseen attack. Starboard bow. 1½ cables.
27th May	08.31	2	8	Starboard bow, surprise attack. 1 cable.
28th May	04.23	1	2	Dive Bomber. Astern, 2½ cables.
	04.47	1	2	Astern of "Southampton".
	04.54	1	4	Port Beam, one cable.
	04.59	1	2	Astern, 1½ cables.
	05.11	1	3	Near "Beagle".
	05.12	3	7	Between "Coventry" and "Beagle".
	05.15	1	1	Starboard Beam. 2 cables.
	05.16	1	2	Starboard beam. 1-2 cables.
28th May	05.17	5	LN	All round "Coventry" and "Southampton".
	05.23	3	12	Dropped on land (French army quarters).

Date	Time	No. A/C	Of Bombs	Remarks
	05.25	1	4	Starboard Beam.
	05.39	2	4	Near "Southampton".
	05.44	2	4	Starboard Beam, close.
	05.47	3	12	All round "Coventry", "Beagle", and "Southampton".
	05.49	2	4	Starboard quarter, 1-2 cables.
	05.50	1	4	Starboard side of "Cairo".
	05.52 to 06.18	24	54	Approximate numbers. Some bombs near each ship, a few near Allied Forces at Narvik. Shrapnel from one bomb killing 1 rating in "Coventry", and wounding 2 in "Southampton".
	11.30	1	2	Starboard quarter. Machine gunned also. This A/C brought down by Hurricanes.
	16.38	1	2	Port Quarter, close.
	16.53	1	3	Near "Delight".
	19.33	1	2	Starboard beam, 2 cables.
	19.34	1	2	Starboard bow, less than one cable.
	19.38	1	1	Large bomb starboard bow. Shrapnel through foremost funnel.
29th May	09.53	3	8	Dropped on shore, near "Balteako".
	15.33	2	4	Large bombs, starboard quarter, 3 cables.
	20.14	3	8	Starboard side. Distant.

375   Total

CHAPTER EIGHT

REGROUPING FOR THE LONE STAND

As Italy had joined Germany in the war, the enemy now controlled most of the European coast, both Atlantic and Mediterranean. We had lost the French fleet, and had to reckon on the possibility of it being used against us. H-force had been scraped up and sent to Gibraltar hastily to help restore the balance. What would be the role of the Flak ships?

But first, there was a holiday for "Coventry". While one watch was on leave, the other explored the Tyneside towns, chiefly Newcastle. Strawberries were plentiful in the shops, which also sold tinned cream to go with them. The Y.M.C.A. at Newcastle always gave a good welcome and a wonderful tea. The plentiful meals of the next few weeks, when a service man could get a plate of eggs and bacon at every canteen, were to be the last such meals in the U.K. for many years to come. The parks of Newcastle were at their best in early summer, and in the evenings there were good theatre and cinema programmes.

However, on the 29th June "Coventry" left hospitable Wallsend for Scapa, and on arrival there next day, moved to a telephone buoy connected by direct line to the Admiralty, because she was R.D.F. Guardship. New gun barrels had been fitted at Wallsend. The sea was choppy, and mooring took longer than usual. Everyone concerned was drenched with spray, and the Blacksmith and A.B. Barnes took an involuntary bath. On hearing of this the first Lieutenant, now Lieutenant Commander Dalrymple-Hay, ordered that when the whaler returned, the crew should come to the ward room for a drink; and Captain Gilmour similarly arranged to entertain the Blacksmith and A.B. Barnes. "Jimmy" explained that he had been in France for a project involving placing mines in the Rhine, and showed us leaflets which explained to Frenchmen how they were being used to fight the battles of others. These leaflets had, of course, been dropped by the Luftwaffe. Much later, some of us would read that the fluvial mine plan called "Royal Marine", which was to synchronise with a scheme of mining the Norwegian leads to sink German iron ore freighters, (this plan was called "Wilfred"), had at the last minute been vetoed by the French Government.

On the 6th July we left Scapa in the direction of Stavanger, a port on the coast of Norway, for an area whence the submarine "Shark", having sustained damage which left her unable to submerge, had sent an urgent appeal for protection from the inevitable air attack. Once clear of Scapa "action stations", by now just a grim purposeful preparation, was ordered. With us, was the cruiser "Southampton" and some attendant destroyers. As we ploughed full speed over the rollers there were intermittent but frequent bursts of sunshine, but no low cloud; a poor prospect for "Shark". When we arrived in the area from whence "Shark" had signalled, our advanced searching destroyers were under attack from aircraft flying at 7,000 feet, so "Coventry" opened fire. The effect of our shells forced the enemy to aim his bombs from a much higher level, 12,000 to 15,000 feet, than the pilots normally preferred. They were Heinkels, at which we fired on fourteen separate occasions, shooting 739 four inch shells. Most of the bombs were aimed at the destroyers, which had very poor anti-aircarft armament. The destroyer "Flame" was straddled, and one rating killed. A salvo of six bombs aimed at "Coventry" fell about 150 yards from the starboard quarter, and a stick of eight small bombs fell between "Coventry" and the cruiser "Southampton". A few sticks of bombs fell so wide that observers from the bridge were unable to guess for whom they were intended. At length the sky was clear of enemy aircraft, and we turned for home with gloomy reflections that our errand had been futile.

Next day, we escorted "Flame" back to Rosyth. This gave one watch a run ashore, in which they were able to visit Dunfermline, and stroll in Carnegie Park, where the peacocks stole the scene. Then it was back to Scapa, but the following day we left to escort mine layers through the Pentland Firth. Here, on a sunny forenoon, we came across a Dutch merchantman drifting and forsaken. At first glance it might have been the opening scene for a mystery of the sea. So much evidence of sudden interrupted life, in a silent wilderness of water. But she was so low in the water that a torpedo hit was readily surmised. Most disconcerting was the circumstance that no survivors could be seen, though it was evident that a boat had been launched.

Leaving the mine layers at a port on the west coast, we returned to Scapa. Gunnery practise was ordered for the next day, but thick fog made it impracticable. To compensate for this loss of a chance to increase the efficiency of the ship's company, "Jimmy", who regularly prefaced his daily orders with a news bulletin, included a homily about the need for maintaining the customary high standard of the Navy in personal cleanliness and neat dress, when the pressure of long hours at action stations had relaxed. He rebuked the tendency to levity when engaged in such evolutions as "tow-ship", or "collision stations". But his fury had chiefly risen on becoming aware that foul language was being used aboard, and he warned that the Captain would visit with exemplary punishment any man heard uttering certain Anglo-Saxon words. For several of the ensuing days the most frequently heard expletive was "confound it", (or you), but a habit once formed is not quickly conquered.

On return from our frustrated training expedition we found an air alert in force as we entered harbour. No attack developed however.

Whilst at Scapa, the First Lieutenant gave shore leave as often, and for as long as he possibly could. As the weather was consistently sunny, a variety of pleasant excursions could be made. A large number of men went straight away to the beer canteen at Flotta, clutching the ration tickets which would enable them to buy three pints. An experience concerning a destroyer leaving Ponta Delgada some two and a half years later emphasised to me the wisdom of the ration system. After forty-eight hours alongside, which international law decreed as the maximum time a neutral could allow a belligerent that had suffered from storm damage to shelter in the neutral harbour, two ancient, four funnel ex U.S. Destroyers emerged to escort a convoy of three tankers. Many of the destroyers personnel were mentally blank after consuming crude alcohol from wine bottles that had been peddled by bum boat men. The duty signalman was utterly "hors de combat". Ironically, the Officer of the Watch, an R.N.R. Commander, who had drunk his fill of quality liqueur, was unusually alert, and whilst carrying on with his own duties shouted the signalled intelligence for record by notebook. But a call to action stations would almost certainly have been a prelude to annihilation. Alternatively one could stroll in glorious open country, and drawing on Shetland experience, knock on the door of a house and ask if light refreshment could be provided on a commercial basis. Invariably it was, and on a generous scale. The lady of the house might lament that tea was scarce, and the sailor realise, if he anticipated passing that way again, that his mess had an abundance of tea.

Having, as it were, "spoiled" the seamen, the First Lieutenant one day conceived a great desire to paint the ship as rapidly as possible. Consequently, he addressed the hands in the most embarrassed and apologetic manner, imploring co-operation, and explaining that shore leave was impossible until the job was done. In the sunshine the hands worked readily and even with remarkable goodwill; undoubtedly engendered by the gesture of the younger officers, who all took a turn in squatting on a stage over the side and wielding a paintbrush with noticeable efficiency.

Toward the end of July, we escorted a convoy to Aberdeen, then made a very quick turn round, supposed by rumour to have occurred following intelligence that a German invasion impended. These were days when the press made frequent reference, in moods that varied from farce, through the pseudo-scientific to high tragedy, to "Hitler's secret weapon". We have seen that our fighting services had a secret weapon in "R.D.F.", but in addition, many inventions were born of the necessity imposed by shortage of suitable short range quick firing guns to protect ships from the dive bomber. The Oerlikon gun, having been tested aboard "Coventry" before 1939, was judged to be the best available, and ordered on a modest scale, was coming from Switzerland in small infrequent shipments. But as soon as Italy joined with Germany, this sole source dried up. It was a long time before an alternative source of supply was opened to meet our needs. During this period, merchant ships were using devices which included barrage balloons, wire trailing rockets, and even quite innocuous fireworks. One of the captial ships at Scapa, however, mounted a really imaginative deterrent. This was demonstrated on a fine sunny morning, by the carelessness of a person or persons unknown, to all who happened to be looking that way. A single sharp report shattered the silence so that all heads turned to look. For a few seconds there was surprise and baffled wonder, then a shower of small parachutes were seen descending. To add to the pleasing effect of these graceful objects, swaying slightly and falling prettily at a variety of speeds, the grenades they were carrying exploded at irregular intervals. Rumour had it that the consequences of this accident involved calling out of some Home Guard units, and an extended period of "jankers" for a luckless Royal Marine.

An event of significance to the "R.D.F." pioneers, was the arrival of technicians to overhaul and test the apparatus they used. It was found that the transmitter aerial feeders were crossed. This may have slightly affected the efficiency. But the current opinion is, that the high Scandinavian mountains rich in iron compounds, were mostly to blame for poor R.D.F. results in Norway.
In the last week of July we left Scapa with the mine layers again, this time in the region of the Irish sea. Quite frequently, during the mine laying operation, a mine hit bottom and exploded.

This operation completed, we took a southerly course on parting from the minelayers. Next day an exciting event, not observed by the majority of the ship's company, was the launching from a U-boat of two torpedos for "Coventry". Fortunately, one passed ahead and the other astern of us. Continuing south, we rounded Lands End. Whilst rolling in the Channel, a group of aircraft were sighted. With guns at the ready, a challenge was flashed but ignored. Then we loosed a salvo. At once several verey lights soared above the aircraft, and it was then realised that these were our own Fairey Battle Bombers homeward bound from the Continent. On the 28th July we moored off Plymouth Hoe, then proceeded to the dockyard, all in wonderful sunshine. To the surprise and delight of the ship's company, more home leave was announced. The departing men were addressed by Captain Gilmour on the subject of careless talk, and his final point was "Too much talk that our ship is going "south" could lead to our meeting a "Scharnhorst", and I don't suppose that anybody really wants that!"

To each watch, home leave in the finest of weather went all too quickly; as did the corresponding days of shore leave in Plymouth. Rationing had only just been mentioned, and there were countless ways of wiling away pleasant summer afternoons and evenings ashore. Once again the First Lieutenant gave generous leave, and at the same time, urged on below decks the painting that was clearly intended to make the mess decks more comfortable in a hot climate.

Plymouth was filled with every variety of foreign naval rating, Scandinavian, Netherlands and Poles, with a small contingent of the French. The news of the sinking of French ships at Oran, and their capture at Malta and Portsmouth, had doubtless not improved the temper of the last mentioned. Indeed a rating recently drafted to "Coventry", who had taken part in the Portsmouth event, proudly displayed evidence that plunder is the only aim of war", in the shape of a clinometer that was quite useless to him. I recall a pleasant warm evening, when hundreds of matelots were strolling in a polyglot throng near Devonport, when a small group of Frenchmen became conspicuous by their uninhibited behaviour. A small and dapper petty officer of the Polish Navy straightway turned aside to reprimand them, choosing a giant of a man as the first to feel the lash of his tongue. There was a shout of "Marine Francaise" as a ready fist bowled over the figure of foreign authority, and in an amazingly short time the French group were lost in the crowd.

In time we moved back again to the mooring off the Hoe, where occurred an event due to "Norway conditioning". A constant anti-aircraft guard was maintained on the mole about two miles from shore. Here a considerably battery of short range weapons had been mounted. And on one of those fine warm days, many of the ship's company, having eaten dinner, retired to the fo'c'sle to doze in the sun until they were piped to fall in. The deck was practically carpeted with men who had "got their heads down". At this hallowed time, the duty guns crews on the Mole, by contrast, were closed up at all guns to show their skill in shooting at a sleeve target, towed by a truly courageous pilot. The target came in view, and the battery of assorted machine guns clattered into frantic chorus. The dozers, shocked into "Bomb Alley" recollection, staggered to their feet in a blind and heedless stampede for cover. The onlooker, well aware that no danger existed, was entertained by a comedy beyond the best efforts of the world's greatest dramatists or clowns. Plymouth was at this time subject to some air raids by night, but not to concentrated attacks.

On the 19th August we left the Hoe on a westerly course. In the cool breeze and rolling swell of the Channel we became accustomed to sea routine, not omitting "For exercise only "Action Stations". There was no occurrence of general interest until we sighted Lands End, that desolate promontory so worthy of it's name. We proceeded with unbroken routine through that day and night. Next morning we were in the Irish Sea, on a northerly course, and experienced no alarms other than those raised for exercise.

Next morning we anchored at Greenock, and were all very interested to see H.M.S. "Bonaventure", She was a newly built cruiser, and her main armament of twin mounted 5.25" guns used fixed ammunition, and were so mounted that the guns were equally well served for air or surface targets. P.O. Goldring, the "Gunnery Instructor' or "G.I." was most enthusiastic about the ship and anticipated great things of her. There were two days of shore leave in Greenock, which were enjoyed to the full. The ship's company felt that it might be some time before we should next "step ashore" in Great Britain. Many indeed would never do so again. So these days were used to the full. Even after the lapse of a score of years, A.B. Foster, at a "Coventry" reunion, could recall the wonderful steak he ate at the Adelphi Hotel, preparatory to exploring Glasgow. All the more did he relish spending the night at the same hotel; in the morning being deferentially called for breakfast, at a table laid with silverware. And all this for 7s. 6d.

On the 23rd August "Coventry" sailed from hospitable Greenock with a small convoy Atlantic bound, and for hour after hour ploughed on. The attendant destroyers patrolled on the flanks of the convoy, and gun's crews watched them intently. The enemy did not disturb us. Next day the grey sea mists and clouds were less obvious. There was a clearer sky, the rollers had a greenish tinge, and "Coventry" was riding the heavy swell of the Bay of Biscay. In the lines of ships following the lay of the Portuguese coast, most conspicuous were the destroyers. Their fluttering ensigns, with the flash of the scarlet cross, were in contrast to the universal colour scheme of grey and green.

On this day clocks were put back an hour. The following morning we sighted the ships of 'H' force, "Renown", "Valiant", and "Ark Royal", with the cruiser "Sheffield", and aircraft carrier "Illustrious". Part of the convoy would proceed on the Cape Town route, but "Coventry" and "Illustrious" were to be part of convoy "Hats". The object of this convoy was to give a modicum of air reconnaissance, air striking, and air defence potential, to Admiral Cunningham's Eastern Mediterranean fleet based at Alexandria.

CHAPTER NINE

MARE NOSTRUM

Soon, we should be passing the Pillars of Hercules, on to a sea where the Fleet was being called upon to emulate the feats of that mythical hero. Late in the afternoon the Malta bound ships had detached, and manoeuvred into convoy formation with the ships of "H" Force. From the "Illustrious", fighters were taking off for training exercises.

In the pleasant sunshine two Fulmar Aircraft were entertaining sightseers on "Coventry's" upper deck, and possibly distracting lookouts, as they practised "dog fight" tactics. Onlookers gasped as both planes closed rapidly, head on to within an ace of collision, before disengaging on opposed wheeling courses. In minutes they had completed their orbits, and once more raced toward each other at a combined speed exceeding six hundred miles an hour. Fascinated, the watchers caught their breath as they anticipated the avoiding manoeuvre. At the last moment it began. But a blinding flash and a shower of splinters announced misjudgement, and a suicidal collision. Then the sky seemed full of falling wreckage.

At once the bosun's mate was piping "Away lifeboats crew!", and in minutes the sea boat, with Lieutenant Law, the gunnery officer in charge, was being lowered whilst the crew adjusted their life belts. "Put in the drain plug!" yelled Leading Seaman Chapman from the well deck to the stroke, and the action was performed just in time. Dropped neatly on top of the swell, the boat quickly gathered way, as the oarsmen pulled with the fervour of a racing crew. As they neared a patch of floating debris, a bright orange lifebelt was spotted, and in seconds the whaler was there. At once the floating airman was hauled in board, and with a rapid manoeuvre the boat moved off to where a second lifebelt was showing. Once again a body was hauled in board. As the rubbery forms, devoid of all human shape were gently laid in the bottom boards, no one needed telling that both were dead. In silence we returned to "Coventry", where the seaboat was recovered and secured, and our charges carried quickly to the sick bay. All too soon our opinion was confirmed.

Next day, at midday, the funeral service was read, and the bodies returned to the sea. All warships in the convoy joined in "funeral formation", a manoeuvre which resulted in every ship in turn passing over the burial position. The gloom of the occasion was considerable, but gave way to speculation on the immediate future, when Gibraltar was sighted on the 27th August. We went to the Mole for oil, expecting prompt departure. Much had changed in the Mediterranean, which we had known last year as a pleasant training area. There was no longer a friendly French Fleet. A small part of that fleet now lay immobilised at Alexandria, thanks to the diplomacy of Admiral Cunningham. But at Oran there had been naval action in which battleship "Bretagne" and destroyer "Mogador" had been sunk, battleship "Provence" damaged, and some twelve hundred French seamen killed. There were still powerful modern ships at Dakar, under Vichy control.

The Italians were now declared enemies. Their airforce was alone numerous enough to dominate the Mediterranean, in addition to which there was a respectable navy of fast, modern ships, including a shoal of submarines. Fortunately, they had the disadvantage of a restricted supply of oil fuel.

Heavy Italian air raids on Malta had quickly proved the pre-war theory that the Island would not be suitable as a main fleet base. But one hour after the Italian declaration of war became effective on June 11th, 1940, Admiral Cunningham had started out from Alexandria with "Warspite", "Malaya", and "Eagle", five cruisers, and nine destroyers toward Italy. He swept to within one hundred and twenty miles of the heel of Italy without challenge. On the return trip, an Italian submarine torpedoed the old six-inch gun cruiser "Calypso", which sank with the loss of one man. On July 9th, 1940, the Eastern Mediterranean Fleet covered a convoy from Alexandria to Malta. Off Calabria the Italian Fleet, appeared and shooting started. A hit was quickly scored on the battleship "Cesare", so the Italians made use of their superior speed to go home. As the British Fleet returned, large numbers of Italian aircraft made bombing attacks from a great height. Although the accuracy was considered remarkable by Admiral Cunningham, the only hit scored was on the bridge of the cruiser "Gloucester", where the Captain, six officers, and seven ratings were killed.

On July 19th, H.M.S. "Sydney" sunk the cruiser "Bartolomeo Colleoni" off Cape Spada, North of Crete.

Of little interest to us at the time, was the sinking of the neutral Greek cruiser "Helle" on August 15th by an Italian submarine. At the time, "Helle" was anchored off the island of Tinos, decorated with flags and brightly lit in honour of the Feast of the Assumption.

Once again we secured to the Mole at Gibraltar, but after taking on oil we lingered, and leave was piped for one part of starboard watch. This allowed interested parties to explore the narrow streets, where the most prominent buildings were souvenir shops; and to enjoy a pleasant tea ashore.

On the 30th August, we left Gibraltar with "Calcutta", "Renown", "Illustrious", "Valiant", "Sheffield", and "Ajax". Convoy "Hats" had begun. Next day we were towards the Balearic Islands. We had been undisturbed by the enemy, because radar gave us the ability to quickly locate the enemy spotting planes, and to direct the aircraft carriers' fighters to them. The fighters either drove them off before a report could be made, or shot them down.

When leaving Gibraltar, the Captain had cleared lower deck to explain the operation in which we were engaged. "H" Force was accompanying us to the Sicilian narrows. Here, the Italian Fleet, with the support of aircraft from Cagliari in Sardinia, or from the island of Pantellaria, which was close to the navigable channel, had the best chance to stop us. But in addition to giving cover by it's aircraft carrier, capital ships, and cruisers as far as the narrows, "H" Force would arrange diversions to distract the enemy while we cleared the channel.

The diversions took the form of two destroyers proceeding north of the Balearic Islands, there to transmit radio signals that might give the enemy the impression that a fleet visit to Genoa was in progress. Also, on the night before we entered, and during the most dangerous hours of our passing through the narrows, "Ark Royal's" aircraft would bomb the enemy aerodrome at Cagliari.

At dusk on the 1st September, our convoy was approaching the narrows. We were at action stations all night, and most of the following day, but there was no sign of the enemy. In the morning we duly sighted Gozo, and soon afterwards entered Valetta harbour. There was an air alert at this time, but we spotted no enemy aircraft. Gone were the Daisas with their cheerful Maltese boatmen.

The Eastern Mediterranean Fleet had arrived with three ships from Alexandria, in spite of heavy air attacks. The store ship "Cornwall" had been hit, but both she, and the second store ship "Volo" were now in Valetta harbour, with the oil tanker "Plumleaf", from which we replenished our tanks. South of the island, "Warspite", "Eagle", "Malaya" and "Orion" with attendant destroyers waited ready to accompany us on the journey east.

Towards evening we left Valetta. Next morning we met Admiral Cunningham's fleet. From then on we had our first experience of attack from the Italian air force. The high flying bombers were dropping salvos of bombs in every direction. "Coventry" was seldom the target, but we were constantly shooting at the attackers of our companion ships. Fighters from the carriers were also discouraging the Italians. Compared with out German adversaries in Norway, these people seemed almost harmless; although it will be recalled that we had less air support in Norway, and minimal fighter direction by radar. Also we were not now penned in the fjords. One could not say we were utterly free from anxiety, rather that we were sustained by a certain reassurance. We nevertheless looked forward to sundown and a quieter life. Just as the sun was declining one Italian airman made us sit up. Unnoticed from "Coventry", he divebombed the nearby aircraft carrier "Eagle". While we contemplated the water spouts which his bombs raised very close to "Eagle", the roar of aircraft engines fell on our ears, and we looked up to see an Italian aircraft passing over us. None of our spotters had reported him, and not a gun spoke. I recall clearly seeing the pilot's face, and would swear that he had an expression of bewilderment. As well he might, considering his getaway. Conversely, I , and doubtless several others, were devoutly thankful that it had not occurred to him to strafe us.

Soon after this we left the Fleet, and with "Calcutta" joined a seven knot convoy bound, via the Kithera Channel, for Greek ports.

With this convoy on the next day, towards noon, guns were called to the ready on the approach of a considerable Italian air formation. They attacked convoy ships, but were engaged by fire from "Calcutta" and ourselves. About ten bombs were dropped but all of them missed.

Evening brought relaxation, to be followed by a quiet night.

On the next day we left our convoy, and joined "Sydney", "Liverpool", and "Glasgow", on an easterly course. While we had been with our convoy, the main fleet had by guns and aircraft attacked Italian aerodromes at Leros in the Dodecanese.

On the 6th September, we entered the familiar confines of Alexandria Harbour. There was an air alert, but the enemy's object was reconnaissance.

Once through the defence net our attention was attracted by the modern Vichy cruisers "Duchesne", "Duguay-Trouin", "Suffren", and the old battleship "Lorraine". Conspicuous on the masts of these ships were huge clocks. Knowing men readily explained to their simpler acquaintances that these clocks were there for gun control purposes rather than to enable men on watch to see how long it would be before their relief arrived.

Having exhausted these novel features, our eyes turned to the familiar landmarks remembered from a year ago. There were the Pharos, Ras el Tin, and the extensive coal wharf at Mex. How long, we wondered, before we get off the tram at Mohamed Ali Square. Starboard watch were able to visit their old haunts the same evening, and on return reported minor changes to their port watch friends. Next morning whilst scrubbing decks, we looked around at the felucca boatmen similarly engaged. Soon it was their hour of prayer, and they kneeled on their prayer mats facing east.

To us came the sound of the pipe "Cable party of the starboard watch muster on the fo'c'sle! Special sea duty men to their stations". As the cable rattled into it's locker, port watch realised that Saturday afternoon, which they had anticipated spending ashore, would be occupied with, at the best, normal sea routine. We cruised east without incident, and in darkness arrived at Port Said. The R.N.V.R.'s and H.O.'s looked at some dimly illuminated parts of the harbour with interest. In a very short time we entered the canal, and were gliding forward in silence; our searchlight beam lighting the way ahead. All ships take on a pilot for the navigation of the canal, as a pile up could mean a serious blockade to other traffic lasting weeks. With the canal being our vital life line to the far east, the effect of such a stoppage can be well imagined. The canal is quite narrow and for the most part straight and the roads run alongside. To see another ship moving along the canal is like seeing a ship floating across the desert. The Australian War Memorial stands starkly against the purple sky, the twin towers looking as if a sword had cleft the obelisk apart. Overhead gleamed a myriad of stars, but on neither side could we glimpse any evidence of habitation beyond the canal banks. Infrequently, the light of an electric lamp revealed the outline of an official building, and usually at these places the silhouettes of scurrying white clad figures were vaguely descried.

There was no breeze, and we quickly noticed the hot air of the land. Our search-light attracted a swarm of every size and kind of moth, giving the appearance of a flurry of snow. Within half an hour the novelty of gazing about us had palled, and all off duty hammocks were slung in an upper deck position wherever possible. On turning out at "Lash up and stow" next morning the first job of the upper deck sleeper was to shake out the handful of moths with whom he had spent the night.

All the time it was getting hotter and we rigged a permanent canvas swimming bath and filled it with sea water. Swimming was not really possible, as it was only about ten feet in diameter and four feet in depth, and when some two dozen bathers were in it, there was hardly room to move. But it helped to keep cool. The heat did not in any was discourage the British eternal love of sport. The most popular sport and perhaps the most fiendish game being deck hockey. A few minutes of this would reduce the toughest character to a limp rag. I have often wondered why this game is so strenuous, and can only suppose, that the reason is due to the confined space in which the teams play, one is always in the centre of the game striking out at the puck which can never be many feet away from one, wherever one is playing.

During the time we had been passing through the canal, the families of London members of the ship's company had endured the first of their night bombings from the Luftwaffe.

CHAPTER TEN

RED SEA HOLIDAY

On Sunday morning, at 7 o'clock the 8th September, we arrived at Port Tewfik. For the new sailors it was an occasion to have entered the gate of the Red Sea, with it's sweating temperatures, sharks, and Arab Dhows. But of greater immediate interest were the "buzzes" concerning our next operation. At 1 p.m. we left harbour, and the first excitement was to stream paravanes. The Gulf of Suez was certainly warm enough, but devoid of scenic attraction. There was no spectacular demonstration by the sharks. Later in the day, however, we were interested when it was announced that Mount Sinai was just in view.

Next day we joined a slow convoy, and learned to get used to temperatures of the order of 110 degrees Fahrenheit. The First Lieutenant rigidly enforced the wearing of tropical shirts, (with a double thickness of cloth to protect the spine), and pith helmets. Coventry's drinking water, sedulously dosed with chloride of lime, was revolting, and even "goffers" were little better. Fortunately, the Sick Bay Petty Officer had access to a source of truly potable water, and provided glasses of lemonade at a reasonable price.

Night was appreciably cooler, but next morning we prepared for another day of sweating on this torrid sea. The spry attitude we had acquired coming through the Mediterranean now demanded conscious effort. The sun radiated an over-generous heat which was fully reflected by the lapping waters, and the air was still. At a temperature of 110 degrees, the order "For exercise only, action stations" came to be a relief from boredom. Night came with it's welcome drop in temperature, but it seemed a very short time before we were back to the heat-of-day routine. In late afternoon, we put on speed while our slow convoy carried on to nearby Port Sudan. Later, we overhauled another slow convoy, with which we stayed for two days. During this time we passed abreast of the Italian occupied port of Massawa. It was known that several Italian destroyers were stationed at Massawa, and on "Coventry's" bridge there were hopes that some of them might appear, but they failed to oblige.

When we put on speed, there was a "buzz" that we were bound for Aden. In early morning the rock cliffs of the coast came in sight. From our approach, the legendary port was hardly distinguishable from the sterile rock landfalls we had sometimes glimpsed on the way down. Aden was backed by featureless mountains sitting on the horizon. Indeed, the town occupies the crater of an extinct volcano. Soon, we should realise that in this part of the world green leaves were a wonder to behold. Direct rays from the sun, combined with heat reflected by the rocks, produced the climate of a furnace. Nevertheless, human beings with a minimum of wealth were able to survive there. Many of them laboured in the scorching sun to load coal-burning ships by the crude method of carrying the coal, half-hundredweight at a time, in sisal sacks.

Once in harbour, "Coventry" ratings quickly remarked on the fact that the seamen of H.M.S. "Kimberley", deeply sunburned, were covered by no more than a pair of tropical shorts and the normal canvas cap. The First Lieutenant also noticed it, and in daily orders announced that this rig would be permitted aboard "Coventry" whilst in harbour. At the same time, he advised gradual acclimatization to the sun's rays, to begin when the sun was declining. But by afternoon, we had left harbour and were proceeding further south. The signalmen knew that we were going to meet a convoy.

Next day, we sighted a group of ships, and on joining them, were pleased to find that they were moving fast. This convoy included "Empress of Britain", "Empress of Canada", and "Andes". They carried Anzac soldiers from the Middle East. We were two days with this convoy, bringing it well past Massawa, but no enemy forces appeared. Now it was our turn to put into Port Sudan while the troop ships went north to Suez. There were some "County" class cruisers in the harbour, in their far eastern colours of white with yellow funnels, looking very elegant with their high free board and tall funnels.

Once secured in the harbour, afternoon shore leave was piped. Exploring ashore, the liberty men soon found that the town existed solely for the port and it's commerce. They found that the principal building was a large stone built rectangular edifice housing the market. By afternoon, all perishable provisions had been removed, and the most prominent articles on offer were Manchester cotton goods. A cheap and useful memento, was a white cotton scull cap with orange coloured embroidery, as worn by almost all the men there. From the fashionable quarter of town, however, taxi men rushed with their vehicles to the quay side. Here, the cheery brown faced drivers greeted the sailors like long lost brothers, pressed them to enter the waiting cabs with promises to waft them instantly to the land of hearts desire.

Many took the trip but few were attracted by the bait, after a quick survey of the sordid locality that was journeys end. The denizens, however, were quite ready to entertain with friendly conversation those with purely social interest. Next, the taxi men proposed a visit to the "fuzzy-wuzzy village". Off went the sightseers, to acquaint themselves with the local dwellings, crafts and customs. Here they were beguiled into buying quaint and ancient Arab weapons, that by appearances might have done execution in many a Bedouin skirmish. On return to the ship, these objects were critically appraised by their mess mates, who pronounced them to be of the finest Birmingham workmanship. To several of the liberty-men, however, the best memory of Port Sudan was the "John Collins", served at the "Red Sea Hotel". This mixture of gin and lemonade, suitably iced, could momentarily slake the Red Sea thirst. Prominent in the harbour was the captured Italian submarine "Galileo-Galilei". The records found in this vessel had given the Admiralty enough information to dispose of all eight submarines, (reduced to seven by the loss of Galileo-Galilei), stationed in the Red Sea when Italy entered the war. Three more were subsequently sunk, and the rest tried to reach home via the Cape of Good Hope. Only one of them made it.

Some weeks earlier, Galileo-Galilei had attacked a Red Sea convoy, which was watched over solely by an R.A.F. patrol. Every available British anti-submarine craft subsequently arrived on the spot, and the submarine submerged deeper, kept still, and waited until it seemed certain that the hunting vessels had gone. A survey with the periscope showed that one sub-hunter remained; the sloop "Moonstone", armed with a single 3" gun. At once the Italians surfaced, eager to close in. "Moonstone" promptly opened up with a Lewis gun, scoring hits on the conning tower and killing the Captain. Now "Moonstone" closed in, to capture the submarine and all it's crew.

On the afternoon of Sunday the 15th September, we left Port Sudan with a convoy for Aden. Two days of uneventful steaming followed, and at dusk on the third day, the Perim Light was spotted on our port beam. By morning of Thursday, the 19th September, we were approaching Aden, and half the guns crews were fallen out to recover paravanes, which had been streamed as a precaution against air or submarine placed mines. Half way through this operation the alarm rattlers sounded. At once the towing wires were secured on cleats. The sailors returned to their guns. Three aircraft were in sight, and we got in three salvoes before they aimed their bombs for the convoy. Soon after, splashes appeared, well clear of the target, and the planes were homeward bound. Now came a signal, that a metal fin had been seen to fall from one of the bombs. This, with the evidence of our own spotters, led to the suspicion that these Italians were using artillery projectiles as bombs. Once the sky was clear of aircraft, the paravanes were recovered, and we prepared to enter harbour. There was shore leave that evening, spent by many in enjoying cool drinks, or seeing the film at Shaftos open-air cinema. Others went to the shark proof bathing places.

Next morning we left harbour, and found ourselves going north with a moderately speedy convoy. In that convoy were several ships that had left U.K. with us, parting company near Gibraltar, notably the "Amara". But in the evening we left them to proceed south through the Strait of Bab el Mandeb. On this journey the temperature was exceptional, reaching 120 degrees Fahrenheit. On the 22nd September, a Sunday, we entered harbour at Aden. We should stay a few days to re-fuel, and store ship.

Certain Fleet Reservists, with pre-1914 traditions, had fired the imagination of a few of the R.N.V.R.'s with alluring recitations about the glories of Aden. Able Seaman Risdon and Barnes were consequently anxious to try the view to be had from a peak behind the town known as "Sham.Sham". Having been granted leave to make this excursion, they stepped ashore in the cool of early morning, and by 5.30 a.m. had begun the climb. The sun climbed simultaneously, but faster, and it took two hours of ever more arduous effort, during which the sweat poured, before they rested at the summit. The view was indeed worthwhile, but the rising temperature compelled retreat after only a few minutes of pleasure. The descent took longer than the climb, and growing thirsts made it seem an age. They were thankful to reach Gold Mohur beach, were, protected by shark nets, they could luxuriate in the cool sea.

The majority, however, preferred an afternoon or evening of unhurried leisure, taking a meal at an Indian restaurant, or beer at the canteen. The restaurant meal was usually roast chicken, and personnel stationed at Aden were always keen to talk with men from the ships, preferably "Townies", (men from the same home town), who usually could tell up to date news, so there was no lack of guides. We were somewhat surprised to find in the shops of Aden, tins of best quality American fruit salad—not common at home. Even more surprising, was the poor quality of tins of fruit salad that had been part of the cargo of a captured Italian merchantman. A.B. Durno, an Aberdonian R.D.F. operator, sported a meal at a hotel and ever after remembered the luxury of "iced asparagus tips".

On the morning of the 26th September we left Aden at 09.00 with cruiser "Ajax" to join another considerable convoy of Anzac troops. The convoy included "Empress of Japan", "Orion", and "Oronsay".

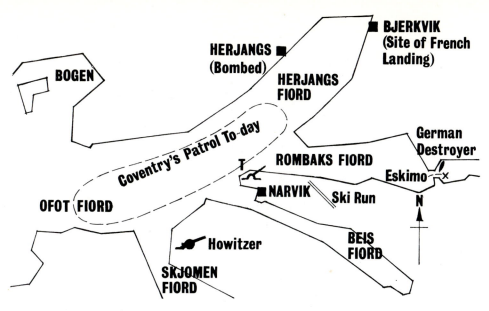

Plan of Narvik Fiord

Bombardment of Narvik Commences

Narvik in Flames

Plate Nine

Evacuation of French Troops from Norway

Fighters Collide—Picking up the Pilots

Spike Sullivan with Salvaged Cockpit

H.M.S. "RAMILLIES"
Grand Harbour Malta

Bargains in Sister Street
A.B. Russell

Baby Octopus and Gash Wallahs

Bum Boat Boy
Port Said

Italian Raids in the Red Sea

Arab Dhows in the Canal

Red Sea Rig
A.B. "Joe Palooka" Mowbray, and A.B. Risdon

Camouflaged "COUNTY CLASS" Cruiser Port Tewfik

Plate Eleven

S.M. 79 Shot Down in Alexandria

French Battleship "LORRAINE"

"BARTOLOMEO COLLEONI" on Fire
Sunk by H.M.A.S. "SYDNEY" off Sicily

H.M.S. "WARSPITE" Straddled

"ARTAGLIERE" Blows Up.
Sunk by H.M.S. "YORK"

Tombstone of Smoke

Cartoon by A.E.L. Laws

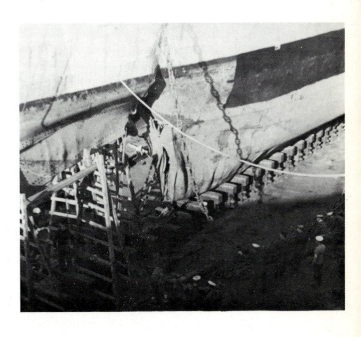

"COVENTRY" in Gabbari Dock Showing Torpedo Damage

Plate Thirteen

Captain's Christmas Day Rounds

H.M.S. "ORION" Avoids Stick of Bombs

H.M.S. "ILLUSTRIOUS" Hit

Plate Fourteen

H.M.S. "COVENTRY" On Patrol

"COVENTRY" Football Team in Alexandria Stadium

Plate Fifteen

Fraternising with the Cretans

Bows Blown Off H.M.S. "LIVERPOOL"
by Torpedo Bombers

Mutiny On Board "ESCAUT"
Boarding Party Approaches.

Sunderland Flying Patrol

Near Miss for H.M.S. "AJAX"
Disembarking Troops in Suda Bay

The Afternoon Watch

Towards the evening of next day we left this convoy. Before doing so the lower deck was cleared, and the First Lieutenant explained that the soldiers in the convoy would soon be fighting in the desert, and he hoped we would give them a good cheer before we left the convoy.

Accordingly, as many men as possible manned the upper deck, and "Coventry" altered course to pass near one of the troopers. When we could clearly see the faces of our Australian companions, a really lusty cheer was made for them. They were delighted, grinning, and waving their hats. If the "Coventry" cheer pleased the Australians, it raised our own morale at the same time. After the fall of France, it had seemed reasonable enough to Navy adherents that enemy landings were most unlikely, though the vague fear of new techniques gnawed at the faith of the more imaginative. Whilst occupied with our Atlantic rendezvous, coming through the Mediterranean, and accompanying Red Sea convoys that were never attacked, we had heard constant radio announcements of the number of Luftwaffe raiders shot down. It was taken for granted that our air force was superior and few were aware of the frightening disparity in the ratio of defenders to attackers. It would be long before we should know what we owed to the sustained courage of a small band of our countrymen, supplemented by equally worthy men from some of the countries already swallowed up by the enemy. Years would pass before it was fully told how their small fleet of superior aircraft, economically directed by radar, daunted the massive Luftwaffe, and turned the will of Hitler from the path of success.

Having refused to consider any possibility of defeat, we had found it irksome to hear of the Italian army's preparations to invade Egypt while our army, it seemed, just looked on. Here was the promise of attack on men, whose navy and airforce had shown them to be lacking in war winning qualities, and the prestige of the Anzacs was a guarantee of success.

At that time, however, our main concern was what awaited us at Tewfik. We entered the Gulf of Suez, once again directing our gaze frequently to Mount Sinai, and proceeding at 20 knots. We did not stay at Tewfik, but straightway entered the Suez Canal. On that warm Sunday afternoon there was ample leisure to look around. Going through the lakes we saw the families of canal officials in picnic and bathing parties. Naturally, the young women in swimsuits attracted most attention. This was the nearest most matelots got to the "Nicey French girl" mentioned in the opening patter of the legion of Arab touts that pestered sailors in the streets of Alexandria.

We passed through the canal in company with one of the Navy's little freak ships—a gunboat with the very appropriate name H.M.S. "Gnat". She consisted of a 6" gun, with an engine room to propel it through the water, and little else. Later we found another unusual Naval craft, H.M.S. "Terror". This ship consisted of a twin 15" gun turret mounted on the forecastle, and the significance of at least two bombarding vessels was not lost on us. Obviously the army were going to make a move, and we were going to soften up any enemy positions, and then cut off the supply columns by bombarding the main road from the west which runs parallel with the coast.

On reaching Port Said by late afternoon, there was some delay, which was turned to advantage by the gulli-gulli man who came aboard to entertain us. And here I would digress to explain the peace time custom of the Mediterranean Fleet in transactions of a similar nature.

It was commonly reported that in the years preceding 1939, a Levantine merchant calling himself Jim Irish had a monopoly of peddling souvenirs and similar articles to the men of the Fleet. As soon as the Flag Ship was in Alexandria Harbour he would appear in a launch, bearing gifts for the Captain of the Flag Ship, and the Master at Arms, and request to come aboard.

The money spent by the much larger force of naval personnel passing through Alexandria in war time, had warranted Jim Irish opening a large emporium ashore. But here there was competition from Khalil Khan, and even lesser men were able to fish the golden shoal.

But our gulli-gulli man was woefully short of capital. He was lean and bare, wearing a threadbare galibieh, and his only other possession was a yard length of steel wire. We were not surprised when, to the accompaniment of a dazzling smile, he requested the loan of a pound note for use in his first trick. There was nobody willing to produce a pound note, but Leading Seaman Morris, a regular Navy man with greying hair, sportingly handed over a ten shilling note.

The gulli-gulli man confirmed the general expectation, by causing the currency note to vanish with a minimum of abracadabra. After that, he rivetted our attention with several skilful demonstrations. Noteworthy was the way in which he thrust the steel wire through both cheeks, with less concern than a sailor lighting a cigarette.

Now came the "piece de resistance", which was a demonstration of escapalogy. In a very short time, a pile of ropes brought from nearby equipment lockers stood ready to hand. Then the gulli-gulli man invited all comers to bind him in such a way that he was unable to escape.

There was no rush from the iron-ship sailors to try their skill. The experience of most of them was limited to turning up a rope on a cleat, racking wire hawsers secured on bollards, or securing a boat's painter to a rail with a round turn and two half hitches. But at length A.B. Peter Gallienne, a Fleet reservist, possibly in service at Jutland, was pushed forward by his cronies. They were the "bosun's party", and had shown considerable skill at special rigging jobs. Gallienne selected a suitable coil of rope, grinned at the gulli-gulli man, and with becoming gravity started to bind him. He proceeded slowly, and avoided straining the ropes, which would have impeded blood circulation. Gallienne's cronies broadcasted knowing smiles, which made it clear that the challenger would regret his challenge. The onlookers inwardly admired the man who could defeat an escapalogist in so humane a manner.

At length the last knot was tied. Gallienne rejoined the audience which moved back to give the waiting performer a good clearance.

The gulli-gulli man assumed a friendly grin, and turned slowly in all directions for viewers to see the complicated cocoon of ropes that pinioned his limbs. Then he sat down, changed to a recumbent position, and began to wriggle.

After two minutes he stood erect, holding over his head the ropes that had bound him. There was considerable applause, which drowned the sarcastic chuckles of those who had not been impressed by Gallienne's effort. To these, bosun's party explained how their champion had mercifully refrained from using certain devilish knots learned on the China station.

The performer had been paid in advance, and smiling happily had begun his triumphal exit, when Leading Seaman Morris hurried forward to reclaim his ten shilling note. The gulli-gulli man's lack of English resulted in communication being slow and misleading, but at length the light dawned. In a flash the ten shilling note reappeared in the conjurers hand, and was quickly returned to the purse in the Leading Seaman's belt.

We left the darkening harbour and very soon were aware only of the darkness between sea and sky, and the chop and splash of the waves.

CHAPTER ELEVEN

MEDITERRANEAN ACTIVITIES

On the morning of the 30th September, we were nearing Alexandria. Our interest quickened as the anti-submarine net at the harbour entrance was opened to admit us, and promptly closed once we were inside. The Fleet was in, and we soon identified "Warspite", and "Malaya". Once again we noticed the Pharos, a common-place erection, said to mark the site of one of the eight wonders of the ancient world. Ras-el-Tin, the palace of King Farouk, came in sight, then the smart headquarters of the Alexandria Yacht Club. Admiral Cunningham was, of course, only too uncomfortably aware that from here, Axis agents had a grand-stand view of the comings and goings of his Fleet. In his autobiography, he relates with relish his action to deceive one staunch Yacht Club member, the Japanese ambassador. Whilst the Fleet was preparing to leave harbour for the operation that would culminate at Matapan, the Admiral went ashore with all the ceremony and luggage normally used when he went for a long week-end, and returned unseen to his ship a few hours later. The Vichy ships were still there, presumably enjoying their long holiday.

"Coventry" was berthed by a concrete mole near the coal wharf. Thus our libertymen would no longer land at No. 14 gate, where the volume of fleet traffic was enough to sustain a money changers booth, in which every evening sat three smiling men each wearing a red fez, very prominent under brilliant illumination. Now we entered through No. 50 gate, which opened on to a sandy district of poverty stricken hovels called Mex.

Each watch had a run ashore, and after the long tram ride, got off to find that Fleet personnel were now a prominent part of the Alexandrian scene, and catering for them was a flourishing industry. Everywhere they were welcomed with smiling faces and flattering comments. The "hostilities only" ratings were for the most part readily captivated by this Levantine charm, but if they admitted this in the hearing of regular sailors, sour comments were made. They remembered the Italo-Abyssinian war days, when it was necessary for men ashore to keep in groups of three at least; and that frequent attempts were then made to steal the boom boats of the flag ship.

A current story of those days indicated a curiously divided loyalty. In the time of the Abyssinian war, ran the tale, if an Italian troop-ship were passing a British warship, the Italians would make insulting gestures, and shout words that to English ears sounded like "Boot-neck". I never heard what these words meant, or what was the standard reply. In this sort of atmosphere at Port Said, a large Italian trooper waited, when a British cruiser arrived, and prepared to moor near them. Commander Woodhouse, who was the First Lieutenant, was eager to impress the Italians with a display of superior seamanship.

Everything, indeed, went remarkably well until the crucial operation. Then an unlucky seaman tripped, and let go a wire hawser. The resulting train of misfortune produced a farce at which the Duce's men guffawed with pleasure.

The following Sunday, after the church parade, the Commander referred to the responsibility of the Fleet vis-a-vis, the Duce's demonstrations, and deplored the poor show of mooring the ship. "As for the man who dropped that hawser", grated the Commander, "he should have broken his leg!!" This comment earned him the reputation of a latter day Captain Bligh. But generally, these incidents had been forgotten by the sailors. Possibly they had not been forgotten by the C-in-C and his officers, who had a burning desire to try conclusions with the Italian Fleet.

Alexandria was a sunny playground for the matelot ashore, and the piastres in which he was now paid, could, judiciously spent, admit him to a variety of pleasures. There were some half dozen cinemas of which I remember the names of only Ritz, Rio and Mohamed-Ali. In some of them the roof could be rolled back during the interval, when white robed waiters would bring in cane tables for refreshments of coffee, ice cream, cakes, beer, or any other drink. At weekends, the polyglot Europeans of moderate means, would come for the family spree. The plump, dark haired Greek girls, with their small round hands, usually smiled playfully at their escorts, while their French opposite numbers, usually fair haired, played the game by looking pretty aloof.

The most popular rendezvous was the Fleet Club, which had been organised by a Fleet Chaplain. The Club's main glory was a beer garden. It was a large, sand floored, and palm shaded quadrangle, with cane tables and chairs well spaced out. When the Fleet was in, many hundreds of matelots came here in the evenings, and the Arab waiters, with red fez and spotless white clothing, had a hectic time administering a generous supply of "Stella" beer. Tombola was played here, and the possibility of large prizes brought a considerable throng of participants.

The much smaller number of thirsty men arriving at the club in the afternoon, would proceed to a small bar having the sign of "The Bug and Gluepot", but as a thirst quencher at this time of day, minerals were generally preferred. In addition there was a restaurant, tailor's shop, and barber's shop, where the U.K. sailor was astonished at the thoroughness and variety of services provided by the Mediterranean barber. For the watch on board, however, there was a reminder that the violence of the enemy did not necessarily stop at the anti-submarine net of the harbour. A new harbour duty had arisen for the seamen. During the hours of darkness they would provide sentries stationed on the upper deck, armed with electric torches and whistles. The sentries were to watch all movement near the ship, and to challenge any boat that came too close. If a boat refused to stop on challenge, they would sound their whistles and direct onto the boat a jet of water from one of the ready rigged hoses.

Lieutenant Commander Dalrymple-Hay had previously explained that ill-disposed persons might attempt to damage our ship with explosives. To many of us this conjured a vision of nothing more terrifying than a Beau Geste type Arab with a home made bomb. There were even facetious suggestions that an unpopular superior returning by felucca at an irregular hour might get an accidental dousing. The threat that made this order necessary was, however, a deadly one. Skilled and daring Italian engineers and frogmen had learned an effective technique for sinking ships by fixing mines to the keel while the ships lay in the fancied security of their own harbours. In time to come, Italian frogmen would so damage "Valiant" and "Queen Elizabeth" that they would sit useless on the bottom of Alexandria harbour for months. Even before then, a similar arm of the Italian Navy would come close to sinking "Coventry". But in October 1940, "Coventry's" sentries were watching and waiting for an enemy who indeed had started out, but had been liquidated before reaching his goal. On August 22nd, Fleet Air Arm Swordfish, had sunk the Italian submarine "Iride", which was bringing the frogmen and their explosives to the eastern Mediterranean.

Sentry duty had it's more pleasant side, however, even during the middle watch. At this hour there was absolute silence and glass calm water; the only moving object was the light of the Fleet patrol launch. Thus for a few minutes before relieving the duty sentry, one could marvel at the spread of stars in the clear Mediterranean sky, and frequently watch the career of a meteorite.

Having spent two pleasant days in harbour, we left with the Fleet in the dawn of the third, wondering what awaited us. The First Lieutenant had explained in his daily orders that "the Fleet did not put to sea for the fun of the thing, but for a definite object", going on to say that wherever possible he would let the ship's company know what was happening. We were informed that the main object of this excursion was to look for Italian supply convoys making for Libya. At sea all was quiet. We were able to identify "Malaya", "Eagle", "Ramillies", and "Ajax". It was possible that aircraft from "Eagle" would bomb Tobruk. The Fleet covered a wide area of sea, and often unseen over the horizon were co-operating units. The occupation of gun's crews was for much of the time to watch the sea, look at the sky and speculate on what the moving R.D.F. aerials were tracking. Any unusual movement of a Fleet unit, or long burst of lamp signalling always aroused interest.

A somewhat unpopular chore of duty gun's crews was to proceed to one of the special lookout positions just below, and on either side of the bridge to spend an hour on look-out for submarine periscopes. Two men occupied each look-out post, and I have subsequently wondered if it would not have been wiser to have only one man there. Because, sad to relate, lookouts were sometimes more interested in telling a form of confessional than in watching for the underwater enemy. One young seaman related how he clicked with an ATS girl at a dance and spent the night with her. His mother received an anonymous letter of accusation and duly reproached him. "Doubtless", I volunteered, "you expressed your regret and assured her that this would never happen again". "No", said he' "I knew that my mother and sister would keep on saying "It's no use being sorry now". "So I said when returning from leave, that I had my own life to lead, and rather than be nagged, I should not be coming home again". "Soon I got a letter assuring me that all was forgiven. Even my father, who I thought was unable to write, sent me a letter asking me not to be foolish". Just then, the words of Lieutenant McKean, Officer of the Watch, came through the speaking tube—"And now, what about looking for a few submarines"?

Our first Mediterranean operation was uneventful, and we entered harbour on October 7th in a very self satisfied frame of mind.

But next morning the Fleet of heavy ships left harbour, and by nightfall we had followed them. The operation was a Malta convoy code named "Decoy", and included the fast merchantmen "Clan

Ferguson", "Clan MacGillivray", and "Lanarkshire". At that time, of course, we were not so well informed, and a few hopefuls had started the eternal buzz about "returning to the U.K." By morning we found the weather cool and squally. Some of the ships company were getting over the stomach infection known as "Gyppy Tummy", and a few were trying to keep down seasickness. But when at sea, gun's crews liked nothing better than stormy weather. Aircraft did not venture out, and submarines took refuge in the depths. The Italian Fleet had not established itself as a serious menace. Stormy weather meant "cruising stations", when guns crews would be allowed to gather in the small shelter rigged for the purpose, there to engage for the most part in riotous social chatter. Three days of normal routine passed, uninterrupted by any sign of the enemy. The last time the Fleet had made this trip, for meeting our "Hats" convoy at Malta, four Italian battleships had appeared, though they did not venture to interfere. It was for this reason that Admiral Cunningham was bringing his whole Fleet on this occasion. The ships with us were "Valiant", "Malaya", "Ramillies", "Eagle". "Illustrious", six cruisers, H.M.S. "Calcutta", and sixteen destroyers.

We entered Valetta harbour under lowering skies. At this point the destroyer "Imperial" struck a mine, but was able to cope with the damage sustained. The formerly busy harbour was almost deserted; but on a precarious perch at the end of a breakwater stood a small crowd of Maltese schoolboys, who, after shouting "hurrah", broke into a well known chorus proclaiming the sexual decadence of Mussolini. We appreciated their welcome and their pluck, but could not then forsee that the fortitude and fighting spirit of people like these lads and their parents, was going to be the main factor in keeping a precarious hold on the Mediterranean, Suez Canal, and North African coast. Later that day we left harbour with some empty merchantmen. Well to the north, a force of cruisers were stationed to intercept any sally by the Italian Fleet. Evening and darkness came without alarm, but during the middle watch there was evidence of gunfire to our north.

By 2 a.m. there was moonlight, and at a distance of one hundred and ten miles north-east of Malta, a flotilla of Italian destroyers was sighted by H.M.S. "Ajax". Two of the destroyers, "Ariel" and "Airone" were sunk by "Ajax", and a third, "Artigliere" seriously damaged. Italian hits on "Ajax" killed two officers and ten ratings, wounding twenty more.

H.M.S. "York" set off at high speed in pursuit of the Italian destroyer, which was now clearly silhouetted in the morning light. She seemed to be holed up forward, and slowing down, as H.M.S. "York" opened fire again. The salvoes appeared to be hitting the bridge, and the stricken destroyer now completely stopped, was doomed. The Italian Commander must have ordered "Abandon Ship", as everywhere sailors were jumping into the sea and swimming away. "York" moved in close and started picking up survivors. When everyone was aboard, the Captain ordered torpedo tubes to be trained on the Italian destroyer, which showed no signs of sinking. "Fire", and the torpedo sped away to it's target. The torpedo struck just forward of the bridge. For a fraction of a second, it seemed as if the warhead had failed to go off, but with a shuddering roar of flame and black smoke the "D'Artiglierre" disintegrated. The smoke plummetted upwards into a great mushroom, and hung in a pall over the placid water. There was a stunned silence, and then routine took over again; men went back to their duties, and H.M.S. "York" headed back towards the other ships, and the convoy proceeded safely on to Malta.

On Sunday, 12th October, we were near Crete, and the day passed without incident. Next day, however, we were several times called to action stations, when snoopers were spotted, but no attack developed. Following this, we, with "Calcutta", were shepherding a number of ships from Greece, which were bound for Port Said. Then it was that Italian high level bombers came to aim their bombs at the merchantmen. We met several successive attacks, and used up a lot of ammunition. These aircraft dropped about thirty bombs, without getting even a near miss.

Towards evening we were advised by signal that the cruiser "Liverpool", having been torpedoed by an aircraft, was stopped and on fire. Forty of the ships company had been killed. Ten minutes later, we, with "Calcutta", were speeding to assist. The Admiral wanted us there before the Italians came to finish the job. The sea was calm, as with straining engines, we flung a great bow wave to either side and raced through the darkness. The gun's crews, sometimes glimpsing the serenity of the sparkling sky, speculated on the fate of "Liverpool". After two or three hours, a patch of faint illumination appeared ahead, which soon grew to a bright flame on the horizon. Eventually we made out the silhouette of "Liverpool", with the bow from stem to "A" turret shattered and blazing furiously. It brought home the consequences of combat even on this calm, co-operative sea.

Within three hours, "Liverpool's" ship's company had controlled the blaze. Meanwhile, the cruiser "Orion" had arrived, and was towing "Liverpool", stern first. The group of ships went towards Alexandria at 9 knots, but after several hours the towing hawser parted. New hawsers were passed, and soon after, the damaged bows fell off and towing became easier. By now the moon had risen,–a splendid opportunity for another wave of torpedo bombers. The bombing of Italian air fields at Leros in the Dodecanese by aircraft of "Illustrious", and "Eagle", on the night before, may have been the cause of our freedom from attack.

Through the next day there was no alarm, and on Wednesday the 16th October we entered Alexandria harbour. The night was moonlit, and most of the Fleet in harbour, so there was an air raid, with the object of dropping mines to seal the fleet in harbour. On these occasions, the Fleet's anti-aircraft guns fired "Blind Barrage" at any target reported by radar within a distance of five miles. The batteries of 4" guns mounted in ships at different points in the harbour would erupt sporadically with ear splitting detonation, followed by a lurid glare, which revealed silhouettes of every class of ship. Sometimes Bofors cannon mounted ashore would clatter in panic, and now and then a fountain of red or green tracer would play. These amazing fire work displays must have been very costly, but presumably, cheaper than ships sunk while concentrated in an easily defined area.

We got a week in harbour; time to notice changes, The "colours" ceremony on the flag ship was now a short affair. In 1939 it had been pleasant to listen as the band played Marseillaise, Brabanconne, Polish, and Egyptian, (the sprightly "King Farouk, King Farouk" . . . .), in addition to our own anthem.

Nevertheless, we still heard the Marseillaise wafted by the breeze now and then from somewhere aboard the "Lorraine".

The Vichy sailors always kept very much to themselves ashore, and mostly frequented a bar called the Petit Trianon.

The shore goers were learning their way about, and passed word of new places to cronies having similar tastes. The bathing beaches of Stanley Bay and Sidi-Bishr were generally very popular, while some frequented the racecourse at the Sporting Club. For those inclined to quiet reflection, Nouzha Gardens held great attraction.

For real local colour, the roller skating rinks of Cleopatra, and Sporting Club, were hard to beat. Between free-for-all sessions, European girls attired in dazzling skating costumes, would, with their partners, dance Tangos to the most entrancing melodies. Now and then the service element, British blue and khaki, the slouch hat of the Aussie, and occasionally the red pom pom of the Vichy matelot would crowd the place out. This was the case on one hot afternoon, and as a result of over-crowding and bumping, an altercation began between a Lancashire lad in khaki and a Vichy Petty Officer. The proprietor went immediately towards them, calmly intoning "what is the matter"? Simultaneously, a public spirited Australian placed himself squarely between the quarrelers a split second before they had decided on a punch up. He received telling blows from each of them, before the surge of impatient skaters scattered the group. The belligerents were swept far apart, and forgot their quarrel in trying to keep their feet. The luckless Australian spent the rest of the afternoon trying to find his hat.

Far more satisfactory than such excitement, however, was the arrival of mail aboard "Coventry", though most of it carried dates just prior to our departure from the U.K. It was nevertheless read several times over.

On Sunday the 27th October, we left Alexandria during a middle watch, and at daylight recognised "Eagle" and "Malaya", in company with smaller ships. Next day we heard that Italy had declared war on Greece but did not fully realise how this would affect us. The following day, towards evening, we were back in Alexandria. Our excursion had been an occasion for some small units of the fleet to bombard Sidi Barrani.

To our surprise we left harbour independently in the forenoon of the next day. After a pleasant two day cruise, we approached land quite new to us. Behind the shore was a view of distant mountains. Our curiosity grew as we entered a pleasant bay from which many green leaved trees could be seen, in contrast to the solitary infrequent palm trees of Alexandria. This was Suda Bay in Crete.

The Captain was soon ashore on official business, and later in the day leave was piped. The bay had very few houses, and a single jetty. Once we got ashore a light rain shower began, a luxury after the heat and sand of Alexandria. Walking along a country road it was delightful to sniff the odour of ploughed fields displaying red soil, and to see the olive gardens. At once we noticed the song of the birds, and were intrigued to see trees laden with lemons. We passed through a small hamlet where the houses were like fortresses. They were built on a knoll by the road, and surrounded by massive stone walls. The inhabitants kept quiet, and eyed us warily.

At length we came to a larger village, where there was a small square and a hostelry. Here we saw soldiers, who turned out to be British Royal Engineers, and there was a bout of greeting and tongue wagging. The engineers were part of a very small unit. They first advised us where koniak could be had, and in the subsequent conversation retailed a lecture delivered to them by their officers. Most memorable feature of the lecture concerned the social attitude to island women, and was summed up in the epigram "If you get involved with a woman here, there can be only one of two possible results, either a merry riotous wedding feast, or a sad and moving funeral". We were protected by the shortness of our stay, being well out to sea that same evening.

CHAPTER TWELVE

DAYS OF SUCCESS

We entered Alexandria harbour at 16.00 hours next day, with a belief that our fortunes in the war had improved. We were pleased with our new port of call. Few questioned the propaganda suggestion that the Greeks had entered the war from a desire to join our good crusade.

But, in fact, Italian forces had begun to provoke Greece; (whose government had neither a formidable air force, nor armoured regiments in it's army), from the moment Mussolini had declared war on Britain. Most flagrant had been the mysterious torpedoing of the Greek cruiser "Helle", by the Italian submarine "Tricheco". It was probably with these events in mind, that the Greek Government turned a blind eye, to the use by the British Fleet of Greek anchorages for tankers holding strategic fuel reserves. The Italians by way of riposte had directed their aircraft to shoot up Greek ships in the vicinity.

Ultimately, the Italians had send a demand to the Greek Prime Minister, General Metaxas, that they occupy certain key areas. This the General had refused, presumably in the belief that the Wehrmacht would not be sent to intervene in his stand against Mussolini. This was the dilemma of a man suffering from cancer of the throat, and soon to die.

The Greeks had not in fact joined us against Germany. They welcomed us as allies against Italy, and permitted the use of Suda Bay as a base, and also allowed the Fleet to convoy their ships leaving the "Free Zone" of Piraeus.

On the morning after the return from our first trip to Suda Bay, we set out again; this time with H.M.S. "Ajax", the netlayer "Protector", oil tankers, and mine-sweepers. There were two days of pleasant cruising, interrupted by a lone Italian snooper aircraft which kept well out of range. On the afternoon of the 1st November, we arrived at Suda Bay, and "Ajax" proceeded to the jetty to unload stores and equipment. We were stationed some distance out in the Bay, where our guns commanded the approaches to the jetty. It was a glorious day, and with memories of our previous visit, we rather envied "Ajax" her berth against the jetty. "Coventry" was at action stations, prying in every direction with R.D.F. There was a sudden chorus of "Alarm enemy aircraft" from the communication numbers. The director indicator clocks ticked furiously and gunlayers and trainers quickly swung their handwheels in an effort to keep up. In seconds, all guns were with the director, loaders stood ready with ammunition, while Officers of Quarters glanced round to see that ready-use lockers were open and clear. Most gun's crews were looking ahead towards a gap in the range of hills beyond the Bay. Then we saw six aircraft of fighter bomber size, racing in line towards "Ajax". A heavy barrage from both "Coventry" and "Ajax" began at once. The destroyers joined in, and there was pandemonium as detonations re-echoed in the confines of the bay. But these Italians were determined, and on they came, keeping low. In spite of the barrage, which included the short range weapons of "Ajax" when they got close, the Italians kept a straight course and aimed several bombs at the cruiser. Soon after this the barrage ceased, and within seconds the attackers had shrunk into the distance. They had made no hits, but had several near misses.

To us anti-aircraft gunners, the efficacy of our fire often seemed doubtful. The first few actions had shown that our weapons would not bring aircraft down "like pheasants". We knew that convoys welcomed us because we kept the attacker high up, and gave him so little leisure for deliberate aim, that he rarely hit a ship. But we judged rather, from the shooting at countless aircraft making a direct attack on our own ship. Besides the exertion of rapid loading, we endured the shocking detonations from the gun barrels; and in Norway, went through the unpleasant and undignified period of taking cover. After all this, the aircraft would fly off apparently unscathed. Official literature encouraged us with information that many a plane that went over the horizon apparently unharmed, had, in fact, sustained serious damage, and never reached home. Indeed, our own ship's radio office would sometimes report after an engagement, that S.O.S. signals from a nearby enemy source at sea level had been received.

Lieutenant Dalrymple-Hay, that outstanding leader and builder of morale, appreciated the feelings of the gunners, and in daily orders made reference to the great day when we should "shoot one down in flames". On this occasion he was delighted to see wreckage fall from one of the fleeing planes, and made sure that all on the bridge should know it. So it was not unnatural that one should overhear in the bathroom that evening the sarcastic voice of a gunner intoning "Yes, and "Jimmy" reckons he saw wreckage fall from one plane". But next day "Jimmy" was triumphant, and wrote in daily orders "Proof that I did see one of the planes damaged has arrived. An Italian air crew has been captured ashore in the direction where our attackers flew yesterday".

Next morning, we sailed with "Ajax". We had hardly cleared the entrance to the Bay, when an alarm brought all guns to the ready, and soon after, five aircraft attacked at high level, splitting their bomb load between "Coventry" and "Ajax". We gave our attackers several salvos, and they in turn dropped bombs which fell wide. "Ajax", however, was near missed once more. When clear of Crete we had an uneventful cruise, and late on the day after, anchored in Alexandria.

Next day we were in Port, with evening shore leave to one watch, but early next morning we left with a seven ship convoy accompanied by "Calcutta", "Ajax", and "Sydney". All day we headed north to Crete without incident, and so continued the second day until "Calcutta", and two merchantmen left us for Suda Bay. "Coventry" and the rest now set course for Malta.

The objective was to supply Malta with another convoy, and to meet reinforcements from Gibraltar ; "Barham", "Berwick", and "Glasgow". The Fleet was covering us, This operation was called "Coat". Next day Italian spotters, in the shape of Cant flying boats, were indicated by "R.D.F.", but Fulmars from "Illustrious" promptly met them and shot them down. One of these large flying boats, damaged by a fighter, plunged through the clouds in full view of surrounding ships. Every gun that could be brought to bear was used to ensure destruction. In a sudden, steep dive, the heavy craft splashed into the rolling swell. The gunners cheered to the echo. And within seconds, the breakers were rolling in the normal pattern ; the Italian flying men and their craft forgotten.

Next day we arrived in Valetta. There was an air alert, but no attack developed. We saw some Blenheim bombers, a hopeful sign of the beginning of air defence of the island,—and of air cover for convoys. Unknown to us, R.A.F. reconnaisance planes now in Malta, were able to make constant reports on the position of the Italian Fleet.

After a day with the Fleet and it's reinforcements, we were Alexandria bound. Our convoy included "Clan Lanarkshire", and "Clan Ferguson". There were two days of uneventful cruising for "Coventry", and back in Alexandria we heard news that probably explained our good fortune. In "Daily Orders" of the 12th November, "Jimmy" confided that "The C in C was looking for the Italian Fleet", going on to deplore the fact that the Italians "liked their bases better than coming out to scrap".

Admiral Cunningham had seen a chance of using aircraft to damage the Italian Fleet, which the Greek Ambassador at Ankara had reported as concentrated in Taranto Harbour in preparation for an attack on Corfu. To make sure that the position of his own Fleet was not reported, the C. in C. exhorted "R.D.F." to locate, and the fighter pilots of "Illustrious" to kill, any enemy aircraft in the vicinity. This was evidently accomplished. The attack on Taranto, named operation "Judgement" was most successful. With twenty one comparatively slow "Swordfish" aircraft from "Illustrious", the Fleet Air Arm sunk three Italian battleships, leaving the enemy with only two that were serviceable.

This news of success, and the safe arrival of our convoy in Alexandria, was somewhat spoiled by our hearing that the City of Coventry had been attacked by the Luftwaffe, and it's Cathedral destroyed. A pack of Brownies from Coventry had earlier sent gifts to cheer up "Coventry" ship's company. Now it was our turn to help the people of the town. A collection was made on board, and when the boxing team was competing at the Fleet Club, a further collection was made. Collection proceeds, with the addition of a grant from the ship's canteen fund, produced over a hundred pounds for helping Luftwaffe victims of Coventry.

After a day to turn round in Alexandria, "Coventry" was again at sea with a convoy to Greece. A day and a night's cruising brought us to Suda Bay, which, with it's anti-submarine net, store ships, and oil tankers, was becoming a respectable naval base. The following day, we left with a convoy for Alexandria, and completed the trip without having any sign of the enemy. Following our arrival we enjoyed the luxury of three days in harbour.

Extract from the Daily Orders.

Wednesday, 20th November 1940, Alexandria.
It is hoped that a football ground may be obtained, and it is suggested that failing any opponent, another match, Probables versus Possibles be played. The M.A.A. should make the necessary arrangements with the Gunnery Office regarding reliefs for the duty watch.

During this time our boxing team, the pride and joy of the First Lieutenant, did well in a contest at the

Fleet Club. Later a football match with H.M.S. "Glasgow" was arranged. This brings to mind that "Glasgow" was later caught napping at Suda Bay by Italian torpedo bombers, the most effective weapon the Italians had. In a subsequent visit to Suda Bay, two soldiers stationed there told me what had happened. During an off-duty stroll, they heard the sound of aircraft engines, and looked up to see two Italian torpedo bombers lining up for an attack on "Glasgow", moored in the Bay, and eagerly waited to see the ship's guns shoot them down. To their disappointment and ultimate horror, the ship's guns stayed immobile and silent. The ship was oblivious of the enemy until a torpedo scored a telling hit astern.

On November 23rd, we left harbour at dusk, and by morning found ourselves with a six-ship convoy. Next day, during the afternoon, R.D.F. reported enemy aircraft, and soon a group of three were spotted. They were Italian torpedo bombers from Rhodes, and we prepared to meet an attack. The Italians wasted no time and came in steadily in spite of our salvos. Having dropped their torpedos they turned away. It was now up to the lookouts of our convoy and it's escort, and the Captains on the bridges of those ships, to observe the track of the torpedoes, and take avoiding action if they could. Some minutes passed; then it was clear that the attack had been unsuccessful.

Towards evening, two of the convoy left us to make for Suda Bay. The escort, with the four remaining; "Lanarkshire", "Clan Ranald", "Clan Ferguson", and "Clan Macaulay", altered course for Malta. This was in connection with convoy "Collar". We were going to meet "Clan Forbes", and "Clan Fraser", which had left Gibraltar with motor transport as cargo. Early next morning we entered a deserted Valetta harbour, and straightway proceeded to a tanker for refuelling. During the morning, there were frequent alerts, but no call for shooting. On the previous night, aircraft from "Illustrious" had bombed the aerodrome at Leros, in the Dodecanese, and simultaneously, aircraft from "Eagle" had attacked Tripoli.

Extract from Daily Orders,
Monday 25th November, 1940. (On Malta Convoy)
Specially painted electric light bulbs have been placed under hatches and in certain parts of the ship which open onto the upper deck. These are being removed and replaced by ordinary bulbs. Flat sweepers are believed to be the guilty parties, during working hours. They remove the coloured ones substituting normal bulbs, so that more light may be obtained in which to work. This is quite natural, but the coloured bulbs are to be replaced before packing up. The Mess Deck Petty Officer is to make himself responsible for seeing that this is done.

We left Malta at noon, and were soon after joined by "Ramillies", "Newcastle" and five destroyers. The main Fleet was covering us from a position south east of Malta. To the north the cruiser force was covering the passage of five empty ships from Malta to Alexandria. The afternoon passed without event, but we had the most dangerous part of the operation to come. In the darkness of that night we should enter the Sicilian Narrows, and next day meet the ships from Gibraltar. At action stations we speeded through the darkness, wondering who was near us, and if any patrol should come upon us. The steady lap of the waves was the only answer to our questions. After some hours of this, we were startled to see on our starboard beam, at perhaps three miles distance, the headlights of a car, evidently travelling on a hilly road. Clearly, we were close to the enemy, but did he know it?

All remained quiet. Dawn showed an empty horizon, and the morning wore on without alarm. At 10.45 ships were seen on the horizon. It was the convoy from Gibraltar, covered by Admiral Somerville's Fleet.

At this time, the Admiral received a report that Italian battleships and heavy cruisers were closing in on him. As he had only ten minutes before learned that an Italian force of five cruisers and five destroyers had been spotted sixty miles to his north east, he directed our convoy closer to the Tunisian coast. "Ark Royal" was ordered to prepare an aircraft striking force against the approaching battleships. At 11.15 a.m. he received a signal warning him that yet a third Italian naval force was approaching.

Thus the stage was set for a battle between Admiral Somerville's two battleships, one aircraft carrier, one 8", and four 6" cruisers, with ten destroyers, and Admiral Angelo Campioni's two battleships, seven 8" cruisers, and sixteen destroyers. While his convoy passed on through the Narrows, Admiral Somerville altered course toward the enemy. At 12.15 the Italian crusers hove in sight of Admiral Somerville's Fleet and started shooting at "Renown" and the British cruisers, which, with the addition of "Ramillies" replied. The shots from the British battleships fell short, and after six salvos, "Renown's" target was lost in smoke. Following this encounter, there was a running fight between the British and Italian cruisers. The Italian shooting was good. "Berwick's" after turret was put out of action, and she received a second hit. "Manchester" straddled the Italian "Lanciere" which was put out of action. At 1 p.m. the two Italian battleships appeared, and heavy shells fell near the cruisers, which consequently retired to bring the Italians in range of "Renown" and "Ramillies". But the Italians were shy of pursuing them.

"Ark Royal's" aircraft, meanwhile, had made a torpedo attack on the battleship "Vittorio Veneto".

The Italians were clearly running home, so Admiral Somerville caught up the convoy and provided cover until dark. Then "Coventry", with "Manchester", "Southampton", and six destroyers, took the convoy through the Narrows, and "Ramillies", "Berwick", and "Newcastle" made for Gibraltar.

It is interesting to recall that, Admiral Somerville's thanks for getting his convoy through, was a Committee of Inquiry from London asking why he had not left the convoy and pursued the Italians into their home waters, where they had the support of a massive air fleet. Indeed, "Ark Royal" had met a very heavy bombing attack some hours after the attempt on the "Vittorio Veneto". Needless to say, the Committee could only endorse the Admiral's action.

On November 28th at 08.00, we rejoined Admiral Cunningham's Fleet off Malta, and on the 30th November were in Alexandria harbour.

Extract from Daily Orders
Saturday, 30th November, 1940.
Breakdowns will be exercised whilst the hands are at action stations. The Gunnery Officer will go round to the various quarters and stations, and detail the supposed damage to the particular parties concerned.

These exercises are being carried out so that the ship's company may be rehearsed in combating such situations as are likely to arise due to enemy action.

It is of the uttermost importance that the ship's company should co-operate. There is to be no skylarking, and each man should try and imagine that the situation as detailed, has actually occurred. A "balls up" and/or omissions, may easily lose a ship. Therefore everybody concerned should pay strict attention to what is going on, and learn as much of the next man's job as possible. If this is done, a ship that would otherwise be lost, can more often than not be saved, and this means not only the ship, but the lives of those in her.

I think that we shall arrive in Alex. on Sunday morning. The 11th. Cruiser Squadron had left us, but the Fleet is somewhere fairly close ahead.

Darts League   Tomorrow's matches . . . . . .

Admiral Somerville's action occurred off Cape Spartivento, the south tip of Sardinia, and "Spartivento" is commemorated as a "Coventry" battle honour. There are two Capes of Spartivento and the Italian name for the action is Cape Teulada.

Admiral Cunningham, commenting on his covering operation from Alexandria, writes, "A feature of this cruise to the Central Mediterranean, and a most unusual one, was that not a single gun was fired by "Warspite", or any of the ship's in company with her, throughout the whole of our seven days at sea".

We had a week in Alexandria, with generous shore leave, and were elated when mail arrived. But those members of the ship's company, whose homes were at Liverpool or Southampton, also had to consider the news that the Luftwaffe had delivered heavy blows there.

On the 11th December we left harbour with the Fleet. The "buzz" was that the desert army was advancing on the Italians, and welcomed the assistance of coastal bombardment by ships. Our enemies camped in confidence at Mersa Matruh, some 150 miles from Alexandria. But on the 7th December, General Wavell's "Desert Rats" and Anzacs, attacked them. The Italians promptly retreated. Action was largely confined to the coastal road, and the gun boats "Aphis", and "Ladybird", with the monitor "Terror", had already helped in starting the Italians on the run. On the day of our leaving Alexandria, the first significant strong point, Sidi Barrani was captured. "Coventry", said the "buzz", would support "Terror", and the battleships bombarding Bardia. This was a reminder of Narvik, but under better conditions.

However, on arrival off the Libyan coast, we stood idle. For some reason the bombardment had been called off, and even on the next day there were no action orders.

The following day was Friday 13th. We had left the main Fleet and were stationed off Mersa Matruh. The date could not pass without a crop of trite remarks with superstitious implications. Possibly it was a lucky day for the Italians, because a sand storm developed to obscure the coast and frustrate any plans of bombardment. On board "Coventry" was a slight feeling of disappointment.

We patrolled rather aimlessly up and down the coast, with nothing to do but to keep a look out for a barge load of Italian prisoners that had drifted to sea during the hurly-burly of the coastal advance. Dusk brought the relaxation of "cruising stations".

Those due for the middle watch were springing into their hammocks; men off duty were relaxing in conversation, reading, letter writing, or having a drink at the "Goffer" Bar. On deck, the guns crews looked now at the darkening sea horizon, now towards the equally featureless coast. Some thought that the lifebelts they were compelled to wear all the time at sea would be a useful pillow if conditions allowed an hour's doze on the upper deck. Then, with a disconcerting suddenness, a violent explosion lifted "Coventry's" bows. Men in hammocks found themselves tumbled onto the mess table or iron deck. In some places cascades of water invaded the mess deck. In confined spaces with few exits, panic and stampede were natural dangers. But the authoritative and soothing voices of senior ratings were at once raised to check such tendencies. In the torpedo workshop, the explosion force dislodged a clock which fell on the head of P.O. Turner. He picked up the clock and noted that the time was 8.50 p.m.

A.B. Foster was sweeping a flat for "First Lieutenant's Rounds" when the ship shuddered, and the noise of explosion sharpened the shock. He guessed that a mine had hit the ship aft, and lost no time in going to his action station at No. 1 gun on the fo'c'sle.

Here he found water running over the deck, and cruising station gun's crew soaked to the skin, and covered in debris. Some of the gun's crew were recovering from the fright of being almost washed over the side.

Just then two more explosions were hard, far off. The moon, in it's first quarter, had just risen.

Through the central communication system, the routine action reports were going to the bridge in the usual rhythm. Lieutenant Commander Dalrymple-Hay had ordered frequent practice of this "collision" routine, and instinctively the ships company calmly organised itself in a matter of minutes.

Cruising station gun's crews remote from the foc'sle, had from the start of their watch been provided and prepared for the ultimate emergency. No alarming list or other signs had given them any reason for anxiety. They, therefore, stood impatiently by the guns, waiting to hear what had happened. To them it seemed unlikely that "abandon ship" would be necessary, and, they reflected, even should that occur, conditions were exceptionally favourable for it. Those most concerned after the impact were the ship-wrights sent to the site of damage. This had been caused by the Italian submarine "Naiade," which by the first glimmer of moonlight had been able to shoot three torpedoes at "Coventry". One had hit us right forward by the stem; another yard forward and it would have missed completely. The second and third torpedoes, going wide of the mark, had exploded at the end of their run. Already six of our destroyers were seeking the Italians for retaliation.

On "Coventry" there had been neither injury nor loss of life. However, the stem was damaged, and several of the steel plates of the ship's side blown completely away. The paint store had been eliminated.

Thanks to the "Blucher" design, a transverse bulkhead was holding back the tons of salt water which would otherwise have rushed in immediately, to drown several men and disable the ship. The ship-wrights lost no time in shoring up this life saving steel wall by using beams and wedges. One hour after the explosion, they were able to advise that "Coventry" could safely proceed, stern first, to Alexandria. Thereupon the ship gathered way in this unusual fashion, and "Collision Stations" relaxed to "Cruising Stations". Now, those who had sprung from their hammocks on the stimulus of alarm, or been thrown from them by the force of the explosion, quickly jumped in again. Returning to the mess decks, they trod warily over the litter of ditty-boxes, broken crockery, and spilt victuals, and were soon asleep.

Meanwhile another drama was being enacted. S.S. "Naiade" was heading back to Taranto underwater, deeming this the most prudent manoeuvre until well clear of the danger area. The Commander of the submarine was more than pleased, and the crew highly elated with their success. A torpedo hit on a large British cruiser did not befall the lot of an Italian submarine every day in the week. This was a notable achievement, as the cruiser was quite clearly dealt a mortal blow, and the last periscope observation had shown the cruiser settling deeply by the bows. Visions of the decorations awarded by Il Duce himself floated pleasantly across the Commanders mind, this sinking could not fail to produce an honour of the highest order. But although Friday the Thirteenth was lucky for some, it was unlucky for others. By the merest chance of fate, the Italians set a course which led them to destruction. Across the shadowy seas, fate in the form of His Majesty's Destroyer "Hyperion", was racing to the scene of the enemy report made by "Coventry"—and her path cut right across the path of the retreating submarine. As the two ships raced towards each other unaware and unsuspecting, the crew of the destroyer were preparing for action. The Captain ordered an Asdic search, and almost immediately an echo was picked up right ahead.

As the "ping" interval reduced itself to zero with the signal, and the object passed under the destroyer, the Captain released his depth charges. For a few seconds, after the soft "plash" of the charges entering the water, there was a hush, and then the whole bed of the ocean seemed to rumble and boil into foaming cauldron climaxed with huge watersprouts. The end came swiftly for the Italian submarine, but fortunately for the crew, the "Hyperion" picked up a large number of survivors, including the commander.

It was a very despondent Italian Commander and crew, battened below decks in the "Hyperion", as she steamed towards Alexandria. But at least he had one consolation, he had sunk an enemy warship, the sacrifice had been worth it, and the Italian High Command would think so also. "Hyperion" entered harbour at dawn, and immediate arrangements were made to transfer the Italians ashore for interrogation. They stumbled on to the upper deck blinking in the sunlight, staring round at the naval base of the enemy Eastern Fleet. But their jaws dropped with sheer disbelief, as they saw their victim of last night safely tied up alongside the harbour wall and apparently unhurt. The Italian Commander would just not believe it, and his chagrin and bitter disappointment could not be dispersed by the sympathy of his crew.

While "Coventry" limped back to Alexandria, we foresaw a longish period in dock for repairs; maybe we should be going to U.K! And Christmas was coming! The middle watchmen started their watch with unaccustomed content. When the morning watch began, there was the prospect of entering Alexandria harbour without preparation for the customary rapid turn round. It was Sunday, and the whole ship's company would enjoy it! Coming through the boom defense we proceeded to our usual berth, with the bows somewhat low in the water, but were quickly moored. It was then announced that our attacker, the submarine "Naiade" had been sunk by H.M.S. "Hyperion". Soon after we crowded on the upper deck to see "Hyperion", and "Mohawk" proceeding to their moorings. "Hyperion" was greeted by prolonged and enthusiastic cheering from "Coventry".

A Sunday afternoon ashore in Alexandria was something to look forward to, and I joined a group that intended to hire a car for exploration. From our group of six, A.B. Reddy, a former fairground and amusement park operative from the Birmingham area, appointed himself negotiator. On nearing the garage, he concealed his party round a corner, so that the garage proprietor should not raise his charges on the basis of their aggregate wealth. The price having been agreed, we were signalled to advance. At this point the hirer suggested that feminine company could be had for a small supplementary charge. This the ever smiling Reddy firmly declined, and we piled into the vehicle which he drove off.

Gaily we left the centre of town, making for Mohamed Ali Square, then down Rue des Soeurs, (Sister Street" to all matelots), bound for fly-blown Mex and the arid wastes beyond. Following a sign post "Sollum", we were soon on the coast road for an exhilarating ride, passing several army vehicles. At length we came to an area where there were several barbed wire enclosures, guarded by a few sentries carrying rifles at the ready. A sentry allowed us to approach the cage, and we found ourselves scrutinising a group of Italian officer prisoners.

One aristocratic and cultured man spoke to us in excellent English, with the apologetic manner he might have used had we arrived as guests at his mansion, and the maid been late with the tea. His first question was "Are you Americans"? Then he enquired how far Wavell's army had advanced, and seemed disappointed that the strong points had fallen so quickly. A.B. Reddy was trying to advance Wavell's army even faster than the B.B.C., explaining sotto voce, "You don't want to give these "B's" any encouragement"! Just then a ruffianly little man in blue naval uniform came near, and our Italian friend said "He is",—here making a sign with his hand to indicate a submarine submerging,—"who has just joined us". So here was a survivor of "Naiade",—one of the men who had tried to send us to a watery grave. He did not look anything like so pleased with life as his army companions, and evidently spoke no English. The sun was shining brightly and there was plenty to see, so we waved them a cheery farewell.

A week later we made another excursion to see Italian prisoners; this time as they arrived in goods wagons near Alexandria station. The object was to acquire souvenirs, and we furnished ourselves with bags of oranges for barter purposes. The Italians must have been very thirsty because they parted with every sort of badge, coin, note, and even forage caps for one of the fruits. One proud young fellow refused any offer for his badges. An older, peasant type, protested when he received only one orange for his currency note, which was of larger denomination than the one for which the man next to him had acquired an orange. A.B. Reddy was interested solely in Lire notes, which he hoped to convert into Egyptian piastres. Among various knick-knacks, I acquired a forage cap with a generous quantity of "desert sand", which gave it topical appeal. Before the next year was out that cap was collecting fresh sand,—at the bottom of the sea near Tobruk.

Next day, tugs towed "Coventry" to Gabbari dry dock. From the harbour this had always seemed a most attractive spot, because nearby, close to a huddle of buildings and grey white walls in the universal dust, were two green trees.

As the water was being pumped out, the dock staff placed beams between the ship's hull and dock side to stay the ship in an upright position. And all those of the ship's company who were able, ran to where they could see the extent of the damage.

There was a gaping hole in the bows, fringed with torn and twisted tongues of rusty steel plate. The junction of stem and keel had been blown clean away. Through the vents hung lengths of chain cable and mooring wires, giving the impression of a monster disembowelled. There would be no doubt about Christmas in harbour. Consequently, the work of clearing the forward mess decks of paint splashes, scattered equipment, clothing, and lashed up hammocks, proceeded cheerfully.

Having received an assurance that new overalls would be issued to replace those irrecoverably soiled in the filthy job of clearing the paint shop, a party of fo'c'sle men started work with a will. As soon as the deck floor was dry, a party of Arab dock labourers walked on, clothed in a motley of British Service apparel, that in most cases included a thick woollen balaclava. The paint room party was immediately warned to be careful about the labourers below them. But all too soon a cascade of blue paint plastered one of the Arabs, not excepting his flourishing beard. Understandably, he was out for blood, and could easily have done more execution among the paint shop party than the "Naiade's" torpedo. However, Lieutenant Commander Robb, R.N.R., turned out to be an exceptional diplomat, and succeeded in restoring friendly relations.

The hopes of a long stay in a more inviting dockyard away from the Med. faded when the local shipwrights began to repair the bow. Nevertheless, shore leave was generous, and it was practically certain that Christmas day would be spent in harbour.

No slackening of the war effort was to occur, however. One morning a platoon of Royal Marines, and a like number of seamen suitably armed, were carried in lorries to a sandy terrain to practise infantry manoeuvres. A.B. Gibson there distinguished himself by tumbling over a sand cliff without injury, and Lieutenant Peyton-Jones R.M. made the acquaintance of Polish army officers camped nearby, who entertained him with a horse riding party. The First Lieutenant found several fixtures for the football and boxing teams, usually in the afternoons, and leave was regularly piped for "supporters". Large groups of supporters invariably left the ship with the athletes, and there were no recriminations if any supporters lost their way to the sporting event.

Christmas Eve was well celebrated at clubs and cabarets strung out from Ramleh, along the Corniche road to Sidi-Bishr. One group could not forget going to the bar of the "Royal Arms" to drink a convivial toast. The barman left the bar for a couple of minutes, inadvertently leaving a newly opened bottle of whisky on the counter. A.B. ('Governor') Holloway seized the opportunity to fill up the glasses of all his companions. Even more than the whisky, they enjoyed the expression on the barman's face when he returned and lifted the almost empty whisky bottle.

On Christmas morning a church service was held. Afterwards some attempt at jollity was made. But in this sandy, foreign locality, with it's scorching sun, the customary Christmas festivities did not catch on. One Petty Officer commandeered an army truck parked unwatched near No. 50 gate, and with his cronies made a lightning trip to the Fleet Club. By afternoon there was somnolence on the mess decks.

Joe Simms, newly emerged from the boys mess, bought a bottle of "Zotos" brandy from an Arab pedlar, took a gulp and offered the bottle to his friend Ramsey, who demurred. "What's up"? said Simms, "Can't you take it"? Ramsey looked at Simms, whose face was flushed, and wetted with copious tears from both eyes. "It looks to me" he said, "as if it's you who can't take it".

Boxing Day was also a holiday, but on the day following, it was announced that repairs were complete, and that the ship would be proceeding to harbour. Before noon, we had left Gabbari. Within two hours we had put to sea to test the repairs.

It was a most suitable day, as a gale warning was in force. Just out of the harbour, the gale worsened and the seas were steep and heavy. Then, consternation! The new bows fell off. At once "Coventry" was put about without warning and the mess decks were soon littered with shattered crockery. There was some anxiety on the bridge while "Coventry" ran before the seas; but eventually we returned safe to Alexandria Harbour.

Next day, Sunday, was spent in traditional Sabbath calm, with the added pleasure of unexpected shore leave. On Monday we returned to Gabbari. Once again the repairers considered the problem. The loss of "Coventry's" anti-aircraft battery would seriously impair the effectiveness of Admiral Cunningham's Fleet, notably in convoy operations. The R.A.F. strength was so low, that the only available air cover was from carrier based planes, necessarily of lesser performance. And there were signs that more determined aeronauts would soon join the massive Italian air fleet, with which the Fleet was successfully contending.

The second repair would be of heavier steel, and the whole area would be strengthened with solid concrete. It was realised that this would result in the bows lying abnormally low in the water, also that the ship would be reduced in speed and seaworthiness.

While the Admiral's staff weighed these matters, the ship's company contended with more personal affairs. There was news that Manchester had suffered a heavy air attack, and the City of London subjected to a rain of fire, cunningly started at low tide of the Thames, when many fire service pumps had no source of supply.

But the citizens of Alexandria were ever active in commercial ventures for the pleasure and comfort of their guests.

As before in Gabbari, shore latrines were established to which sentries were just as necessary, as for any movable object of the slightest value in that neighbourhood. Thus there was a constant traffic of men proceeding between ship and shore. At certain points on this short route, they would be waylaid by Arabs carrying bottled beer in buckets packed with chunks of ice, and invited to indulge in "icy beer".

Such service was unnecessary in view of repeated shore leave. New Year was approaching and would be adequately celebrated. One of the Scots was an employee of the distillers producing Drambuie, and near Hogmanay, he received from his employers a supply sufficient to cheer a small party. Having done so, they proceeded ashore to further celebrations with clansmen from Australia, New Zealand, and South Africa. The Sassenachs were, of course, not behind hand in similar celebrations.

This was a time when pleasure spots ashore were much resorted to. The "Top Hat Club" near Ramleh Square was very popular. More Mediterranean and Gallic in character was the "Brasserie" in Ramleh Square, which sold quality drinks and cakes but had no music or dancing girls.

Late on the scene was a cabaret calling itself the "Paradise Club". It became specially attractive to a leading seaman who was mess caterer. By his catering skill, and an ability to "flannel" the N.A.A.F.I. assistants, he had given the mess not only the most appetising meals, but accumulated considerable "mess savings". He was highly popular, until without consulting his mess, he announced that "mess savings" would not be distributed, but used to provide extras at Christmas. All this amounted to was a bottle of dark wine much decorated with gilt foil which he insisted was "Champagne". "And", confided he in a stage whisper, "not a word about this to anyone. I'm risking my "hook" to bring it aboard"! But certain sharp eyed malcontents in the mess had observed the marked attention he received from one of the girls at the Paradise Club. He was promptly ousted from his position of mess caterer.

Established in the bars and cabarets ashore was a large corps of women comprising every race known to the Mediterranean. Young women were very much in the minority, and the features of the corps ranged from what in daylight was moderately attractive to near repulsive. They were fluent in several Continental tongues, but the only English words they ever uttered were "Buy me drink", or, "What time you go back to your ships"?

Another numerous class in Alexandria then, was that of shoe cleaners. Mostly boys, they would dog a likely customer, and over a distance of half a mile gradually lower their price. If this failed to produce a deal, the potential customer would likely as not, be splattered in black muck.

Nothing was more evident than the miserable state of the fellaheen class. This was brought home forcibly, when a party of us hired a car and drove to Rosetta for the afternoon. The first Egyptians we met were a man and his wife leading a camel. On presenting them with some cigarettes, they readily posed for photographs, and let us mount the camel to be photographed. Further on we came to a village and walked around followed by a numerous crowd. We saw in one house an Egyptian weaving cotton cloth on a hand loom, and he made us welcome to come in and watch. We had just left, when someone said "Here comes the Baksheesh mob! Run for it".

There must have been about one hundred men in that close packed column, which soon caught us up and started begging. What a tremendous effort they had made for the chance of wheedling a penny or twopence! Returning to our car took us past a building where some half a dozen Egyptian policemen were polishing their equipment. On seeing the crowd, the police seized their batons and rushed at the Baksheesh crowd with savage yells. In seconds, every beggar had vanished.

In order to improve morale by following peace time routine where possible, all night leave was given in Alexandria as soon as suitable accommodation had been provided. For six piastres one could either doze fitfully between the thin sheets provided by such imposing establishments as the Grand Hotel Riche; or sleep comfortably in the blankets provided at the Fleet Club Annexe.

Alexandria as a Fleet base certainly had a variety of attractions. The more intellectual were drawn to the bookshop of Grivas, whose young daughters chatted cheerily with the student type, many of whom were invited to gatherings at their home. It took time, of course, to discover all that Alexandria could offer, but "Coventry" was to be based there until sunshine and pleasure palled, and a longing for U.K. arose. In addition to football and boxing teams, "Coventry" boasted a rugby fifteen. The first game was against the R.A.F. at Alexandria Sporting Club, R.A.F. winning. Next, was a contest with R.A.F. at Aboukir air field, when Captain Gilmour played at full back. There was an air raid alert during the game, but no attackers came. The score for this game was fifteen-ten against "Coventry", and as the R.A.F. team included several former "All Blacks", the Coventry players considered that they had done quite well.

At this time we were saddened to learn of the loss of H.M.S. "Hyperion", but following this came news of serious import. During the course of Malta convoy "Excess", the invaluable aircraft carrier "Illustrious" had been put out of action, and limped back to Malta. Two Italian torpedo planes, conspicuously attacking "Warspite", had lured the protecting fighters from over "Illustrious." Then a large force of JU88's and Stukas, had in circular formation, dived on "Illustrious" and made six hits. Next day the Junkers had damaged cruiser "Gloucester", and sunk our companion of Narvik—"Southampton". Neither of these cruisers were fitted with radar. In later years we learned that the "Southampton" attack had occurred when the hands were at tea!

These losses had been inflicted on us by Flieger Korps X, the men who had chased us among the fjords, and had been specially trained for the destruction of ships.

On Monday 20th January, 1941, we once again left Gabbari dock to make a test, which showed that the repair was effective. We were not to exceed 23 knots, or head into tempestuous seas. That day we filled our fuel tanks and sailed toward Greece with a convoy including "Lanarkshire", "Ulster Prince", and "City of Pretoria".

CHAPTER THIRTEEN

TAKING THE STRAIN

On this, our first convoy in a patched up state, the fates were kind. The weather was benign, and the enemy indulgent. Next day all was quiet, and in the hours of darkness we cleared the Kaso Strait. On the following afternoon, Piraeus came in sight. Entering harbour at 16.30, we were quick to examine the more prominent features, and at once found food for thought. There was a fine array of nearly new travelling cranes, all proudly displaying the name of the German manufacturer.

As soon as we were secured, Lt. Commander Dalrymple-Hay had shore leave piped. The readily assembled liberty men were all issued with a small slip of paper bearing type-written Greek words which said "Please show me the way to the free zone". The Master at Arms instructed the liberty men to take care of the slips of paper. "If you get lost", said he, "show that slip to a Greek, and if he can read, (gentle irony here), he will direct you to the ship". Further, he advised them that the main thoroughfare was Omonia Square, then gave a warning about the potency of Koniak. The First Lieutenant himself came to give friendly advice. He explained that the Greeks were not yet at war with Germany, but they would make us welcome. He suggested that the liberty men should consider themselves ambassadors, and take care to behave so that they would be even more welcome on subsequent visits.

Once over the gangway, liberty men hastened to the dock gate, where a crowd of curious Greeks looked them over. At once an assorted collection of would be guides approached the sailors. Guides were practically essential, because Greeks that spoke English were hard to find. The gentleman who attached himself to our group of six, speedily led us to the railway station, and an underground train took us to Athens in a very short time. Without ado, he led us to the Terrasse of a respectable restaurant, and soon had us round the table drinking wine. He explained that he had been a considerable property owner in Constantinople years ago, but the Turks had seized the town and he was consequently penniless. He went on to say that he spoke seven languages, and we thereupon expressed a belief that he must hold a considerable position. We were wrong however. Our guide told us that his qualifications were so impressive that no businessman in Athens would offer him any of the low paid positions that might become available. This revelation infected us with a similar diffidence in some inexplicable manner. By now we felt at home in the town, so we paid for the wine, and gave our friend the gift of drachmae, which he had intimated would be most welcome. To anyone seeking the treasures of Athens he would doubtless have been worth his weight in gold. Sailors ashore, however, are wont to gravitate toward somewhat more brassy entertainments.

It was a surprise to visit a park and find oranges growing on the trees. More surprising still, nobody touched them. At the park gate was a photographer, very similar to the U.K. article.

Very prominent were shooting galleries, where the staff spoke transatlantic English, and there were ingenious targets obviously copied from the Yankees. Scoring a bull might result in a music box playing, the sails of a windmill turning, all sorts of interesting events; and of course a proud and pompous Mussolini starting to grovel in the most indecent attitudes.

Before long we were all wearing little dolls made of beads and little tufts of wool, which represented the kilted Evzones. The Scots were always quick to proclaim their sartorial link with these public heroes. A most popular ditty of the day went to a tune known to us as "The Wood Peckers Song". The name Mussolini was distinguishable at the end of what was clearly a crescendo of contempt. On our return by underground train to Piraeus, a little girl sang this song, at the same time playing a concertina. At the end amid thunderous applause, she passed round a hat.

Next day we were due to leave at noon. The First Lieutenant was anxious that the starboard watch should also get a run ashore. He therefore had leave piped to that watch from 08.00 to 11.30 a.m. Before the liberty men left, he explained to them the risk he was taking, and stressed how he relied on them to be back on time. He concluded by saying "I don't mind whether you come back by train, taxi, on foot or even in a wheelbarrow, but get here on time". The starboard watch made good use of their leave, and ten minutes before leave expired most of them were back. For some reason or other, a large group of Greek naval officers had been invited on board "Coventry", and generously entertained in the ward room. "Jimmy" was walking down the gangway in cordial conversation with two of the guests, who were literally festooned in gold braid. The corporal of the gangway, soon to report to the Officer of the Watch on completing his duty, looked blankly at a number of leave tickets still unclaimed in his box. Only a few minutes to go, and it seemed that "Jimmy's" faith in the liberty men was going to be shaken. Just then, however, an uproar started at the dock gates. The corporal of the gangway, shifted his stand to get a better view through the legs of the battery of travelling cranes. A small crowd of idlers surrounded some moving object of interest that was coming towards him. Then came the revelation. A group of wine merry sailors were pushing a wheelbarrow, in which lounged two comrades looking pathetically stupid and bemused. A small squad of marines was at once ordered to take them into custody. From "Jimmy's" face it was plain that he was not amused.

Once at sea, the First Lieutenant subjected the culprits to irate comments, in which the mildest word was "disgusting". He emphasized these by remarks in daily orders, then let the matter drop.

From Piraeus we joined a convoy in the direction of Suda Bay. The second day was quiet, also the third, by evening of which, we were approaching Kaso Strait. Next day we were for some time with a Port Said convoy, but left it at dusk. On the 27th January, we were back in Alexandria.

We stayed for three days, in which we refuelled and stored ship, and enjoyed shore leave. It was a moonless period, so there were no air raids.

On the last day of the month we left harbour for Piraeus. Forty miles out we spotted a Heinkel H.E.111, and action stations sounded. But no attack developed. Next morning, "Ajax" from a position ahead, reported seventeen Heinkel H.E.111's escorted by Italian fighters. There were, however, no attacks that day. The Germans were presumably just moving in to Rhodes. That night we cleared the Kaso Strait, arriving at Piraeus on Sunday, the 2nd February. There was leave to the port watch from 13.00 to 23.59. Subsequently we were several times in Piraeus, and there follows a selection of ship's company experiences on those occasions. This particular occasion, however, was a few days after the death of General Metaxas, and the First Lieutenant suggested that liberty men should adopt a sympathetic demeanour. We half expected the Greeks at the dockyard gates to be in tears, but they looked very much as on our previous visit.

The death of General Metaxas was going to lead to a very debatable alliance. The Mediterranean Commanders in Chief with only token air power, now had an additional three hundred German aircraft to contend with, but would soon be required to open another front in Greece. Mr. Churchill had forebodings of "Another Norway" but it was now too late to turn back.

The sailors only worry was, that in Athens, satisfying food was less easily found than in Alexandria. But the British club, which was kept going by ladies from the Embassy, served appetising chips, or fried eggs and bacon. Here also, one could buy cheaply a small book explaining the Greek alphabet, translating common public notices, and giving an introduction to the Greek language.

The starboard watch were consistently watch aboard during our Piraeus visits, and there was a rumour that some of them clandestinely broke ship for a local and limited spree in Piraeus itself. They had the good fortune to find a restaurant with abundant roast pork, so there was some relief to otherwise bad luck.

In one Athens cinema a film was being exhibited. It was "Drums along the Mohawk", straight from Hollywood. The dialogue was in American, which was translated for the Greeks by captions projected at the side of the screen; similar to the device used in Alexandria where Arabic, Greek and Italian captions were given. We hoped that the Greeks would not connect us with the cruel and treacherous officers of George III. Even the troopers in the film were pretty mean men. There was time also to visit the theatre, but the show was such, that only a person speaking Greek could appreciate it. Very early, the more intellectual "Coventry" men, either with friends met by letters of introduction from Grivas, the Alexandria bookseller, or by independent enquiry, proceeded to view the glories of the Acropolis and associated ruins. Afterwards, one indignant signalman recounted to me how horrified he was, when a Greek friend interrupted his contemplation of some inspiring sculpture, to point in a deprecatory manner to a scene about one hundred yards away. He turned to see some naval "Ambassadors" in square rig who had mistaken the ruins of the Temple of Victory for a convenient surface for inscribing rhyming doggerel normally reserved for a "Chalet de Necessité". There were a few British soldiers in Athens already. Some of these told us how common it was to be accosted by blatant German agents. The troops had been instructed to refrain from fighting with the agents, to avoid incidents in what was technically a neutral state. On later convoys, when Greece was feeling the weight of the German army, and Luftwaffe , these agents were even bolder. I recall some of us going to an inn, and being joined at the bar by a man who spoke English well. After cursing and ridiculing the Germans, he got round to enquiries about our ship and convoy, not so much a subtle probing, as a questionnaire, to which misleading replies were readily given.

One group of liberty men claimed to have gained entry to a women's prison, where the only fluent English speaker was a charmer, who told the visitors that she was inside for murdering her husband.

Leading Seaman Skelly was somewhat embarrassed on a visit to a public convenience. He had compared the notice carefully with the example in his phrase book, but heard female voices on entry. This explained itself when he saw there was a common entrance to two sections, but on entering the male section, he found it was a lady attendant who proferred toilet paper. On his declining it, her use of the plainest anglo-saxon in a friendly comment on his needs, brought fresh blushes.

Those liberty men ambitious to dally with the Athenian maidens were soon disappointed. Some of them were told that bona fide courting couples required a police permit, to comply with a law that had been made with the object of reassuring soldiers away at the front. The Greek restauranteurs continually recommended Koniak, or Mavrodaphne.

On the morning of the 3rd February, we left Piraeus and sailed in the Crete direction. Two uninterrupted days cruising brought us near Alexandria. Before entering harbour at 13.00 we ran through a heavy sand storm, which made R.D.F. ineffective.

In Alexandria, we spent a pleasant week during which both letters and parcels arrived.

At dusk on Friday the 14th February, we left with a five knot convoy for Benghazi. It included several mine-sweeping corvettes, the monitor "Terror", and a Belgian ship "Escaut", laden with five hundred tons of high octane fuel.

As we left harbour we noticed that the "Pharos" was gone. Royal Engineers had removed it with high explosive, as it was considered a land mark for mine droppers.

The day after, Daily Orders informed us, "We arrive at Benghazi a.m. Tuesday 18th, and shall remain if there is a berth for us. How long this may be is not known. But I think it highly probable that we shall have visitations in some form or another and maybe we shall be lucky enough to bring one or two more, down in flames".

On the next day, afternoon was nearly gone, the sun low in the sky, and gun's crews relaxed. "Escaut" ran up a flag, a common enough action for ships in convoy. But the signalman on "Coventry's" bridge read this one off as, "I have mutiny aboard". This would be a serious problem at any time, but it had arisen on entering an action zone popular with the Luftwaffe.

The Captain decided to send a whaler with an armed party, comprising as few gunners as possible; so the men were called from the ammunition feeders, of which there were four on every gun.

Steadily the whaler neared "Escaut", keenly followed by every pair of eyes not engaged in aircraft spotting duty. What would happen as she neared the mutineers? The whaler was now almost alongside, and still no clash. Then we saw the armed party climbing casually aboard. Within half an hour the whaler minus the armed party, was back and we heard a strange story. It appeared that when the whaler drew near, two quite amiable Belgian seamen were leaning over the taff rail, making it quite clear that they wanted to assist the boarding party. Meanwhile, the officer in command of the armed party had been receiving intelligence by signal lamp. So the painter of the whaler was passed to one of the seamen who secured it. The armed party scrambled aboard, some of the less deft passing their rifles to the Belgian seamen as they negotiated the deck rail. The "mutiny" was a one man act by the chief engineer, who had quarrelled with the skipper about entering the danger zone. After this excitement, were two days of cruising, during which enemy aircraft appeared only on the R.D.F. screen. The third started in a different way. At 07.00 we went to action stations for two aircraft that turned out to be shadowers. We were soon fallen out, and calm restored, but at 09.30 the Captain cleared lower deck, because we were passing through an unswept minefield. 11.08 brought enemy aircraft and action stations. Three Junkers 88, two Heinkel 111, and a Dornier, made steady attacks, mainly on "Coventry". There was the customary bout of shooting, followed by the towering water spouts from heavy bombs, but no damage was done.

At 15.25 three large groups of aircraft beset us. During the intervals between attacks, Able Seaman Padfield, a communication number on No. 6 gun, gave a realistic imitation of an Arab tout intoning "English good, Mussolini finish".

Benghazi harbour was now in sight, and once the enemy had departed, the convoy turned towards the entrance. Outstanding at Benghazi, was the cathedral with its twin domes. We made fast to the mole, wonderfully constructed by Mussolini's modern Romans. The harbour was considerably damaged, and littered with wreckage, including a dredger toppled on its side. Cranes and cargo handling installations were wrecked beyond repair.

"Coventry" was near the entrance at seven o'clock in the evening, when yet another large group of Luftwaffe arrived. The only defence guns were those mounted in the ships. Both sides had a jamboree. The Luftwaffe kept its formation in steady attack, with a mixed shower of mines and bombs. "Coventry" was shaken by two near misses on the starboard side. The corvettes were also selected for attention. In retrospect, one is thankful for the inconspicuous lines of "Escaut".

"Coventry", and the whole escort, were of course, blazing away incessantly during these attacks. The gun's crews intent only on maintaining the fastest possible delivery of well aimed projectiles. The attack was low enough to make short range weapons effective, and many of them scored hits. Anti-aircraft fire ceased as soon as the last bomb was loosed, and the Luftwaffe made for home as steadily as they had come, but not before a detached observer had surveyed the harbour to check results. The bombs had done no damage, but the mines were waiting.

"Coventry", now secured to the mole, while the corvettes moved toward the entrance. A mine exploded near the quarter of the leading corvette, raising a tremendous geyser. The corvette had been put out of action, so the remaining corvettes anchored where they were.

Once secured, the party from "Escaut" came aboard. Whether they were more pleased to rejoin their friends, or to put as much distance as possible between themselves and "Escaut's" cargo of high octane fuel was not discussed. As it was necessary to man only a quarter of the guns through the night, a large number of men looked forward to "all night in". But this pleasure was spoiled by the explosion of several mines at irregular intervals.

Next morning at six a.m., the Luftwaffe brought us to action stations. A Heinkel torpedo plane had attacked corvette K.40 with two torpedoes, and aimed uncomfortably close, but K.40 was jubilant because she had shot down the Heinkel. Two survivors swam from the Heinkel wreck, and a boat from K.40 took them from the sea. During questioning the survivors said that they recognised "Coventry" as a ship they had seen in Norway.

At 11.56 more Luftwaffe attackers came, but in the face of the concentrated fire from all the ships, had no success. They came back at 13.09, and although they were once more repelled, we realised that these repeated attacks were fast reducing our ammunition. No one was sorry when we prepared to leave harbour at three o'clock in the afternoon. The reason was that our convoy had no hope of unloading at Benghazi, and had been ordered to Tobruk. Benghazi was nearer to the axis bases in Sicily and Tripoli, than to our own base at Alexandria. No anti-aircraft guns could be spared for port defence, neither was it possible to provide a patrol of fighters.

We had not cleared the harbour, before the Luftwaffe came back. Our guns swung round, following the director. Right aft, two leading seamen stood by the bollards to release wire springs. Some Arab dock labourers had arrived, to carry stores from us to the corvette, and our hastened departure compelled a similar action for them.

The only way to the mole was via the stern wires, by holding to the upper one and shuffling sideways along the lower hawser. Half way across, the leader lost his nerve. His companions restored it, by means of vigorous kicks in the buttocks.

As yet, no-one had opened fire, and we were passing close to "Terror," where every member of the crew seemed to have his own Breda gun. "What's up"! they yelled, "Can't you take it"? "Coventry" men yelled back the standard answer. "You can have the bastard"! Two years later, in Royal Naval Barracks, I overheard a bearded Royal Fleet Reservist telling his version of this incident. But he improved the story by saying "And what do you think the Captain of the "Coventry" signalled to our Captain?". "You can have the . . . ."

The attack was a sharp and concentrated affair, and I can recall the satisfaction I felt, when observing one large bomb leave the plane, obviously in the direction of another ship. This group of Luftwaffe scored no hits, but one of their dive bombers failed to pull out of it's dive, and took the fatal plunge. We certainly admired "Terror's" ships company, left there to stick it out.

Extract from Daily Orders
Wednesday, 20th February, 1941

We part company with this convoy at 00.00, proceeding to a spot about 120 miles off Malta to pick up another, part of which we escort to Alex. Where we shall arrive (D.V.), in about four days time.

I was pleased to see at least some of the Between Deck Parties lying down, when I went round. It is essential that those not actually doing a job of work, should do so—None of these parties should put foot on deck unless they are told that they may. Contact bombs shower splinters—Nobody wants to die, or get messed up—so keep under cover. Furthermore, if any of the Between Deck Parties are on deck without orders or permission, they are absenting themselves from their place of duty—a serious enough offence at any time.

On convoy next day we read the comment of our elated First Lieutenant.

"We had our excitement and no mistake. All must agree that Benghazi is not exactly a dull place—we were lucky to come out whole, and without casualties. We fired a considerable number of rounds from both long and short range weapons—the first in anger since November. One gathers a little here and a little bit there—mostly buzzes, perhaps,—but "Terror" will have it that our pompom got one of the reception committee on the 18th. Anyway, whatever we might or might not have brought down—we did take in, protect, and bring out of Benghazi a convoy—in spite of very heavy air attacks. These attacks were broken up, and chiefly by us. Let us hope that although not as lucky as "Peony", in that we did not see one come down, that we may have been the means of stopping one or two from getting home.—I think we have.

The "Stewart" had an exciting passage when on her way to join up with us, having been machine gunned and bombed pretty heavily—and was also lucky to get away with it.

Extract from Daily Orders
Saturday, 22nd February, 1941
We had our excitement this day, and it is to be hoped that we were not responsible for putting down a Fulmar—Anyway, if this did unfortunately happen to be the case, the fault was in no way ours. Under such circumstances one must open fire without loss of time.

R.A.1 Signalled that fighters had brought down one Heinkel and damaged another—whether this includes the torpedo bomber we got mixed up with or not, one cannot say. The "Clan Macaulay" says she thinks she hit one, as they found a piece of aeroplane fabric on their deck after the first attack.

It is regretted that Gun's Crews did not get their tea brought to them. Arrangements have been made to obviate similar omissions. Supply parties are being organised so that they can supply food as well as ammunition to the Gun's Crews, should circumstances make this necessary.

Extract from Daily Orders
Monday, 24th February, 1941
What our movements are to be in future is not definitely known yet. It looks, however, that we may have to go into dock for about a 24 hour spell to get the old bows patched up.

Extract from Daily Orders
Wednesday, 26th February, 1941
The other day a Savoia was observed to launch torpedoes—avoiding action was taken. The Savoia, and two other aircraft, were then seen approaching the ship, very low over the water. The pom-pom was ordered to open fire, which it did, and fired at the leading aircraft, the Savoia. It so happened that the other two were Fulmars, and not hostile. These aircraft were fired upon. Nevertheless, the order to open fire was rightly given, and in the mix-up even if one of our shells did hit one of our own aircraft, we cannot be blamed.

It is understood that the "Eagle" lost no Fulmars.

Seamen's Messes are getting slack about their stool covers. Leading Hands are reminded that each Mess has four covers, of which two should be in use, and two clean,—the latter to be shipped for Saturday's Mess Deck Rounds.

Sport.

It may be that our boxing team, in conjunction with "Perth", may be called upon to fight on Thursday. The match will be against a shoreside representative team, some of whom, I believe, are pretty hot. Mr. Wolfe, the Times correspondent out here, will arrange the matches,—and I am assured that there will be no funny business.

Near Tobruk we left our convoy and turned toward Malta. On the 21st February at 07.00, we were one hundred and forty miles from Malta on our way to meet a convoy there. At 12.30 p.m. we opened fire on a Heinkel spotter.

At 15.30 we joined the convoy, a fast one including "Clan Macaulay" and "Breconshire". From then we were at action stations until nightfall, repelling repeated high level attacks, and an occasional dive bomber. "Clan Macaulay" was subjected to a dive bombing attack from a Heinkel, and the bomb struck the funnel. One can well imagine the feelings of the pilot when the bomb went through the funnel, and plunged into the sea without exploding. The following day was uneventful, and on Sunday, 23rd February, we reached Alexandria.

The First Lieutenant was a firm believer in shore leave as a morale booster, and although the early evening was already spent, had leave piped the moment we were moored. Further, he had ordered that on the first night in port after prolonged sea duty, "men under punishment", (about three or four unfortunates as a rule), should be allowed ashore.

Almost as fast as the change of scene on a revue stage, a drove of faultlessly dressed liberty men appeared, were promptly inspected, and soon after sat in the large launch maintained in harbour for regular duty of this kind. As it glided close to the wharf, impatient men, for once heedless of the warning orders of G.I.'s and of Sergeants of Marines, leapt ashore, and ran for the gates which had been opened wide by a grinning Egyptian policeman. The orderly majority was not long in catching them up, and when an Alexandria bound tram was seen approaching the stop at the end of the cobbled lane, a breathless stampede began.

Thanks to co-operation by the tram conductor, a sweating, panting, hoard of red faced men in white suits covered the tandem tram like a swarm of ants, filled every cranny, and subsequently gave a concert of hard breathing. A solitary matelot rejoicing in the name of "Dutch Holland", arrived there too late, but was so determined, that he climbed on to the roof of the tram, and clinging to the pole of the overhead conductor arm, rode thus to Mohammed Ali Square.

On the afternoon of the 27th February, we left with a convoy of slow Greek ships, some for Piraeus, and some for Port Said. Next day we ran into a storm, much to the satisfaction of the gun's crews. The following day we were approaching Piraeus, when worsening weather produced seas beyond the safe limit for our weakened bows. The Captain was obliged to put about and run before the sea. Through the night the storm increased, and next day the convoy had to scatter. "Coventry" received orders to proceed to Alexandria at the best speed consistent with safety.

Extract from Daily Orders
Saturday, 1st March, 1941
It was decided that our bow would not stand up to the sea. Furthermore, the convoy was scattering all over the place owing to the weather, and as we could not be of much assistance to them, the Captain determined to turn round. What will happen ultimately depends on circumstances—if the weather moderates we shall most probably go after them, and eventually arrive in Piraeus.
It is regretted that no warning was given before the ship turned round during the afternoon yesterday. Fortunately no casualties occurred. Messes whose crockery was broken, should give a list of breakages to the Mess Deck Officer by Stand Easy time, today. Every effort will be made to make good their deficiencies.

Monday 3rd March, 1941
A lot of unnecessary discomfort and flooding was caused during our last trip through defective clips to hatchways and weather deck openings, which had not been brought to the notice of the Shipwrights Dept.

It is the duty of any rating who knows of, or finds any defect, to report it at once to his Divisional P.O., who is to bring it to the notice of the Chief Shipwright, so that repairs can be carried out as soon as possible.

We arrived in harbour late next day. On the morrow, speculation arose when the ship's company in suitable parties, went ashore for testing gas masks in a room where tear gas had been placed. Certain of the ship's company were roped in for vaccination.

Next afternoon we left harbour, and at dusk joined a convoy. The following morning we were heading for Crete, and at 11.26 an aircraft alarm sent us to action stations. This had lasted twenty minutes when we were "fallen out", with the explanation that a fast convoy ahead of us was under attack by the aircraft that had been detected by our radar. At 12.28 we were again called to action stations. Four

Italian aircraft at a moderate height aimed bombs at us, but missed with a comfortable margin. At 13.08 we fell out, but at 13.27 were called again to deal with two more Italians. The action and subsequent standing by, kept us fully alert for an hour. There was about twenty minutes resumption of routine, then several bombers made more shooting necessary, and kept the guns manned for an hour. After 16.00 two more aircraft attacked, but did not take long to drop their bombs and make for home. As usual during continuous action stations, the First Lieutenant arranged for tea and sandwiches to be brought to the gun's crews. At 17.10, a torpedo bomber made a serious attempt in face of our barrage. His tin fish however, missed ahead.

That night we cleared the Kaso Strait, and it was obvious to us that Greek convoys from now on would be no pleasure cruise. Early next day we were called to action stations for a Savoia 79, that in the end showed no hostile intent, but half an hour later a torpedo bomber came on in face of our fire and launched a torpedo, which again missed ahead.

There was a quiet period until 14.13, when we came racing to action stations on a report of three aircraft. Now, there was a pleasant anti-climax, following the announcement that the three aircraft were our own Wellingtons.

Next day at noon, we entered Piraeus harbour with the first convoy of troops for Greece; Australians were prominent. We secured alongside for enough time to unload a large number of boxes holding tin plate squares. What the military use of these would be, we could not guess. Then we proceeded to anchor in the Bay, whilst "Ajax", "Orion", and "Perth", went alongside to disembark troops. At mid-afternoon, we left with a Port Said convoy. Next day was quiet, and brought us to the Kaso Strait by nightfall. The day after was also quiet, and we left our convoy at dusk. The following morning at 06.00 we entered Alexandria Harbour.

Here, we saw "Formidable", which had come to replace "Illustrious". The arrival of "Formidable" had been delayed because there had been mines in the Suez Canal. The Luftwaffe, now at Rhodes, were most industrious at canal mine laying, hoping thus to prevent the arrival of fleet replacements or reinforcements. Next afternoon, we left harbour and joined a large convoy of twenty-three merchant men for Piraeus, our biggest convoy yet. The day closed with the onset of stormy weather. If the bridge was anxious, the gun's crews at least were elated.

By next morning we were through the Kaso Strait, and the sea was rising. Through the dull dark day, we ploughed on with the convoy; but at midnight received orders to leave it, and accompany a convoy returning to Alexandria.

By now wind speed exceeded 80 miles an hour, and "Coventry" was once again forced to run before the gales. Missing the entrance to Suda Bay, we hoved to all night; but with the coming of daylight, made towards the Bay. I recall that on this occasion I was a lookout in the air defence platform. Next to me was Royal Marine Betteridge, who remarked cheerfully, "Well, if she does turn over, we'll be thrown clear". In that sea, it would not have mattered very much. It was Sunday the 15th March when we came through the anti-submarine nets at Suda. There was shore leave from 13.30. We remained in Suda Bay for two days, during which an unusual sporting event took place. One evening, the First Lieutenant paid a social visit to the sloop "Moonstone", which had earlier covered itself with glory whilst on a Red Sea patrol. The "Moonstone's" Commander boasted of the ship's whalers crew, and Jimmy promptly suggested that they race against a "Coventry" crew next morning. Back aboard "Coventry" he realised that he had no trained whalers crew, but A.B. Sullivan, working in the Ward Room, had heard of the dilemma, and told the First Lieutenant that there was aboard, a former racing crew of R.N.V.R. London!

Orders were promptly given for the whaler and crew to be ready after breakfast next morning, but by morning light it was seen that "Moonstone" had left the harbour. Lieutenant Dalrymple Hay thereupon decided that there should be a whaler race between seamen and marines, and the crews in their boats were towed to a point a mile from "Coventry".

The starting pistol was solemnly fired, and Captain Peyton Jones in the motor boat was keenly watching as the whalers leapt forward in true racing style. But two minutes later he was shouting "Action stations" and urging us back to the ship. The seamen won by a short head, and both crews scrambled aboard to their action stations, the guns being already directed at an Italian spotter. The spotter kept out of range, and ultimately went off. Subsequently however, relays of spotters using the same tactics kept us at the guns all morning.

On Wednesday the 19th March at 08.00, we left Suda Bay, but not before we had opened fire on a snooper. We accompanied a convoy which "Calcutta" was returning to Alexandria. There was no interruption of routine, and we left this convoy at dusk. Next morning we joined a Piraeus bound convoy. Although the weather was deteriorating, we sighted several aircraft, many of them shadowers, but had no attacks. On an unexpected change of orders, we left this convoy. Usual wireless telegraphy activity suggested a fleet operation.

Next morning found us clearing the Kithera Strait, and during the day we joined the Fleet, Malta bound, with "City of Lincoln", "City of Karachi", "Clan Macaulay", and "Perthshire". It was a quiet day. The day after brought us with the Fleet to within one hundred miles of the Italian main land, but the enemy was apparently unable to spot us.

In the evening, however, we, with "Carlisle", were detached to meet a north bound convoy for Piraeus. On Sunday, the 23rd March, we spent a routine day until 16.23, when an Italian S.M. 79 arrived for snooping. Afterwards, we were attacked by a Junkers 88.

We met the Piraeus convoy next day. At 14.27 we went to action stations for Italian shadowers. At 17.21, and again at 17.52, a trio of Italian planes attacked with torpedos which fortunately missed. After 7 o'clock, five high level bombers arrived to attack the centre of the convoy. Every available gun was turned on them, and none of their bombs found a target.

Well into dusk, and almost darkness, torpedo planes pestered the convoy. R.D.F. followed them, and spotters for a time could just make them out. The question was, could they see the ships well enough to attack? Gunfire would doubtless have been welcomed by them to illuminate the targets, but none of the convoy escort obliged; and at length, complete darkness allowed our convoy to cruise unmolested.

Morning of the next day was a quiet one without aircraft alarm, and we were gratified that the afternoon was peaceful as well, so much so, that the First Lieutenant arranged for a game in the intertop deck hockey competition to take place. At dusk we parted from the convoy, and near midnight we were entering Suda Bay, with the object of taking oil from the Norwegian Tanker "Pericles".

The starboard sea boat was to be turned in on it's davits, and the First Lieutenant was urging the seamen to make haste. In his impatience he shone a torch towards the davits in the belief that illumination would speed the work. The chorus of righteous curses and admonitions that this drew from the anonymous darkness stayed in his memory for many months. Nevertheless, "Coventry" went swiftly past the boom defence, and was able to secure to the oiler at once. Within minutes the oil tanks were filling, and all except the duty part of the watch were in their hammocks with the prospect of "all night in".

From that contented slumber they were rudely awakened by the roar of an explosion. "Coventry" leapt from the water, while the alarm rattlers chattered, and everyone, in many cases carrying their outer garments, ran to action stations. Even as they ran, "Coventry" was under way and increasing speed, headed for the open sea by the cold light of dawn. Quickly everyone was fully clothed and settled in to routine and intelligence of recent events was collated.

At the beginning of the morning watch, the duty part, in charge of the Gunner, W.O. Smees, had begun to cast off from the oiler. Mysteriously, the drone of a petrol motor broke the silence. "What's that"? snapped the Gunner, as the men on deck, peering into the murk barely descried a motor boat heading for "Coventry". One imaginative youth was just about to volunteer "A jolly-boat with a special message for the Skipper"? when the boat flashed a few feet in front of our shakily repaired bows, smashed into the oil tanker "Pericles", and erupted with a force that made the whole bay shudder.

Once again, "Coventry" had got away with it. "Pericles" oil was nevertheless still available for the Fleet. Subsequently, damaged "Pericles" left Suda for a repair port, but ran into a storm and foundered.

Later, we learned that the 8" cruiser "York" had also been hit, sinking in shallow water to leave about a foot of freeboard. This successful Italian operation had been carried out by six men, brought with their explosive craft into Suda Bay by torpedo boats. The inadequate boom defence they had easily cleared.

In "York", a Stoker Petty Officer on duty in the boiler room, had a terrifying experience. Getting on his feet, he was pleased to find that he had suffered no damage beyond severe bruising. But all lights had been extinguished, and he was uncomfortably aware of flood water up to his ankles, so he hastened towards the door. His heart sank when he found that the door would not budge to his most desperate tugging, and his hands sought over the steel plates for some opening that might save him from this death trap, for the water was rising. Fairly quickly he found a small ventilating louvre, wrenched off the cover plate, and was just able to get his fingers through. The water was now up to his knees, and his only resource was to yell for help. By the time the water level had reached his waist, he counted the five overall buttons from there to his collar, and redoubled his yelling for help. Then he realised that the number of overall buttons to his collar was now four. Suddenly came hope, as a hand grabbed his fingers. Faintly he heard a voice "Are you all right? We're bringing an acetylene cutter to get you out!"

On the floor of the gangway above, the minimum opening required for a man to pass through had been chalked, and a welder worked grimly to melt the steel. The imploring voice from below urged speed, and said that now the water was two overall buttons below his collar. There was a quarter of the circumference of the circle to go, and from the beginning, the sizzling flame had been urged at full efficiency. Only one button now, shouted the agonised voice of the trapped man, while the grim calm men above watched the flame start it's last inch. Two men knelt ready for the moment to prise out the steel disc, hoping it would come before the rising water extinguished their comrade's life. At last the hole was made! An arm was thrust into the shrinking air space below, a hand encountered a head of hair which was straightway hauled through the opening, then other hands seized the stokers overalls, and he was laid, trembling, on the iron deck.

He went subsequently to Hospital in Alexandria, where in the "Mc Noon" ward of the 64th General he ultimately recovered. One of his companions was a lad who survived the sinking of the South African Whaler "Southern Floe". For weeks this man, whether walking, eating, or sitting, remained in a cowering attitude, his eyes still staring in terror at the roaring Stuka.

With considerable resource, "York" had been beached; but as there was no steam to drive the generators that gave gun-training power, she was useless. Several courageous divers were killed by the effect of bombing as they worked to raise the cruiser, which eventually became a total wreck.

Thus, Admiral Cunningham had lost the only eight-inch gun cruiser in his Fleet.

Thankful for our good luck at Suda Bay, we were subsequently gratified to spend the early morning uninterrupted by aircraft alarm, despite the fact that we had just joined a considerable convoy. The only escort, besides "Coventry", was two destroyers. The latter were virtually unarmed against high level air attack, and very poorly provided with short range weapons. At mid morning, we had a reminder of the persistance of the Luftwaffe, when three JU88's arrived to attack the convoy. It was the convoy rather than "Coventry" that drew their attention.

Fortunately, our shooting was sufficiently good, to prevent them scoring even a near miss with the dozen or so bombs they unloaded. Thereafter, quietness reigned, and by turns both watches were able to eat the midday meal in peace. The same good fortune continued in the afternoon, and the First Lieutenant judged it a splendid opportunity for playing the semi-final of the deck hockey tournament.

Gun's crews, not on lookout duty, leant over the armour plate fences and cheered their teams. The struggle had reached a crucial stage when a bosuns mate started piping "Enemy aircraft approaching", in a "matter of fact" manner. The pipe had hardly been made all round the ship, when he was back in a hurry piping, "A large number of enemy aircraft approaching". But before he finished the second call, the alarm rattlers went. In seconds all guns were following the director, the doors of the ready use ammunition lockers opened, and everyone ready. Guided by the radar aerial we stared to port, and soon half a dozen black dots appeared. Almost at once they multiplied to eight or nine, then a flock, (in fact, twenty four), of Junkers 88 long range dive bombers.

A concentrated attack on "Coventry" was the immediate thought, and the prospect of survival was bleak. The only hope was exceptionally rapid shooting, and it proved that this reaction moved the entire ship's company. Viewed from the air, here were a large number of valuable cargo ships whose only defence against a dive bomber was a machine gun, that would not be effective until the dive was nearly completed.

Doubtless the pilots had been briefed to destroy the cargo ships first, because, singly and in pairs, they set course for the dispersed merchant ships. Lieutenant Commander Robb R.N.R. in 'B' director, was afterwards reported to have been in a fury as he repeatedly loosed a salvo at one Junker about to dive, then quickly changed aim to help another of the ship's manned by his brother officers of the mercantile marine.

Both directors kept all guns shooting at an unprecedented rate, and almost before we realised, the Junkers, having loosed their bombs, were going home. To our great delight, not a single ship had been hit. One only had been damaged by a near miss, but could still maintain convoy speed and keep station. The destroyers, though unsuitably armed for high angle shooting, had enthusiastically seconded the efforts of "Coventry".

A further cause for satisfaction, was that radar and the ship's W.T. had evidence that six Junkers were soon afterwards stationary at sea level, and signalling for rescue.

Dusk and nightfall were trebly welcomed when they closed this eventful day, but there was more to come. During the middle watch, the main Fleet passed us at high speed. We wondered if the Italian Fleet had started to threaten the Greek convoys. "Warspite", "Valiant", "Barham", and "Formidable", with the co-operation of cruisers, and nine destroyers, would meet the threat. Next morning, we entered Alexandria Harbour, and there was jubilation when mail arrived. There was no shore leave, however, that evening. But while we were sleeping, the Fleet sunk the 8 inch Italian cruisers "Zara", "Pola", and "Fiume", with destroyers "Alfieri", and "Carducci". Two thousand, four hundred Italians perished thereby.

CHAPTER FOURTEEN

IN AND OUT OF GREECE

On Saturday, the 29th March, we left harbour to join a slow convoy. Rumour said that several Italian warships had been sunk. This to us seemed a natural enough event. But it would not reduce air attacks. At dawn next day we met some eight knot ships from Port Said, and quiet continued, thanks to fighter aircraft from "Formidable".

But when we were near Crete, at dusk, we were shaken by a salvo of bombs exploding fifty yards astern. An enemy aircraft had, unnoticed, flown right over us.

After dark, we saw falling flares and gun flashes astern, where, fifteen miles back, the convoy of "Perth" and "Ajax" was under attack. In the morning we went alongside the wharf at Piraeus. We stayed three days, during which all-night leave was given. Somehow the atmosphere ashore was changing. Public jubilation had once been noticeable, and bars and restaurants full, with frequent allusion made to victories over Italians. But lately we met only the professional gaiety of barkeepers and restauranteurs. The shooting galleries were slack, fewer people walked the streets, and no-one sold Evzone dolls. There was more difficulty in finding a meal.

The Greek man in the street, after all, would not be sailing with a convoy. He knew that the Germans were active in Yugoslavia, and of the huge armies, and masses of modern weapons that came with them. He had seen the British contingent land; noticed the token air force, and small armoured regiment. The whole lot had passed through Athens in two or three days. His preoccupation might have been to ponder how life would be when the Germans took over. Official history confirms that the Greek campaign was a withdrawal from start to finish.

On the 4th April, before noon, we were leaving Piraeus harbour, when the alarm rattlers sounded. We closed up quickly, to the sound of Greek shore batteries firing. While we wondered about the unaccustomed slowness of our own lookouts, it was announced that the aircraft approaching were our own Spitfires.

There was no further excitement until the next morning, near Crete, when a high flying Italian was spotted. Action stations sounded, and with a few salvos, we shook him up before he released his bombs at high level. They missed wide. At midday during dinner, we scrambled to the guns again for another high flyer, but it did not attack.

Next day was Sunday, and routine proceeded quietly. But on that day we heard that the anticipated invasion of Yugoslavia and Greece by the Germans had begun.

By Monday we were off Alexandria, and here joined a Piraeus convoy. The day passed without alarm, but we heard broadcast, news that the Germans were advancing in both Greece and Libya. At that time, German troops were never mentioned as doing anything other than advancing. Tuesday was a quiet day, also Wednesday, but during the morning a signal mentioned an air raid on Athens.

At 11.00, we were approaching Piraeus. On coming near, we looked eagerly for familiar landmarks, but looked in vain. A confused jumble of wreckage, and here and there drifting smoke, was all that could be seen. The Port in fact no longer existed.

The explanation was that on the 7th April, the Luftwaffe had dropped mines and bombs into the harbour, setting ablaze "Clan Ferguson", which was unloading there. Part of the cargo had been two hundred and fifty tons of high explosives, stowed beneath the general cargo. The attempt of a British naval officer, to tow "Clan Ferguson" away from the harbour, had been frustrated by the Greek harbour authorities. "Ajax", and "Calcutta", also in harbour, escaped miraculously.

Thus vanished the only modern port for our forces, the only port indeed which the Greek Government had allowed us to use. Even then, our military convoys unloaded under the scrutiny of German diplomatic staff, and the British General Wilson was not even allowed to announce his presence in the country, or welcome his troops landing. At this time, however, our thoughts were about the cheerful and friendly persons we had known at the harbour, like the man on the gate, or the proprietor of the little wine shop opposite.

We left this area for the open sea, but returned at dark. At 20.00 there had been a call to action stations for an air raid alert, but it was some time before the enemy arrived to attack Athens, which was some miles from us.

First, we noticed the search light beams combing the sky, and soon we heard the oft repeated dull thud of exploding bombs. Anti-aircraft guns were in action, but there were not many of them. On the other hand, streams of tracer bullets, looking like coloured fountains, showed that short range weapons were plentiful and widely used. We also noticed that the defenders had no monopoly of these weapons. One low flying aircraft put a jet of tracer straight down a searchlight beam; on another occasion an upward red stream of tracer was suddenly doubled by a return stream. Then an aircraft gleamed in a searchlight beam relatively close to us, and all guns were trained on it. No shore guns were engaging the target, and the plane flew heedless towards us. Even when a second beam crossed the first to floodlight the target, no avoiding manoeuvre was made. Here was a sitting target at unbelievably close range. When every available gun was bearing, a salvo was loosed, and the aircraft vanished. The searchlights returned to the routine sweep. Next day, we cruised aimlessly in the open sea, and attracted no attention from enemy aircraft. The following day was Good Friday, the 11th April, and we entered Suda Bay to go alongside an oil tanker.

Daily Orders included this comment:

"Owing to circumstances, we have not known from one minute to the next what was to happen to us. Nor do we know what will happen after, or during today. Anyway, be prepared for anything.

Owing to the uncertainty of our movements, it has been impossible to issue Orders during the last day or so, but it has been an interesting experience. We fired about 250 rounds the night before last, and I think tickled up at least one. The shore side searchlights were damned good, and it is understood that pieces of two planes were found inside the nets. We can lay no claim to these however.

News has not been over cheerful of late—don't get downhearted. The High-ups know what they are doing, and glum faces won't help. Keep your chins up, and remember somehow or another there will always be an England."

Refuelling completed, the Captain cleared the lower deck to explain that we should "steam north with a fast convoy, before returning to Alexandria". Soon afterward, we joined the transport "Glenore", and three destroyers, all making nineteen knots.

It was satisfying to be travelling at this speed after so many slow convoys, and we were curious about our destination, never doubting that it would be some interesting haven. Now we were in the Aegean, and noticed several mountains and rock girt islands. Here and there we noticed an odd brilliance reflected from some of the buildings, and it was explained to us that this occurred because many of the houses and farm buildings in these islands were built of marble.

In the afternoon, there was action alarm for a low flying aircraft; a Dornier, that flew steadily toward us until the guns opened up. Then it diverged slightly to reveal Roumanian markings, and continued on it's course away from us.

By evening we had come in sight of land. There we could see a few houses, and in the distance, a ploughman driving his furrow over a field of black soil. There were heavy low clouds, and a slight drizzle. The temperature was considerably below what we had become used to. Leading Seaman Price looked enquiringly at Lt. Commander Robb who was passing, and said "Mudros, Sir?". "Yes", rejoined the officer, "How did you know"? "I was here in 1928 with the "Skate" sir", explained Price.

Why were we here at this port of the Island of Lemnos, fifty miles by sea from the Dardanelles, of bitter memory? The object was to evacuate several thousand soldiers of the Herts and Bucks regiments. Already the Yugoslav army had been beaten, and the Greek forces were on the point of collapse.

The destroyers patrolled the entrance of Mudros Bay, making anti-submarine sweeps. "Coventry" remained at action stations, and at dark the embarkation of troops began. The gun's crews found it very chilly business. All the troops were embarked by dawn, which was about 6 a.m. There had been no panic; it was even suggested that some delay had occurred because the troops would not move until they had finished the beer in the canteen.

At around 6.45 a.m. we were all under way, when there was an alarm for a high flying aircraft. Gun's crews expected the worst, but no attack came. There were no regrets as the island receded.

At 10.30 a.m., R.D.F. reported a very large group of aircraft, strung out over thirty miles, and forty miles away on our port beam. Fortunately they stayed on course, but eventually crossed our path fifty miles ahead, whence they made for the mainland of Greece. Later we heard that this was a seventy bomber expedition which devastated the port of Volos.

For us, there was the good fortune of a rapid cruise on a beautiful day, with frequent interesting land falls on either side. The enemy did not find us.

In the small hours on Monday the 14th April, we cleared the Kaso Strait, and were back to the familiar Mediterranean climate. Steaming without incident, we used the day and carried on through a quiet night, arriving at Alexandria at 06.00 next morning. Our operation had been successful, but here we were on another evacuation. And, according to the news, the Germans in North Africa, with a new General called Rommel, had now gone past Tobruk; though the Australians were holding out in the town.

Most gloomy thoughts were forgotten, however, as soon as shore leave was piped. The indefatigable tourists, Able Seaman Risdon and Barnes, were wandering through one of the more respectable streets of Alexandria, when they saw a sign indicating a Turkish bath. In a mood to appreciate such a luxury they walked briskly to the entrance. Boldly they knocked on the door. It was opened by a huge dark woman clad in a white coat, who after eyeing them with distaste, let them in and showed them in to a cubicle. Once undressed, they donned bath robes, and were motioned toward the vapour cabinets. Then the giantess, to their considerable embarrassment whisked off their bath robes, and drove them before her. With complete indifference she led each one to a cabinet where once seated, he was firmly clamped with only his head emerging. Then she pulled the lever of the steam valve hard over, so that almost at once they gasped, and the sweat ran off them. After what seemed an age, she came back to release them, and with a curt nod indicated where they should go. There she scoured them both, and none too gently, with a scrubbing brush, leaving them to take a shower and dry off. Now came the massage, but only Barnes braved it. The lady pummelled and battered him over a considerable period from every angle, so that he was ultimately reduced to the state of a limp rag. And now for the very first time she smiled.

As the bathers sat and relaxed, sipping a welcome cup of tea, conversation began, and in this way they learned that the lady was by birth a Turk, and that she ardently espoused the German cause. Here entered another Briton who had endured the treatment. When the amazon had departed, he announced himself as a sergeant in a commando regiment, and congratulated himself on enjoying the comfort of ship accommodation and sea transport, between spells of action on land.

"Coventry", would soon be seeing something of this sort of thing. The assault ships "Glenearn", "Glenroy", and "Glengyle", with a force of commandos had just got through the canal, now clear of mines, and arrived at Alexandria. Mr. Churchill had wanted these men to seize nothing less than Pantellaria by an operation of this kind; but the Chiefs of Staff had been obliged to point out the scarcity of both men and weapons. The Chiefs of Staff were, on the other hand, ready to try and capture the Dodecanese Islands.

At mid-afternoon, on the 16th April, we left Alexandria harbour. Well at sea, we joined "Glengyle" and set course for Bardia. Commandos would land at Bardia that night, and make a general nuisance of themselves. They would re-embark by dawn and both ships return to Alexandria.

There was suppressed excitement at the prospect of this novel operation. Ploughing through an increasingly choppy sea, we reflected that continued action stations might be relieved by some pyrotechnic spectacle. But on reaching the landfall, we turned round for home almost at once. The seas were too heavy to expect both landing and recovery of the special craft devised for this form of attack.

On the 18th April, we were in Alexandria harbour and shore leave was piped. The Fleet had left harbour with the object of bombarding Tripoli. This was the port receiving supplies and reinforcements to nourish the advancing Afrika Corps. Already destroyers had been stationed at Malta for stopping Axis convoys from Italy. One of these convoys had been recently annihilated, but at the cost of losing our destroyer "Mohawk".

Men ashore in Alexandria were suddenly recalled to the ship, chiefly by notices posted in the Fleet Club. It seemed pretty ominous in those times, when the initiative seemed to be with the Axis. On board there was great speculation, and almost a sense of relief, when we left harbour at 03.00 on the 19th April. With daylight, we could see that we were once again protecting "Glengyle", and we were indeed to have another go at Bardia. The daylight passed without any alarm or remarkable event, and at 22.00 we made our landfall. We could just make out a dark and desolate shore. Staying at action stations, we imagined the landing craft packed with men, leaving "Glengyle" for a long silent trip over the water in utter blackness. At first we waited eagerly for the noise of explosion, and the glow of fire. But after an hour of dull frustration we got fed up with it, and those gunners not on duty as communication men, or lookouts, began to doze. When dawn broke we were able to pick out details of the coast. Then we saw "Glengyle", and landing craft being hoisted aboard. Soon a lamp signal was made from "Glengyle", and we began to move. Just then a signal lamp ashore blinked, and "Glengyle" made a short acknowledgement. One of the landing parties had returned to the beach too late. Operational orders had required the ships to leave the coast immediately before dawn, and there had already been a half hour's delay.

At increasing speed we made for the open sea, regretting the party left behind, but aircraft would no doubt be pursuing us as soon as light allowed, and it would be folly to risk the entire expedition. Full light came, and we reached the normal hour of "stand easy", but no aircraft reports or alarms. What a pity about the party we had left! Noon came, and aircraft were sighted. All guns trained on directors, but the aircraft ignored us. During the afternoon, R.D.F. reported several aircraft, but none came to attack. With dusk tension relaxed, and soon we were speeding through friendly darkness to Alexandria. A very good trip had it not been for the stragglers left behind.

Several weeks later, daily orders contained a news item to the effect that, these stragglers had first hidden in a cave by the shore, then made their way with the help of Arab guides to British army lines. Years later we learned that the raiders had found very little enemy property to destroy at Bardia.

Next day was spent in Alexandria harbour, and a new kind of mail was delivered, the air-graph. This system of sending micro film by air, and printing the letters at the delivery area for distribution, was most welcome. On the 23rd April, Captain Gilmour left the ship for hospital. The same day, Lt. Commander Dalrymple Hay, First Leiutenant and Acting Captain, cleared lower deck after we had left harbour at 06.00. His purpose was to explain that it had become necessary to evacuate our army from Greece, and that we were even now proceeding to do so. Although nobody was really surprised, official confirmation that the so far unbeaten Wehrmacht had once again pushed out our troops, dampened the spirits of many.

For the Fleet Staff Officers, the problem was to lift the troops without the use of harbour facilities, and to contrive that once at sea, the ships were not sunk by the horde of Luftwaffe planes. Our air strength was less than half a dozen fighter planes. All the weapons and transport, brought from the Western Desert to Greece, would be destroyed.

The evacuation plan was to lift the army from seven main beaches, which were served by good roads. Embarkation would take place after dark, and the ships leave in good time, so that they were out of range of most of the enemy aircraft when daylight came.

Concerned solely with our present surroundings, and the few facts revealed by the Acting Captain, "Coventry's" ship's company started this operation in a similar frame of mind to those that had gone before; expecting to proceed to their destination, meet some enemy aircraft attacks, and return to harbour. Once out of sight of land, we met the transports, S.S. "Pennland", and S.S. "Thurland Castle". Unladen, they rode high out of the water. We were proceeding at 13 knots in glorious weather. R.D.F. reported no aircraft, and none were spotted, so we were at "defence stations", with half the guns manned. In such conditions there was no sense of urgency, and for two days we cruised uneventfully.

On Friday the 25th April, we were north of Crete, and air defence lookouts were very much on the alert. At mid afternoon there was a slight stir on the bridge, when the Officer of the Watch received an R.D.F. report. Within seconds, the off duty watch, some of them roused from dozing, were doubling to action stations, urged on by the alarm rattlers. Immediately, all guns followed the director, and were aiming at extreme elevation into the sun. And there we glimpsed two gleaming objects, Junkers 88's approaching on a bombing run. Two salvos met them before the bombs were seen falling. Thereupon the aircraft made off, and there were none to follow. We had time to look about us. It was evident that "Pennland" had been hit. Indeed, two hits on the fo'c'sle had started a fire; also compass platform, and steering machinery, were damaged. We were fascinated by the lookout in the crows nest, descending by devious diversionary routes, which must have broken all time records for reaching deck level. There had been a near miss amidships, and the main hold was flooded. With destroyer "Griffin" standing by, "Pennland" turned back. As the distance between us was increased, we reflected that this was the first time we had seen the enemy damage one of our charges. Eventually "Pennland" dropped from sight over the horizon. We should never see her again, for at 6 p.m. the same day, Junkers 88's returned to sink her. "Griffin" picked up thirty survivors. The loss of "Pennland" meant that we had insufficient capacity to lift over six thousand Australians, one thousand of them wounded, who would be waiting for us at the beach of Megara, about twenty miles west of Athens. Destroyers "Hasty", "Havoc", and "Decoy", received orders to take the place of "Pennland".

Unaware of any occurrence beyond the apparent minor damage to "Pennland", we carried on, remaining at action stations and doubly alert. Preparations had begun aboard for the reception of the soldiers, and manning the boats that would bring them from the shore. Dusk brought the customery relaxation, and darkness a feeling akin to security. We knew there was an exceptional night's work before us, and began to realise it when we nosed into a mountain locked bay, edged toward the shore, and dropped anchor. Immediately the power boats and whalers were lowered.

From the shore we heard intermittent detonations, that announced the destruction of transport, guns and other equipment. Splendid vehicles that we could ill afford to lose were being blown up, rather than allowing this war material to fall into enemy hands. Apart from this, there was silence. No lights were seen, but now and then we saw the glow of fires ashore.

Within half an hour our boats returned, filled with Australian soldiers. At once they were ushered to the mess decks, where ample meals and unlimited tea were waiting. The boats continued to ferry in silence, and just before 04.00 on Saturday the 26th April, the ships had taken five thousand nine hundred men from the shore. Five hundred men, for reasons never explained, were left behind. This despite the efforts of Leading Seaman Gardiner, who refused to leave the beach until he had made a thorough search for any possible stragglers, and only just made it back to the ship as the anchor broke surface.

At 04.00 the evacuating ships got under way, and once clear of the bay, made the greatest possible speed through the darkness. The ships were "Coventry", "Thurland Castle", "Havoc", "Decoy", "Wryneck", "Hasty", "Water Hen", and "Vendetta". One at a time, gun's crews were allowed below for washing and toilet needs. On the mess decks they met the Australians, who were in wonderful form, and unable to find enough words in praise of the Royal Navy. With beatific smiles they guzzled tea, and one soldier said, "You don't realise how wonderful that stuff tastes—we haven't had any for weeks. We found out that as soon as we started a fire, the Stukas were on us". Said another, proffering a blue woollen jersey to a sailor, "You take this mate. It might be some good to you, but whenever I wore it, the bloody Stuka pilots sorted me out for special attention".

The hate for Stuka pilots was exemplified by three grinning men who proudly displayed some very greasy currency notes. "See that fat", said one of them, "It boiled out of one of the bastard's that we managed to shoot down".

Exceptional, was the story of a rather quiet man who said, "I am sixty, and I lowered my age to join up. But I reckon I am more of a burden to my mates than a help". The Australians could not sufficiently curse the fates, that had put them against an enemy who pinned them to the ground with Stukas, while they never saw a single aircraft fighting for them.

And the retreat to the beaches had shown that it was also insecure behind the front line. One column was approaching a cross roads, and the leaders had been instructed to go straight on. But as they came near, they saw a British Military Policeman equipped for traffic control, directing them to the left.

The officer in charge halted the column, and sent to the rear for confirmation. A few minutes later, an investigation squad came running up to lay hold of the "M.P.", but during the excitement he had vanished.

Daybreak roused us to realisation that the quiet calm of this cool morning would not last long. In the thin mist, we saw that our convoy had grown, by the addition of ships from Raphtis. With full light, several Australians came on the upper deck, armed with Bren guns, and anxious to do execution. At about 8 a.m., a group of twelve aircraft came toward us, and all guns in the convoy threw up a concerted barrage. Although the attackers were nowhere approaching the field of fire of close range weapons, the Australians with Bren guns blazed away. "Coventry" was contributing an upward torrent of projectiles, and the Heinkels were missing satisfactorily as the convoy stood on to the south, when "Coventry's" luck failed. There was an order to cease fire, and two minutes later stretcher bearers came among the gun deck carrying a torpedo-man, Petty Officer Bannell, He was chalk white, and his eyes glazed. From his lips rose bubbles of crimson blood. "He's finished", muttered a nearby Australian, and this was only too true.

Here was the worst tragedy. This man had been killed by a steel splinter from a "Coventry" projectile. Our gun barrels had worn beyond the safety limit, and from time to time, the propellant cordite would be unable to give the projectile enough muzzle velocity. The result was a premature burst of the shell, which in this case had been not far from the gun muzzle. In these circumstances, the guns would be used only in the event of a very heavy air attack. Fortunately, subsequent attacks were from single scattered aircraft. The pom pom joined in wherever possible, but the 4" guns were silent.

Late in the afternoon as we were approaching Crete, R.D.F. reported a group of fifteen aircraft. Miraculously, British fighters from Crete were available to break the formation and destroy some of the aircraft.

The two that subsequently found the convoy made half-hearted attacks that failed. At 17.00 that day, we entered Suda Bay. Our Australians, with considerable expressions of good will, took their leave from us in launches which ferried them ashore. We went straight to an oiler. The first concern of the Captain, was to have the gunners party recover from the ship's boats, a vast quantity of .303 ammunition.

On the morrow, which was Sunday, we left Suda Bay at 11.00. Later we passed "Calcutta", with a large group of ships including "Orion", and "Perth", which had taken troops from Nauplia. Here, the Dutch ship "Slamat", which delayed an hour after receiving the order to leave the beach, had been sunk.

Some of "Calcutta's" convoy joined us as we headed for Alexandria through the Kaso Straight. In the later afternoon, we went to action stations for five Junker 88's, which came into attack. With all guns, except the two known or suspected to have produced a premature shell burst, we raised an effective barrage, and had the satisfaction of seeing ample evidence of bombs that had missed. Afterwards we sighted "Phoebe", standing by the sinking "Costa Rica", that had lifted troops from Kalamata the previous night. Thus, the last notable event of a most exceptional sabbath.

From our special correspondent off Greece, Wednesday

A complete picture of the evacuation of our forces from Greece, was given to me today by the captain of the anti-aircraft cruiser "Calcutta", who was also at Dunkirk, and at Andalsnes in Norway when the British troops left. "Dunkirk", he said, "just organised itself into success, but this evacuation was properly organised from the start, and in my view was entirely successful. It provided me personally with some remarkable coincidences, as, for instance, the colonel whom I'd last seen in exactly the same place in our wardroom when I had taken him off from Andalsnes in Norway. Evacuation began in earnest on the night of April 24th–25th. The whole thing was different from Dunkirk in this–the task of transporting the men from shore to ship was slower, as they were heavily laden, not only with their personal arms, but also with all their equipment".

Not a Single Light

"But they were not tired and exhausted. Most of them had been resting under trees throughout the day, waiting for us to pick them up when darkness fell. All these operations were carried out without a single light, and as far as I know not a life was lost accidentally".

The first convoy, of which the "Calcutta" formed part, included three transports and smaller escorting craft. In the afternoon of April 24th it split up into two groups. The "Calcutta", with one transport, went under the cover of darkness to the small port of Raphtis, south-east of Athens, while the other transports with the destroyers went to Nauplia, at the head of the Gulf of Nauplia. "We embarked 700 men", said the captain "while our transport took on 5,000. Meanwhile one of the transports sent to Nauplia ran aground, and was subsequently so heavily dive-bombed that she became a total wreck". "The other one, however, and the destroyers took on as many as they could, and kept their rendezvous with us at eight next morning in the Aegean. At 11.00 that morning three Junkers 87's came over us and made a sharp and accurate attack, but we all escaped damage and disembarked 13,500 troops".

Another A.A. cruiser, H.M.S. "Coventry", with some destroyers and a merchantman, embarked 5,500 men from Megara, a little port between Athens and Corinth. The next day the "Calcutta" returned to Greece for further evacuation. "I took three merchantmen with me", said the captain, "and hugging the coast, made for Nauplia. The rest of the ships in my convoy, with the escorting destroyers, went on to Raphtis and another similar fishing port, Raphina. "At four that afternoon, after we had separated, we had a sharp attack from Junkers 87's, and 88's, attacking in two waves of nine machines. They hit one of my transports in the engine room, disabling her, while a second vessel was hit by a small bomb but not badly damaged."

"When it was over I ordered the destroyer "Griffin" to stand by the crippled transport, which was towed safely into port. With the other two I arrived at Nauplia about 10 o'clock. I took 960 men aboard, while the destroyers "Hotspur" and "Isis", took 500 and 400 respectively.

"So far the weather had been perfect, but that night the wind got up, with a choppy sea which made boat work most difficult". "The cruisers "Orion" and "Perth", with the destroyer "Stuart", appeared in the bay before midnight and embarked men from the nearby port of Tolon. I imagine these ships took on about 2,500 men. Further west, the cruiser "Phoebe" at the head of another group was evacuating men from the port of Kalamata.

"I was most anxious to be going, as by this time the Germans had occupied the aerodrome of Argos only a few miles north of Nauplia."

"At seven o'clock on the morning of April 27th, bombers came over, and they did not leave us until 10 a.m. We were shooting so accurately that again and again we put them off. About 7.15 one transport was hit and began sinking. I ordered the destroyer "Diamond" alongside to take off the troops, and about 9 a.m. three more destroyers, the "Wryneck", "Vampire", and "Voyager", joined us in the battle with the dive-bombers, so I detached the "Wryneck" to help with the rescue work.

"In about three hours the "Calcutta" fired about 1,200 round of 4-inch shells, and I cannot tell how many thousand rounds of pom-pom and machine-gun ammunition. All this time I still had my 960 troops aboard, which made the vessel heavy and not easy to handle. The "Coventry" came out to relieve me, enabling me to disembark them, and return to the convoy by the afternoon. One more transport was sunk, but we were able to get all the survivors safely ashore. Then with 14 vessels we set out and arrived without further incident yesterday".

The captain paid tribute to the calmness and courage of the troops, which not only allowed the difficult embarkation operations to be carried out as scheduled, but enabled the ships heavily laden with men to be fought resolutely and with conspicuous success in face of determined dive-bombing attacks.

We arrived at Alexandria on Tuesday the 29th April at 08.00, and mail was waiting for us. Soon after, we went alongside to have guns rebarrelled, and in due course shore leave for the port watch was piped. Any disturbing thoughts we might have had whilst at Suda Bay were soon dispelled.

After a day alongside the wharf, we moved back to the mole near No. 50 gate with new gun barrels. On the 1st May, Lt. Commander Dalrymple-Hay celebrated the day with orders to paint ship; quite a satisfactory occupation in contrast to our recent employment. He nevertheless continued his policy of maximum shore leave during the four more days we remained in harbour.

During this time there were several night air attacks, with the usual object of mining the harbour entrance and navigable channel to bottle up the fleet. One load of high explosive, poorly aimed, landed in the Sister Street area, devastating a wide area of slums and brothels, and causing considerable casualties. Next morning a large contingent of the Egyptian Army arrived by lorry and did an amazingly quick job of cleaning up.

We left harbour on the 6th May with the Fleet, Malta bound. The departure from the port was long drawn out while mine sweepers cleared the navigable channels. This time the operation was a major Malta convoy known as "Tiger". Five merchantmen were coming from Gibralter carrying tanks, and with them rein-forcements for Admiral Cunningham in the shape of battleships "Queen Elizabeth", and Cruisers "Naiad", and "Fiji". With us from Alexandria would come four large ships laden with provisions, also two large tankers.

Next day at sea, visibility was unusually poor, owing to the existence of a heavy sand storm. On this day the Commander-in-Chief received a report from Malta that destroyers there could not leave harbour to meet him. The harbour had been completely mined in, and all Malta minesweepers had been sunk or damaged. This problem was referred to the Fleet Torpedo Officer, Commander W.P. Carne, who solved it by directing that a channel through the mines be cleared by blasting with depth charges. Commander Carne soon after became "Coventry's" captain. On the 7th May, the weather worsened, not that anybody worried, because it was keeping enemy aircraft away. Next day the weather continued to oblige. During this period "Ajax", and three destroyers had made a night call at Benghazi to shoot up the port. They had there destroyed a ship carrying motor transport, and blown up an ammunition ship.

At 07.00 on May 9th, "Coventry" was near Malta, when two Savoia 79's were seen a mile away. After one salvo they sheered off. Later that day the provision ships and tankers from Alexandria entered Valletta harbour, and we met "Clan Chattan", "Clan Lamont", "Clan Campbell", and "New Zealand Star" from Gibraltar. "Empire Song" which started out with them had earlier been sunk by a mine.

Radar showed several enemy aircraft nosing around, but no action occurred. We were delighted when it was broadcast that a Fulmar from "Formidable" had just shot down a Junkers 88. Otherwise the day was remarkable only for cool and cloudy weather. On Saturday 10th May, we were getting near home, but R.D.F. was reporting considerable numbers of enemy aircraft. "Coventry" was at action stations all day, and the (acting) Captain carried out his customary practice on these occasions of having tea and sandwiches served to gun's crews. Frequently our guns followed the director on a target, but it was not necessary to open fire. Night came, with clear weather and bright moonlight.

Then R.D.F. began to report considerable numbers of enemy aircraft. At 9 p.m. we met a determined attack; also during the middle watch of the 12th May, the alarm rattlers roused us to action stations. After drawing several salvos from "Coventry", "Calcutta", and "Carlisle", which surrounded the convoy, the enemy made an attempt on the covering Fleet. We enjoyed the spectacle of the Fleet's tremendous anti-aircraft barrage. All the more because the enemy scored no hits. Arriving in Alexandria in late afternoon on May 12th, we were quickly revived by the pipe of "Leave to the port watch". During the recent operation, we had heard a broadcast about Rudolf Hess landing in Scotland from a plane; but nobody could imagine this having any pronounced effect on the war.

CHAPTER FIFTEEN

THE ATTEMPT TO HOLD CRETE

The Royal Navy was very glad to have been on hand to help the Anzacs. Subsequently the Australians responded by giving every sailor a bottle of Australian beer, while New Zealanders made a contribution to the Royal Naval Benevolent Trust. The Commander-in-Chief had less time, however, for enjoying these complimentary ceremonies, because the war situation was worsening.

He was concerned because the enemy air strength grew steadily, while we had no more than enough fighter planes to keep the Luftwaffe clear of Egypt. The Fleet reserve of anti-aircraft ammunition was running low. From their bases in Cyrenaica, the Luftwaffe was harrying the Fleet. Once established in Crete, they might make Malta convoys uneconomic, if not impossible.

There was enough evidence to show that the Germans were reaching for Crete. They had prepared "Operation Merkur", in which thirteen thousand paratroops and nine thousand mountain soldiers, provided with five hundred transport aircraft, seventy two gliders, fifty two reconnaisance aircraft, supported by four hundred and thirty bombers, and two hundred and thirty fighters, would, under the command of Generals Lohr and Student, make the attempt.

To repulse them was a garrison of thirty two thousand lightly armed and hastily organised men, with less than a dozen fighter planes. Ships bringing stores and weapons to General Freyburg at Suda Bay, were usually bombed and sunk there by the Luftwaffe, as they waited in the queue for unloading at the small jetty. Some reinforcements were, however, landed under cover of darkness by cruisers "Gloucester", and "Fiji", at Heraklion on the night of May 15th., and by "Glengyle"at Tymbaki on the 18th May.

After reaching Alexandria with the "Tiger" convoy, "Coventry" enjoyed a few days in harbour to take on stores and refuel, also to give recreational leave. Every night there was action when the enemy aircraft arrived with mines for sealing the harbour approach.

Leaving harbour on the 17th May, we reached the Crete coast after two days, there to patrol with "Phoebe", "Dido", and destroyers. The Luftwaffe were by now, bombing the three Crete airfields as a prelude to invasion. Every day the soldiers saw their handful of fighters going up to tackle very heavy odds, to be ultimately eliminated. The Fleet had been placed on station to interfere, though "Formidable's" aircraft could give no protection, because the squadrons were repairing damage sustained during the Tripoli bombardment and operation "Tiger". The ships were handicapped by the need, to return four hundred and forty miles to Alexandria, for replenishing fuel and ammunition. For several days two battleships had been waiting west of Crete for the Italian Fleet.

During our passage from Alexandria, there had been no alarm or action, but once near Crete the presence of the Luftwaffe was felt.

At mid-day a signal was received from the hospital ship "Aba", just clear of the Crete coast. Although conspicuously marked with red crosses according to international convention, she was being attacked by Stuka dive bombers. "Coventry" and "Phoebe", with destroyers, set off at full speed to give protection. The magic of Mediterranean sunshine was utterly wasted for us, as the ships bows purposefully clove the blue sea, while hundreds of pairs of eyes combed the skies for hostile aircraft. Lt. Commander Dalrymple-Hay was still acting captain. An hour went by, then another, and we were somewhat pessimistic about the value of our mission. But at about 5 p.m. in the afternoon we sighted "Aba", and almost at once we received a signal that all was well. We were getting quite close and there were thoughts of resuming patrol, when R.D.F. reported enemy aircraft approaching. With "Dido" we were steering closer to "Aba", when the lookouts caught the gleam of a high flying aircraft, seemingly on reconnaisance. Seconds later came a warning shout that eight Stukas were approaching. All eyes and all guns turned to them. Every aircraft had a yellow painted nose,—doubtless "golden" in German eyes. This decoration was a mark of distinction awarded by Reichs Marschall Herman Goering.

Lt. Commander Dalrymple-Hay wanted to be close behind "Aba", where the eight barrelled pom pom would be most effective against the diving Stukas. As "Coventry" dashed in he signalled "Dido" to keep clear, oblivious of the fact that he was speaking to the flag ship of Admiral Glennie. He intended to shuttle to and fro behind "Aba", on a course at 90 degrees to her fore and aft line, whence each of "Coventry's" gun directors would throw a four gun broadside in the enemy's face.

The Stukas closed in, and circled, before attacking in pairs, each from opposite directions.

The gun's crews, projectiles in hand, watched the barrels following the targets with that tense attitude always maintained in that silent period between "Alarm aircraft", and opening fire; and prepared for the difficult feat of loading with the gun almost perpendicular. The first Stuka to nose down was engaged by "A" director, and a split second later, "B" director was similarly engaged. Barking steadily with ear shattering detonation, the 4" guns were soon joined by the pom pom rattling forward, and the crackle of the 0.5" Vickers aft. Diving steadily through the barrage, engines roaring and rigging screaming, the Stukas levelled out just above main mast height, then swooped upward as their bombs plummeted towards us.

Already engaging the next attackers, the gun's crews were only half aware of the roar and shock of explosion, and the subsequent leaping salt water which fell to drench them. The Gunnery Officer, weighing the frequent reports of lookouts against aircraft that were attacking, indicated targets to whichever director happened to be not engaged at the time.

In the forward, or "A" director, the close packed team led by Lt. Commander Robb were alert for the more wary attackers that chose to come from astern where fewer 4" guns could bear, and there was no pom pom. Petty Officer Alfred Sephton was the layer, Corporal of Marines Symmons, the trainer, and A.B. Stanley Fisher manned communications. Also in the director was Chief Petty Officer Davenport, operating the visual height finder, an optical instrument which incidentally gave a close up view of the enemy.

Very early a Stuka found the weak point of the 4" barrage, and dived where only one 4" gun could be brought to bear; but that gun placed a projectile, which was seen to burst right under the nose of the Stuka. "Coventry's" 0.5" Vickers at once spat bullets at the aircraft, then Chief Petty Officer Davenport saw flame from the Stuka's cannon.

Almost immediately Petty Officer Sephton, the director layer said "Dave, I've been hit in the stomach". "How bad John? Can you keep on"? To which came the ominous reply "I can hardly see". Chief Petty Officer Davenport said to the trainer, "You must carry on firing Bill, John has been hit".

Stanley Fisher, on communications, felt a blow in the lower part of the back, and was soon after alarmed to realise that he could not feel the slightest sensation below the waist. The headphones prevented him from hearing anything but the voice of gun control, and his view of Petty Officer Sephton was limited, for the pair were seated back to back. But he was aware that Petty Officer Sephton, would now and then slump forward with his head against the director telescope, then brace himself upright, and that C.P.O. Davenport was moving the elevator wheel. There was no slackening of gunfire. The Stuka swooped up, the bomb clearly a miss, but the murderous cannon bullets had been effective.

On the gun deck, ready use ammunition lockers were ablaze, and several guns crew members had been hit. Marine Provost, and Lt. Hartnell, heedless of burns, snatched blazing cartridges from ammunition lockers set on fire by the cannon shells, and jettisoned them; the wounded gunners, finding themselves not incapacitated, staunched the blood and kept their guns firing.

When all the Stukas were flying away, and no further enemy reported, cease fire was ordered. An opportunity for Lt. Commander Robb to summon a first aid party, and call for the gun layer of the after gun to replace Petty Officer Sephton in the director.

When asked about his injuries, Petty Officer Sephton insisted that Able Seaman Fisher be first lowered to the first aid party. Able Seaman Fisher, after being assisted through the director hatchway, descended the iron ladder by taking his weight with his arms. Fortunately feeling was returning to his legs, and on reaching the deck, he stumbled toward the first aid party, and was somewhat irritated to hear a shout of "Fisher, you're bleeding".

By now Petty Officer Sephton was unconcious, and C.P.O. Davenport lowered him to the arms of the waiting stretcher bearers, who carried him to the sick bay.

With wounded men replaced, "A" director reported "ready" to the Gunnery Officer. Two bullets had perforated the height finder, and had torn the jacket of Lt. Commander Robb.

By now there were no reports of enemy aircraft, and the captain relaxed to "defence stations".

Now the sick bay staff could concentrate on helping the wounded. Petty Officer Sephton was so grievously wounded that little could be done. Then there was the question of removing the bullet from Able Seaman Fisher. When the serious cases had been relieved, the men with painful flesh wounds arrived for dressings. In view of the lull in activity, Lt. Commander Dalrymple-Hay requested the Admiral's permission to return to Alexandria, so that the two seriously wounded men could be moved to hospital, and this was granted. Indeed, a senior staff officer was with the waiting ambulance when "Coventry" arrived.

Extract from "Daily Orders"
H.M.S. Coventry, 18th May, 1941.

Since coming to this ship I have learned to like her, and those in her, more and more. I hope everybody is, and has been, happy. We have had cause, during the lazy times of war, to be proud of the results achieved by our ship's company on their showing, at whatever particular game was being played, no matter what the odds against us may have been.

Yesterday's attack was not, I am sure, the heaviest that the ship has sustained in the past. It was, however, a very difficult one to break up, the sun affording excellent cover from out of which to dive almost unseen to the attack. In fact, there was little or no time within which to fix a target, or get all guns to bear. There is one noteworthy aspect of the engagement—the excellent fire discipline. Acts of excessive bravery too, were not lacking. Lieutenant Hartnell completely disregarding personal risk, jumped down from his action station on to a burning Ready Use Locker, and threw ignited ammunition over the side. Petty Officer Sephton and A.B. Fisher, although wounded (the former most grievously) carried on at their jobs in spite of pain and weakness. Marine Thomas, burned extremely badly by ignited cordite, refused to go for attention until the attack had ended. Petty Officer Goldring, happily not much hurt, though hit about three times, tied himself up and kept away from the Sick Bay, because they were busy. What examples to all of us of bravery and devotion to duty.

As I have stated, in lazy times of war, we have been able to crow about our prowess at sport. And now, when grim war times are upon us, the ship's company have every right to be proud of their splendid showing and fire discipline. They were sorely tried, and not found wanting.

I am proud to have had the honour of commanding this ship, even if it be only temporarily. I regret however, that so much grief has come upon us during this short and eventful time. Particularly the loss of Petty Officer Bannell, and the severe dangerous wounds now sustained by Petty Officer Sephton.

Let us sincerely thank God that things have not been worse, and pray that we may suffer no more casualties or hurts, and that our wounded may soon be well. And that by God's Grace and Mercy we may all pull through to enjoy times of lasting peace with our dear ones.

Dalrymple Hay

Lieutenant Commander, R.N.
In Command.

N.B. Since writing the above, I have learned that Petty Officer Bidgood, Corp. Day, A.B. Cabrin, A.B. Brown, all of whom were hurt, refused to go away for treatment, and I think that the ship's company should know of this. Also that the Doctors' put in untiring work in patching up people.

I am glad to say that P.O. Sephton, although still dangerously ill and by no means out of the wood, is progressing favourably, and there is now some chance of saving him, slender though it may be.

Petty Officer Sephton, however, did not last the night. This news spread slowly through the ship and was received with great sorrow. The operational conditions throughout the Crete campaign were such, that those engaged were aware of little beyond the urgencies of action stations, and a craving for sleep when darkness arrived, and absence of the enemy permitted. But Petty Officer Sephton, in charge of the main top division, had helped many a reservist to settle down in those first weeks afloat, when every-thing seemed to be planned for discomfort. He had never assumed an air of superiority, or professional aloofness. His acceptable advice and cheerful tolerance, had speeded the formation of a well knit ship's company.

From our Special Correspondent off Crete, Monday.

Another attack by German dive-bombers on a hospital ship brought us hurrying to the scene of the outrage. We had received a message from the hospital ship "Aba" that several bombers, after circling her, had dropped eight heavy bombs which, fortunately for the helpless wounded she was carrying aboard, all fell wide of the mark. We were a formation of destroyers with A.A. ships patrolling some 120 miles south when the call for help came, and putting on all speed we reached the scene shortly after another German plane had circled the ship at a height of only 1,300 ft. With her hull glistening white, the red crosses marking her at every angle of view, the "Aba" was a conspicuous sight which no reconnaissance pilot could mistake. Nevertheless we had been escorting the ship only a short time when the object of this reconnaissance was made clear. A formation of eight dive-bombers was seen approaching, and the destroyers immediately opened up with an umbrella barrage over the hospital ship.

As our own forward guns swivelled round they were just able to bear over the target, and round after round screamed over our heads, as on the bridge we ducked under the terrific crack and blast of their firing. With my own ears plugged heavily with special wax, it was a shattering experience, especially when the tornado of hot air whisked off my steel helmet. Still those shells bursting high in the blue sky were obviously an even more shattering ordeal for the Germans, who changed their tactics, immediately broke up, and made individual bombing attacks on the A.A. cruisers. With fierce fire these experienced vessels deterred them again and again. As we counted the aeroplanes manoeuvring in the sky like a bunch of frightened seagulls, the captain remarked to me "These blokes haven't got guts like those fellows we used to see". It was the same captain from whose bridge I had watched the bombing of the "Illustrious" on January 10th, and frankly I had waited with trepidation for a repetition on a smaller scale of that hair-raising performance we had then watched together.

Eight Machines in Attack.

Out of eight machines which circled about us only two put any dash into their attack. One turned several times like a fluttering leaf, then dived so steeply that it appeared absolutely vertical. As he flattened out the pompoms of an A.A. cruiser spat viciously after him. At the same time columns of water leapt into the air astern of the vessel and rose to a height above her masthead. By this time others, who had attempted shallower dives, dropping their bombs indiscriminately into the sea, were darting about just over the water, in an effort to get so low that none of the guns of the ships could bear on them.

One seemed winged, and our signal yeoman was certain that it struck the water. For my part my eyes were glued in those few seconds to another dive-bomber which was certainly pressing his attack. He appeared out of control, so directly did he plummet on to the second A.A. cruiser.

A splutter of pompom fire hid the plane from our view. From where we stood it seemed probable this fellow, too, was winged. After that the raid collapsed suddenly.

Next morning, while the ship's company was at defence stations, the burial service was read, and the man who had made such a success of life on the sea went to it's depths.

His mother would soon receive one of those telegrams, dreaded throughout the United Kingdom. Later would come news of the award of a Victoria Cross, the first given in the Mediterranean Fleet during the 1939 war.

During the two days of steaming to Alexandria, we had no sight of enemy aircraft, but on arrival we learned that a German invasion of Crete had begun.

The Commanders-in-Chief had anticipated such an event, which was expected to be supported by the Italian Fleet. Accordingly two battleships had for some days waited west of Crete, while forces of cruisers and destroyers patrolled likely stretches of the Crete coast at night. These ships had no fighter protection, and readily attracted the Luftwaffe. First casualty was one of the patrolling destroyers, H.M.S. "Juno", which was hit by high level bombers, and sank in two minutes at dawn on the 21st May.

Later in the day, air reconnaissance reported a fleet of small craft making for Suda Bay. They were in fact, fishing craft called "Caiques", with a few small steamers, all crammed with German soldiers. Battleships "Warspite", and "Valiant", commanded by Admiral Rawlings, waited in vain west of Crete. The only part the Italian navy played in the operation, was to accompany the caiques with a few motor torpedo boats.

At 11.30 p.m. on the 22nd May, Admiral Glennie, with cruisers "Dido", "Ajax", "Orion" and destroyers "Janus", "Kimberley", "Hasty", and "Hereward", came upon a large convoy of caiques, with motor torpedo boat escort, approaching Canea. There were two hours of ramming and shooting. On the fo'c'sle of "Ajax", Lt. Commander B. B. Junor, formerly First Lt. of "Coventry", worked like a demon with a Lewis gun, and enemy losses mounted. The Italians loosed their torpedoes, but scored no hits on the attacking cruisers and destroyers.

By morning light next day, Rear Admiral King, patrolling north of Heraklion with cruisers "Naiad", "Perth", "Calcutta", and "Carlisle", and destroyers "Kandahar", "Kingston", and "Nubian", sighted several caiques, and notwithstanding heavy Luftwaffe attacks, scattered and sunk them annihilating the entire force. Admiral Cunningham estimated that four thousand Germans were drowned when the invasion caiques were sunk.

In daylight, the Admirals of both patrol forces found themselves beset by the Luftwaffe, and were perforce prodigal with anti-aircraft ammunition. Admiral Glennie therefore decided to withdraw from the area north of Crete, and made towards the west of Crete Group, commanded by Admiral Rawlings. Admiral King's force made for the Kithera Channel, being continuously bombed for three and a half hours en route. "Carlisle" was hit, and the Captain killed. At 12.10 p.m., Admiral King's ships sighted those of Admiral Rawlings, returning from the west through the Kithera Channel. All ships had by now spent well over half their anti-aircraft ammunition, and at this point disaster overtook them. The destroyer "Greyhound" was hit, and sank in fifteen minutes. "Kandahar", and "Kingston" stayed to pick up survivors, while "Fiji" and "Gloucester" waited to hold off the Luftwaffe. The Luftwaffe mercilessly machine gunned all survivors; enraged no doubt by what had happened to their caique convoys.

Soon, the anti-aircraft ammunition of "Fiji" and "Gloucester" was dangerously low, so they were ordered to join the main force. In half an hour, the Fleet saw them catching up, all guns belching flame. Then several bombs hit "Gloucester", leaving her completely disabled and stopped. "Fiji" still shooting, threw carley floats overboard to assist the hapless survivors, and pressed on to rejoin the Fleet.

An hour later, "Valiant" was hit, but not seriously damaged. But by 6.45 p.m., "Fiji" had been reduced to using practice ammunition. Then a single M.E. 109 stopped her with a near miss, and started an inrush of water. Half an hour later, three bombs hitting over the boiler room, administered the "coup de grace", "Kandahar" and "Kingston" dropped life rafts, then manoeuvred at high speed to avoid the bombs of the Luftwaffe. Returning after dark, they picked up five hundred and twenty three "Fiji" survivors.

During that afternoon, Lord Louis Mountbatten's destroyer flotilla had arrived on the scene from Malta. During the night he had sunk several caiques, also bombarded Maleme Airfield, which was by now in the hands of the Germans. Next morning, "Kashmir", and Lord Louis' own ship the, "Kelly" were sunk by the Luftwaffe. "Kipling" picked up the survivors, and during attacks in the forenoon dodged eighty bombs. By next morning, when seventy miles from Alexandria her fuel ran out, but she was towed into harbour.

While the ships were returning to replenish fuel tanks and magazines, the Germans had delivered an airborne attack on Maleme airfield, which had been pressed home regardless of loss. Once holding a landing ground, German reinforcements poured in. With overwhelming air support, the invaders now had the mastery. While the Fleet reorganised for extricating the garrison, German landings of heavy weapons and tanks were made by sea.

In the desperate days before defeat and evacuation were accepted, we in "Coventry" took part in an attempt to land troops.

On the 25th May we left harbour, and once at sea found ourselves escorting the assault ship "Glenroy", in company with destroyers "Stuart", and "Jaguar". Our object was to land at Tymbaki on the south coast, troops who would cross the mountains to Suda Bay. Next day, in the early morning, R.D.F. reported hostile aircraft, and within minutes bombs were dropping among the convoy. The barrage was rapid, and none of their bombs hit. During the day, R.D.F. produced several alarming reports, but no aircraft chose to attack. Toward evening, however, we saw a squadron of dive bombers coming for us. The barrage was heavy, the pom pom busy, and not one of the bombs hit, but the Stukas strafed "Glenroy". Three landing craft were damaged, and a dump of petrol cans on the upper deck set ablaze. The dive bombers had just turned for home, when six torpedo bombers were sighted. Their attacks were, fortunately, precipitate, and their tin fish easily avoided. But now "Glenroy" had to cope with the fire. She turned round to bring the wind aft, and jettisoned one of the landing craft. We were relieved to see the blaze being controlled, but it was slow work, consuming hours of valuable time. We went into the night as seas started to rise.

Several hours of darkness had been lost, and there were fewer landing craft for ferrying the troops, so a swift and sure landing of eight hundred troops was impracticable, and we were ordered to return to Alexandria. From early next morning, there were intermittent alarms, and several attacks successfully beaten off. But by the late afternoon we had reached the area covered by our fighters based in Egypt. It was then that Captain Waller of the Royal Australian Navy, sent from the destroyer "Stuart", a signal that cheered the hearts of the R.D.F. operators. It ran "Please give our grateful thanks and bouquets to your aerial 'ping' men". Just an hour before this, the decision had been made to evacuate Crete. As in the Greek evacuation, the only practicable policy was to destroy weapons, and bring back as many men as possible. The fighting raged in the airfield areas of Maleme, Retimo, and Heraklion, the only areas of flat land in Crete's mountainous terrain.

The evacuation of Crete would proceed on the lines of the Greek evacuation. The troops would be lifted in the darkness, and ships would leave in time to get beyond reach of the Luftwaffe by daylight. Some ships were now running at less than full efficiency, because operational duty had prevented routine maintenance. There were to be evacuation points at Sphakia, Plaka Bay, Heraklion Harbour, and Tymbaki. All were difficult to approach; and operations were further complicated because communication with the garrison was becoming confused, and the estimates of numbers of men to be lifted from the various points were being constantly altered.

The first lift was from Heraklion on the night of the 28th, May, when four thousand soldiers were embarked by cruisers "Orion", and "Dido", with destroyers "Decoy,'" "Jackal", "Hotspur", "Kimberley", and "Hereward". "Ajax" had set out with them, but returned before reaching Heraklion, because of damage by a near miss. "Imperial", similarly damaged, had carried on to embark four hundred men. Having done so, the steering gear failed. The troops were rapidly transferred to "Hotspur", which also had the duty of sinking "Imperial". Thus the home run started ninety minutes late, and daylight found the ships well within Luftwaffe range. "Hereward" was sunk. "Dido" sustained a hit on 'B' turret, whilst "Orion" suffered several hits, reducing the mess decks to shambles, with two hundred and sixty men killed and two hundred and eighty wounded.

On that same night, destroyers "Napier", "Nizam", "Kelvin", and "Kandahar", were able to land rations and small arms at Sphakia, and to bring away seven hundred men, returning undamaged.

"Coventry" left Alexandria on the night of the 28th May with "Glengyle", and cruisers "Phoebe", "Perth", and "Calcutta", and destroyers "Jervis", "Janus", and "Hasty". We ploughed through the rushing waters at our best speed; gun's crews found spots sheltered from the breeze, and peered into the black void unavailingly. Tomorrow promised to be hectic, and it was reassuring to have the supporting fire of the other cruisers. Dawn came quietly, and with increasing daylight, R.D.F. swept more warily, and lookouts used increasing concentration. At about 10.00 a.m. R.D.F. reported enemy aircraft. Guns followed the director on to the radar bearing, and the crews gazed skywards for an early sight of the enemy. Then a single JU88 came in view. Without pausing, it came straight for the convoy on an attack run. Once in range, the combined ships guns met it with a roaring barrage. The enemy did not falter, but completed his attack. A stick of bombs fell near "Perth", but did no damage. Afternoon was quiet, and having gone through the critical dusk period into darkness, we looked forward to repeating our Megara operation. But when we arrived at 11.30 p.m. "Coventry" and "Calcutta" were ordered to seaward, whilst the rest approached the shore. Destroyers embarked some of the soldiers, while landing craft ferried others to "Glengyle" and the cruisers. Whilst at action stations in the darkness and the silence of the sea, confidence grew.

At 3.20 a.m. on the 30th May, we saw the other ships suddenly near us, heading for the open sea. Soon we were in formation, Alexandria bound, and wondering what morning light would bring. Even more so perhaps, the six thousand soldiers that had been embarked.

Dawn came and went. In the early morning light we hastened on, intent on the traverse of the R D F aerials. Around breakfast time came the first attack by a dozen JU'88's. Our combined barrage kept them up, and the bombs missed. Half an hour later came a similar attack. "Perth" was hit, but did not slacken speed. At midday, came the third attack, and near misses on "Perth", also on the destroyer "Jaguar" which had joined us at Sphakia. But during the afternoon and onwards, R.D.F. reported one or two friendly fighters. There were no more alarms. Later we heard that two pursuing Junkers had been shot down by our fighters. Back in harbour we had time to be grateful for our luck. That night, "Napier", "Nizam", "Kelvin" and "Kandahar", once again left harbour for Sphakia, where they embarked a further fourteen hundred men from Crete, and with fighter cover on the return journey came back safely. "Napier", however, had been slowed down by a near miss from a Junker 88. On May 31st at 6 a.m. our lookouts saw a number of ships leaving harbour. They were "Phoebe", "Abdiel", "Kimberley", "Hotspur", and "Jackal", making the last trip to Sphakia. At dawn the next day, those same ships were returning with four thousand troops. In that very dawn, we were roused by the pipe of "Cable Party" and "Special sea duty men", to be followed by "hands to action stations". By now "Coventry" was commanded by Captain W.P. Carne, the erstwhile Fleet Torpedo Officer who had showed such resource when Valetta Harbour approaches had been mined in, and there were no mine sweepers available.

The chill breeze and grey light of early morning were comfortable enough in view of the deadly birds that might swoop from a sunny blue sky. We were going to meet the last evacuation convoy, and wondered when we should sight those hardy ships, and what attention the enemy would give us. Close behind us was our sister ship "Calcutta", with her complement of predominantly R.N.V.R. London gunners.

The normal breakfast hour had passed quietly:–(the enemy made a practice of appearing at meal times). The sun was now brilliant, and everyone on the upper deck was an enthusiastic lookout on this abnormal Sunday morning. On the bridge, Captain Carne had just noticed that it was 9 a.m., and he had reckoned the ship to be eighty-five miles north of Alexandria, when an R.D.F. report was made to him of hostile aircraft approaching from the North. The alert was broadcast, and lookouts and gun's crews, in fact, everyone on the upper deck, strained their eyes; mindful that aircraft always tried to attack out of the sun.

The minutes dragged by without further R.D.F., or lookouts reports. A quarter of an hour passed, with hundreds of pairs of eyes vainly seeking sight of the enemy.

Captain Carne was suddenly conscious of a yell by his Yeoman of Signals "aircraft overhead sir; bombs falling"!

A glance confirmed this, and "Alter course starboard" was immediately ordered. By now, the scream of the bombs made us all, only too uncomfortably aware, that the enemy had got in first. Simultaneously, the ship listed and the pitch of the engines rose, as "Coventry" altered course. Then came the shock and the roar of detonation as bombs exploded and the lofty ascending columns of salt water reassured us that it was a miss–but only just. Gun's crews were on director pointers to meet the inevitable follow-up, when a series of harsher explosions came from astern. "Calcutta" had been hit.

While we watched, she ploughed straight under, amid a welter of steam and smoke. "Calcutta's" stern rose high in the air for a few minutes, and we could clearly see our comrades abandoning ship by all the swiftest means available. The men below had five minutes to get clear of gunnery plotting rooms, magazines, and boiler rooms, using rope ladders in some cases where the iron stairs had collapsed. Then "Calcutta" settled momentarily level in the clear water, before her bows rose vertically, and she plunged stern first, to the depths. Very soon came evidence of boilers exploding, as the sea bubbled and foamed over the spot. Thus two Junkers 88's had sunk "Calcutta" and all but sunk "Coventry".

By now, radar reported a clear screen. All boats were lowered, and scrambling nets dropped down the ship's side, as we moved towards the survivors. Some were swimming vigorously in our direction. Here and there floated bodies in grotesque attitudes. The boats brought in the injured men mostly. Some white faced and silent, some in pain and oozing blood. Many were thickly covered with oil. Quite a few were torn by the agony of severe burns, exposed to air and salt water.

With the utmost despatch, consistent with humane regard and care for the injured, survivors were brought aboard. Injured men to the sick bay, the rest to the mess deck for recovery. Many a greeting was exchanged, with an acquaintance of "President" days. The number of survivors, returned to Alexandria, totalled two hundred and fifty-five. The voyage back to Alexandria was a time for bitter reflection. There was, however, great satisfaction when we saw that last convoy from Sphakia enter harbour. They had made a relatively quiet return to Alexandria, and during the latter part of it, had enjoyed that rare blessing, R.A.F. fighter protection. The ships had brought back four thousand men, but had been forced to leave a large number behind.

The Crete operation had considerably reduced the effectiveness of the Fleet, and well over two thousand sailors had been killed. Never again would they fill the Beer Garden at the Fleet Club, shout "A house" at Tombola, or throng the cabarets of the Corniche Road; but grievous news was on it's way to thousands more in all directions. Of the thirty-two thousand man garrison in Crete, eighteen hundred had been killed and twelve thousand left behind, the majority of them to become prisoners of war.

During the ten days fighting, the Germans had lost four thousand men, killed or missing, in addition to the estimated four thousand drowned, when the invasion fleets were sunk.

While the struggle had been in progress, the Mediterranean Chiefs of Staff had been faced with the Iraq revolt of Raschid Ali, and the invitation by Vichy General Dentz, to the Germans,–to occupy Syria.

CHAPTER SIXTEEN

TEN DAYS FROM THE RECOLLECTIONS OF
CAPTAIN CARNE R.N.

In May 1941, I had been nearly three years in the Mediterranean Fleet, serving as Fleet Torpedo Officer on the C-in-C's staff. My relief had just arrived, when I was sent for by the Admiral, I thought to say good-bye. But after I had reported to him that I had turned over my duties as F.T.O. to my "relief", he turned to me and told me that the captain of the "Coventry" was being invalided home to England. He went on to say, that he didn't know whether the Admiralty were going to promote me in June, but if in the meantime I liked to remain on the station, he would appoint me to the "Coventry" with the rank of acting captain.

He went on to add that he realised that I had been away from England for a long time, that I had a young family growing up, and that if I preferred to go home he would quite understand. However, I didn't hesitate, my last chance to be promoted would be in the following June, and I knew that I would stand a much better chance if I was already an acting captain in command of a ship. So I immediately accepted his offer, and he told me to join my new ship the next morning. He would make the necessary signals at once.

When I joined the "Coventry" the next morning, she was tucked in alongside the dockyard wall surrounded by other ships. During the forenoon, my predecessor was introducing me to my new officers, making out confidential reports, and generally finishing off in a hurry all those things which have to be done when one gives up a command. Before noon we were interrupted by a signal directing "Coventry" and two frigates to escort one of the Glen ships to Crete, sailing at 23.00 that night.

I spent the rest of the day finding out the particulars of this operation, (the Glen ship was loaded with stores for the Army in Crete, on the assumption that the battle for the island was to continue), and arranging to get the assistance of a tug to get me clear of the dockyard. I saw the tugmaster to explain to him that this was my first command, and he promised to give me a good tow, stern first, out into the centre of the harbour, from where I could get a clear run.

When I went up on the bridge at 23.00 to take the ship to sea for the first time, the night was very dark, and I was filled with trepidation. However, in the event everything went very well, the tug towed us gently out into the harbour, the "Coventry" behaved perfectly, and we slid out through the boom and then the Great Pass, with no difficulty at all. Soon after 01.00 we were clear of the swept channel, formed up in our cruising formation, and had set course for Crete. I was free to get a little rest, feeling rather pleased with myself, but rather weary after a long day. Had I realised how strenuous the next ten days were going to be, I should not have been so complacent.

After dawn action stations, half the ship's company fell out. After the bugle calls and pipes repeated on the loud speakers of the "Warspite", there appeared to be rather an air of casualness about the "Coventry". However, I need not have worried. During the forenoon many aircraft were reported by our radar, R.D.F. as we called it in those days. If any aircraft came within twenty miles of us, a whisper down the improvised loud speaker system to "stand to", brought every man to his action station at once. It was clear that the "Coventry's" crew had learnt their lesson, and were not to be caught napping.

I don't think any of the aircraft reported by our radar that forenoon were hostile, but it was clear from intercepted signals that there was a great deal of enemy activity in the vicinity of Crete, and of course one assumed that all aircraft were hostile until they had been definitely recognised as friendly.

During the afternoon we intercepted a high priority signal from the Admiralty to the C-in-C Med: (I feel sure this signal should have been made in the C-in-C's cypher and that we were not intended to read it). It caused me much worry, as it started by agreeing to some proposal of the C-in-C's which was not in our possession, and then went on to say that all forces should be withdrawn to Alexandria except "Coventry", who should continue to the northward.

No further signal came from the C-in—C, and as dusk approached I had to make up my mind what to do during the night. I felt certain that the C-in-C would not allow me to go on to Crete entirely unsupported. From intercepted signals I knew that our forces had received considerable damage, and were retiring on Alexandria. If I went straight back I should arrive before dawn, and have to hang about in the way of the other forces returning from Crete.

One thing I had learnt from Cunningham during my service in the "Warspite" was, never to make a manoeuvring signal at night, except in an emergency. Before dusk he always made a night policy signal, detailing exactly what was to be done during the night and, if an alteration of course was involved, ships were directed to alter to the new course at a definite time without signal.

Before dusk closed down on us, therefore, I made a night policy signal to my little force, directing them to alter course without further signal at midnight, onto a course which would bring us back close to Alexandria during the following forenoon.

At a quarter to midnight I was on the bridge for the alteration of course. Up to that time no signal had been received from the C-in-C, and I was considerably worried in my mind as to whether I had anticipated the Admiral's intentions correctly. However, at five minutes to midnight, the wireless office rang up to say that there was a high priority signal for "Coventry" from the C-in-C just received, that they were deciphering. When a few minutes later it arrived on the bridge, it was to the effect that I was to bring my convoy back to Alexandria. So it appeared that I had read my Admiral's mind correctly.

During "stand to" the next morning, before it was properly light, the radar picked up an aircraft approaching from the direction of Crete, and apparently quite low. It appeared to be going to pass about five miles clear of us, when it suddenly altered course directly toward the convoy. I was about to order "open fire", when it fired a recognition signal, and it turned out to be an R.A.F. bomber. It circled close around the "Coventry", asking by Aldis lamp for it's position. We gave it a position, and it disappeared in the direction of the coast of Egypt, which was then only some thirty miles distant.

To my surprise, it appeared again after about ten minutes, and without making any further signal it "ditched" close alongside the "Coventry" and sank rapidly, but not before the crew escaped in a rubber dinghy.

The two frigates were on either bow of the convoy, operating their asdics with "Coventry" zig-zagging astern. I did not wish to remove a frigate from the screen, so I decided to pick up the survivors with the "Coventry". Before we could get the way off the ship we had considerably overshot the position of the rubber dinghy, and had to turn and come back to it.

When we had got the survivors out of the rubber dinghy, the Gunnery Officer asked if he could exercise one of the four barrelled 0.5" machine guns, by sinking it. As I had never seen one of these weapons in use I was interested to see how effective it could be, so I told him to get on with it but to be quick, as I was not anxious to remain stopped. I had a feeling that there might be a submarine about.

Actually the demonstration by the 0.5" machine gun was very disappointing, it took several bursts at a range of little more than a cable, to sink the rubber dinghy. They were disappointing guns, much to unhandy for close range work, and too limited in range to be effective at more distant targets.

The pilot of the aircraft informed me that they had been sent to bomb Maleme airfield, which by this time was being used by the Germans. They had got lost, and didn't know where they had dropped their bombs. After we had given them their position they had gone on for about ten miles, but not having sighted the Egyptian coast, and being down to their last few pints of fuel, had decided that they had better return to us and ditch alongside, rather than risk running out of fuel completely, before they were over Egypt.

No further incidents occurred during our return to Alexandria. We were ordered to berth astern of the "Calcutta", alongside a small breakwater close inside the boom, where the two A.A. cruisers were in a good position to use their guns in the event of an aerial attack on Alexandria. To get alongside this breakwater, one had to turn the ship 180 degrees, and approach it from the landward side with the sea breeze blowing one off. Not an easy place to get alongside, fortunately the "Coventry" had been there several times before, knew the drill with the boats, and I had an experienced navigating officer to assist me in manoeuvring the ship. But I gave a sigh of relief when we were safely alongside.

As soon as we were secured, I went along the breakwater to call on the captain of the "Calcutta", Captain "Bunny" Lees, who gave me a number of helpful tips as to the best way of approaching our berth on the breakwater, and also told me of his recent experiences at sea. He had been with the forces to the North of Crete, and had been engaged with enemy aircraft on several occasions.

I could have done with a good night's rest that night, but before I could go to bed an air raid developed, and kept us up for a long time. "Coventry" opened fire on several occasions to reinforce the barrage.

But standing on the bridge it was difficult to differentiate between the reports, and to decide whether they were all of the same aircraft, or of several different ones.

The next day I arranged to have a mooring board on the bridge, with a number of coloured pins with which different aircraft could be plotted. I gave this duty to Lt. Commander Reece, who soon became very good at producing a clear picture of what was happening. I remember that during a subsequent night raid on Alex: after we had been closed up for well over an hour, and had opened fire half a dozen times ourselves, while there had been a great deal of shooting around the harbour; I asked him how the attack was developing. He replied that he thought there were twelve enemy aircraft, and that so far eleven had attacked. He was quite right, there was one more burst of firing when the last enemy attacked, and then we got the all clear.

Early the next morning we received orders to prepare for sea, followed shortly after, by the orders for the operation. Once again we were to escort the same Glen ship to Crete with stores for the army, but in place of the two frigates, on this occasion the anti-submarine screen consisted of three Australian destroyers, including the flotilla leader "Stuart" commanded by Captain "Heck" Waller. As Captain Waller was the senior officer, he was in command of the whole force.

We were due to leave harbour at 18.30. At 18.00 I was already in my sea going clothes, waiting in my day cabin for the First Lieutenant to report "Ready for Sea", and listening to the 6.0 p.m. B.B.C. news. (Owing to the use of double summer time in England, British summer time corresponded to the Eastern Mediterranean time we were using). I was horrified to hear an announcement from the Admiralty that the "Hood" had been sunk during the previous day. This news seemed to be a very bad omen, just as we were setting out on what must prove to be a pretty hazardous enterprise. I suddenly remembered that the day was my forty third birthday. These two facts, the bad news coming on my birthday, cast a gloom over me, but I realised that it was important that I did not give any indication of my inward feelings. In the privacy of my cabin I pulled myself together, so that when a few minutes later the First Lieutenant reported that we were all ready for sea, I was able to walk up to the bridge without, I hope, giving any indication of my inward thoughts.

Our passage that night was uneventful, and at dawn it appeared that we should arrive with our convoy at Sphakia, where she was to discharge her cargo soon after dark. But air activity developed early in the day, and the radar was constantly reporting echoes. "Coventry" was the only ship in the force with radar, so that we were constantly passing reports to the "Stuart" to keep the senior officer up-to-date with the situation.

While most of these reports referred to hostile aircraft attacking other forces, (it was the day that the "Formidable" was bombed), two attacks developed on our force during daylight hours. Neither of these caused any damage, though one bomb fell unpleasantly close to the "Coventry" with that increasing whistling noise which is so unnerving.

It was during one of these attacks, that we noticed that some of the shells from one of the starboard guns were firing prematurely, indicating that the gun was becoming dangerously worn, and must be changed at the first opportunity.

Towards dusk, as we were getting close to Crete, a much more serious attack developed, by a number of aircraft which continued for a considerable time in the rapidly failing light, firstly by bombers, and then by at least one torpedo plane. "Coventry" was steaming close astern of the Glen ship, to cover her as far as possible with our A.A. armament, while the destroyers were on a comparatively close anti-submarine screen. As each aircraft came in to attack, we passed radar bearings and ranges to the destroyers, who endeavoured to back up our barrage with their A.A. guns. Then, when the hostile aircraft got really close and was about to release it's bomb, the destroyers fired a barrage of shrapnel from their 4.7 inch guns to burst over the convoy.

The Australian destroyers were magnificent, switching their barrages to follow "Coventry", so that each opponent as he came in to attack was met by a considerable barrage, which, if not very accurate, must have been very frightening.

It was the rapid and continuous fire which we developed, to which I put down the fact that the force emerged almost, though not quite, immune. Early on the Glen ship was hit well aft, and a large quantity of cased petrol stowed on deck over her after holds, was set on fire. This blazed up, making an excellent aiming mark in the dusk for the enemy.

The petrol was in four gallon tins, about a dozen tins to a case, stowed conveniently to pass it rapidly over the side when we arrived at our destination. Somehow the crew of the Glen ship managed to shove each burning case over the side. At intervals of two or three minutes, another flaming case would fall into the sea, to make a pool of burning petrol which silhouetted the "Coventry" as we steamed past. Every moment I thought the Glen was bound to burst into flames and become a total wreck. But somehow they contained the fire to the petrol and eventually got rid of the last case.

I cannot remember how long this attack lasted, but at the time it seemed to be interminable, and made all the more dramatic by the failing light, which enhanced the glare from the flaming petrol, and the gun flashes and the flashes in the sky from the bursting shells. It was towards the end of the attack, when the last of the cased petrol was being pushed over the side, that the radar picked up an echo very low down and unpleasantly close. We got off a salvo or two at it, but almost at once, the plane, whatever it was, turned away and was lost off the screen. I originally thought it was a torpedo plane coming in to make it's attack, but it did not appear to come sufficiently close to deliver a torpedo attack. I came to the conclusion that it was an aircraft that had delivered it's load of bombs, and was circling around endeavouring to see the results of it's attack. I dismissed the idea of a torpedo attack, as there seemed to be more important things to think about.

However, a few minutes later the ship was considerably shaken by an underwater explosion, and looking aft we saw an upsurge in the wake, very similar to that caused by a depth charge. At that moment there were no aircraft overhead so it could not have been caused by a bomb, further the disturbance was quite different to that caused by a bomb. I had little doubt but that the explosion was caused by some form of torpedo, which had been dropped by the low flying aircraft. There had been various very vague intelligence reports, of the enemy developing a torpedo which turned into the wake of the target and followed it up. Could this explosion be something on that line which had fired prematurely? Anyway that was something for my successor, as Fleet Torpedo Officer to worry about, all I had to do was to make a note of the known facts and report them which, in due course, I did.

As darkness closed down, and the radar reported that the screen was at last clear, I was wondering what should be our next move. Besides losing all her cased petrol, was the Glen ship seriously damaged? Was it worth while going on to land such stores as remained? I was glad I was not senior officer, and had not to make a decision on this question. But I need not have worried, shortly after we received a signal recalling us to Alexandria. Apparently the policy had been changed, instead of continuing the battle for Crete, it had been decided to withdraw all forces.

I cannot remember whether we were actually attacked during the next day as we made our way back across the Mediterranean, but I remember that the air was full of aircraft which we were reporting all day long to the "Stuart". Every radar report was passed out by ten inch light, and from time to time I sent "Stuart" a situation report as I had appreciated the situation from my mooring board. I think these reports were useful and appreciated, as the last signal "Stuart" made to me as we went into Alexandria harbour, was one to congratulate me on the efficiency of what he called my "aerial ping men". I think we deserved that little pat on the back, our radar had given us early warning of every attack and, during the dusk attack, had enabled us to put up an effective barrage as each attack developed, and so allowed us to escape with little damage.

Arrived in Alexandria that evening, we went to our usual berth on the breakwater and fuelled, and early the next morning, ammunition lighters came alongside to replace the rounds we had fired. At the same time another lighter arrived with a 4 inch gun, to replace the worn one which had caused so many prematures. Each projectile had to be fused before it was stowed away, after which we could have done with a little rest, but that was not to be thought of. Long before we had finished ammunitioning we received orders to raise steam, and be ready to leave harbour that evening.

During the afternoon I was summoned on board the "Phoebe", in which ship Admiral King, (who was to command the next operation), had hoisted his flag. As "Calcutta" was also to form part of the force, Captain Lees and I went together.

Admiral King explained that the object of the operation, was to lift off from Sphakia, as many men as possible. What remained of the army in Crete were retreating towards Sphakia, and it was anticipated that by tomorrow night there would be several thousand men ready for embarkation. In order that our approach to the coast, and retreat from it, should be carried out as far as possible under cover of darkness, he intended to arrive off Sphakia at 01.00 the day after tomorrow, and leave at 04.00, any men not embarked by then were to be left behind.

The force consisted of two cruisers, the "Phoebe", and the Australian cruiser "Perth", two anti-aircraft cruisers "Calcutta" and "Coventry", another Glen ship called the "Glengyle", fitted with a number of landing craft, and an anti-submarine screen of destroyers. On arrival off Sphakia, the "Glengyle" was to anchor as close in as possible without further orders, lower her landing craft, and start ferrying off men to the "Glengyle", "Phoebe" and "Perth", who would anchor close alongside. Destroyers were to assist as far as their boats would allow, but it was intended that the main lift should be by the "Glengyle", whose landing craft were much more suitable than ship's boats.

During the operation of embarking the soldiers, "Calcutta" and "Coventry" were to patrol close off the anchorage as a defence against attack by aircraft. Admiral King thought that the enemy would anticipate an operation to embark troops from Sphakia, and would endeavour to interfere.

When he had explained his intentions, Admiral King asked us if we had any questions or suggestions. Nobody had much to say, we were all weary ourselves, and were only too well aware that our ships companies were exhausted and badly in need of a decent rest. The Admiral had explained that the position of the army in Crete was desperate, if we could not get them away, they would have to surrender. So obviously we had to go and make as good a show as possible, but nobody looked forward to the operation one little bit.

The captain of the "Phoebe", Captain "Granny" Grantham, tried to put a more cheerful look on the conference by giving us each a whisky and soda. I was sitting near the outboard bulkhead under a scuttle, which was fitted with a scuttle chute, through which came a pleasant cool breeze. The "Phoebe" was preparing for sea, and in furling the quarterdeck awning, someone caught a rope in the scuttle chute and tipped it inboard. As the chute fell, it hit my right arm, causing me to upset most of my whisky and soda over my nice clean, white uniform, that I had put on to call on the Admiral. Captain Grantham was most distressed and apologetic, and wanted to lend me one of his own white uniforms. But I refused to accept his offer, thinking that if nothing worse than a scuttle chute fell on me during the next two days, I shouldn't do too badly.

On our arrival in harbour, I had been informed that my experienced navigating officer was to be relieved, and as I returned from the "Phoebe" the new navigating officer came to report to me. I was distressed at losing my experienced navigator who had been a great help to me, but I need not have worried. His relief, Lieutenant Kerrush R.A.N. proved to be a skilful navigator, and to have the cheerful courage which one had learnt to expect from the Australian Naval Officers serving in the Mediterranean.

We sailed at dusk that evening, and by the next morning were well on our way to Crete. As far as I remember we were attacked twice that day, and I have little doubt but that we were reported. Admiral King steered a course as though we were making for the Western Med: and then as darkness fell, altered course directly for Sphakia. The defence we put up during the day was successful, and the force approached Crete undamaged.

The night was very dark, under cover of which, some seven thousand men were embarked in the "Glengyle", "Phoebe", and "Perth". "Calcutta" and "Coventry", patrolled along a line ten miles long close off the coast, but there was no interference by the enemy. The force left Sphakia at 04.00 and proceeded at "Glengyle's" best speed, which was about 18½ knots. "Calcutta" and "Coventry" followed up astern, and rejoined the convoy at daylight, the A.A. cruisers taking station on either bow of the "Glengyle", while the "Phoebe" and "Perth" were on either quarter.

We were reported soon after daylight, and the expected attack arrived early in the forenoon watch. The enemy consisted of ten, or a dozen planes, and came in from astern. "Glengyle" zig-zagged madly. I told Kerrush to keep close to her port bow, which he did to such good measure, that once we must have been within half a cable of her. "Calcutta" was in a similar position on her starboard bow, so that as each plane attacked from astern, we put up a very effective barrage which few of the enemy penetrated. They preferred to drop their bombs on the cruisers.

We made full use of our multiple pom-pom, which, with the several pom-poms in the "Glengyle", and "Calcutta's" close range weapons, put up a formidable close range barrage. As the enemy came in, they were engaged first by "Phoebe" and "Perth", and then by the 4" guns of "Coventry" and "Calcutta". Few pressed their attacks, but preferred to diverge either to port or starboard and release their bombs over the cruisers or destroyers. "Perth" during one zig-zag, allowed herself to become slightly detached from the rest of the force, and immediately became the target of two or three of the enemy, one of which succeeded in putting a bomb into her forward boiler room. Although her full speed was considerably reduced, she was still able to keep up with the force, and our retreat on Alexandria was not therefore delayed.

Once again it was shown that if a number of ship's kept well together, had good warning of an attack and the visibility to see the target, and fired hard and fast, only the most determined enemy would press his attack sufficiently close to have a good chance of obtaining a hit. Unfortunately it was not always possible to ensure early warning and good visibility, on which a rapid volume of fire was dependent. Our next trip to Crete showed only too clearly, that if these conditions were not present, then a determined and skilful enemy could cause us great loss.

The remainder of our voyage back to Alexandria was without incident, and we again secured at the detached breakwater astern of the "Calcutta", in the small hours of the next morning. Early in the day an oiler came alongside, followed by a lighter full of ammunition, from which we replaced those rounds which had been fired. The speed with which these stores were placed alongside was a good indication that we should be required for service again very shortly.

Soon after breakfast, Captain Lees walked along the breakwater and suggested we should both visit the C-in-C's office, as he expressed it, "to find out the form". During the almost continuous series of operations during the previous month, all ship's boats had suffered considerably, and there had been no opportunity for repair and maintenance. "Calcutta" had not got a power boat that was reasonably reliable. "Coventry's" motor boat was under repair, but the First Lieutenant had lowered the motor cutter, which appeared to be running satisfactorily. So we both went in that boat.

Arrived at the office, we were immediately shown into the C-in-C, who wanted an account of our last operation, expressed himself very disappointed that we could not report having seen any of the enemy fall into the sea, and told us that we must fire harder and faster, and a damned sight straighter. What was the good of an A.A. cruiser if she could not shoot down every hostile aircraft that came in range? Then he went on to talk a little about the whole series of operations, of how the army were up against impossible odds and that we must do our best to get as many of them out of Crete as possible.

Lees said that we had lost 60,000 men during the first day of the battle of the Somme, was it worthwhile to lose the whole of the Mediterranean Fleet for the 30,000 men in Crete? The Admiral turned on him at once, and repeated that remark which he made on more than one occasion during those tense and trying days, namely, that it takes three years to build a ship, but three hundred years to build a tradition. The Navy always stands by the Army, and we were not going to break a tradition now.

Then he went on to say that there would be a few more men to be collected from Sphakia that night, and that he had sent his only available destroyers to pick them up. He wanted "Calcutta" and "Coventry" to go to sea at 01.00 and meet the destroyers roughly halfway to Crete, and come back with them to give additional A.A. support. Further he had arranged with the R.A.F. that we should have fighter cover. Two fighters with long range tanks would cover us during our return to Alexandria. After which, he said, with one of his more cheerful laughs, we might be allowed a day or so in harbour to refurbish ourselves.

So we made our way back to our ships, neither of us feeling very cheerful, to find that the operational signal had arrived. I desperately wanted to rest, but a lot of paper work had arrived, some of which my secretary was very insistant that I should deal with before we sailed. The First Lieutenant wanted me to see requestmen, and various officers wanted to talk to me and, indeed, I wanted to talk to them. So far I had had very little chance of getting to know any of my officers, but come what may, I was determined to go to bed early, and get a little sleep before we sailed at 01.00. Vain hope, I had hardly got to sleep, before I was awakened to be told that a preliminary air raid warning signal had been received.

Scrambling into my clothes, I hurried up to the bridge, only to be faced with a long wait. The actual raid did not develop until after 23.00. We opened fire on several occasions. The enemy attacked with one plane at a time, with considerable gaps between each attack. It was nearly 01.00 before we received the all clear, and we were just singling up our wires preparatory to slipping, when R.A.L. closed the port.

During the raid, splashes had been seen in the Great Pass, which might have been magnetic mines. No ship's were, therefore, allowed out through the boom until these splashes had been investigated. It was after 04.00 before we were given permission to sail, and it was not until 05.30 that we were clear of the swept channel and steady on our course for Crete. Then it was time for dawn action stations, after which it was too late to think of sleep, so I shaved and dressed and had an early breakfast.

The sun had come up into a clear cloudless sky, and there was every promise of a hot Eastern Mediterranean summer day, in fact, by 09.00 it was already very hot when the radar first picked up an echo, fine on our port quarter roughly in the direction of Alexandria. My first reaction was that the R.A.F. fighters had not heard that we had sailed three hours late from Alex; and had therefore come out too early. As soon as we received the report of the echo on the bridge, we repeated it by ten inch light to the "Calcutta", who was not fitted with radar.

We were doing a No. 10 zig-zag, which meant that at 09.10 we both altered twenty degrees to starboard together, which brought "Coventry" fine on "Calcutta's" starboard quarter, and, more important, brought the echo of the approaching aircraft dead astern in the funnel haze, and straight up sun.

The echo continued to come straight towards us, and at a range of about ten miles was observed to be two aircraft, obviously the two fighters from Alexandria.

The sun was a flaming orb in a sky of burnished brass as we stared through the dancing funnel haze to catch a glimpse of the approaching aircraft, who came steadily on straight for us. I cannot remember, at which moment I became suspicious, I did become suspicious, but not nearly soon enough, as I was too tired for my brain to work quickly. Of course being R.A.F. planes they would not have I.F.F., but surely they would indicate their friendly character before coming too close, either fire a recognition signal, or make a circuit around us outside gun range, so that we could identify them. All our guns were trained in the direction of the approaching aircraft, but the director could see nothing.

The radar had the echo absolutely firm, reports were coming up to the bridge every 15/20 seconds, and were being passed on to the "Calcutta" as fast as the ten inch light could transmit them. I could see that "Calcutta" had all her guns trained on the bearing of the approaching aircraft, but she did not open fire or make any alteration of course signal. I had every lookout on the bridge, signalmen, Officer of the Watch, and navigator searching the sky astern of us. Nobody saw anything until the Chief Yeoman, (I had already learnt that he had the eyes of a hawk and was a most reliable man), who was searching the sky through his signalman's telescope shouted, "It's a J.U.", Immediately I gave the order "starboard 25". (When steaming 22 knots as we were on this occasion we found that for all practical purposes, the ship answered her helm as quickly on 25 degrees of rudder, as on 35 degrees, and did not lose so much way). Stepping to the starboard side of the compass platform, I shouted up the voicepipe to the foretop to "Open Fire", and then ran to the after end of the wing of the bridge, to try and get a view clear of the funnel haze.

Immediately I saw the leading enemy aircraft coming straight towards us, now well into her dive and looking terribly menacing. Almost at once she let drive with her machine guns. The first rounds hit the sea just clear of the port quarter. Then the splashes from the following rounds moved up the port side, just missing the ship. Watching them they seemed to move quite slowly, though I don't suppose that there was much more than a second between the first and last splash.

I had been passed over from promotion the preceding December by another officer on the C-in-C's staff. On promotion, he had been appointed to command an A.A. cruiser, and had been killed a month or so previously by a machine gun bullet, when his ship was shot up by a diving aircraft. Had I not been passed over for promotion, I should certainly have been in his place. I had been congratulating myself, that if I had had to wait for my promotion, at least I was still alive. Now as I watched death approaching me across the water, it passed through my mind that, after all, I was to suffer the same fate.

But I had just got the wheel over in time and the "Coventry", witch that she was then, and always, was swinging fast, too fast for the enemy to adjust his aim. His machine gun bullets just missed us, and a second or so later when the bombs arrived, they were also just clear of the port side, but the centre one of three was sufficiently close to drench the port waist with spray.

An officer who was in the port waist subsequently told me that the bomb fell seventeen feet from the ship's side. How he measured the distance so accurately I cannot imagine, but at least his estimate indicates that the bomb was much too close. The force of it's explosion gave that jerk to the ship, which gives the impression that the whole ship is being lifted.

The aircraft passed close overhead, I shouted myself hoarse for someone to open fire with something, but our close range weapons were as ponderous as the 4 inch guns, and had no hope of catching up with a diving aircraft at that short range. If only we had an oerlikon, or single barrelled bofors, we might have done something, but an eight barrelled pom-pom was still lumbering around from right astern to right ahead when the enemy was nearly over the horizon.

In the meantime the second aircraft was attacking "Calcutta". Lees had seen "Coventry" start to swing, and had immediately put his own wheel over to conform, but the slight delay had not given "Calcutta" time to alter course appreciably, and she was hit by two bombs straight up her centre line.

It was at once obvious that "Calcutta" was seriously damaged. My first reaction was that the attack must be reported, it looked as though "Calcutta's" wireless might well be out of action, therefore it was up to me to make the necessary signal. I shouted to Slawson to make the signal "Am being Bombed". In those days there was a single group for this signal, I think it was O.E.A.B., it was a group we used to see frequently at that time. I think I said to Slawson "O.E.A.B. Calcutta hit" and followed it up by telling Kerrush to give our position, who had foreseen this requirement, and was already taking it off the chart.

I hurriedly took the wheel off and brought "Coventry" back close to "Calcutta", who, it was at once clear, was slowing and was down by the bows. All this time the radar was reporting aircraft. Actually I think the two aircraft that attacked us had separated and circled round to see the effect of their attack. The radar kept picking them up on different bearings, which gave me the impression there were more aircraft waiting to attack.

Soon it was clear that the "Calcutta's" crew were preparing to abandon their ship. They started to lower boats but there was no time, the fo'c'sle was nearly under water, her stern came up, so that one of her propellors could be seen. Then men started jumping over the side; I saw one who seemed to fall into the propellor. Then suddenly she was gone, and there was nothing to see but a large pool of oil fuel, in which were one or two carley rafts and flotta nets that they had succeeded in launching, and a large number of heads bobbing in the oily water.

I told Kerrush to circle round the survivors and reduce speed, we were still doing 22 knots. Obviously we would have to stop and pick up survivors, but were we going to be attacked again? I tried to get a picture from the radar of what aircraft were in the vicinity, at the same time sending for the First Lieutenant and directing him to prepare to pick up survivors, but he must do it with the repair parties. With the menace of air attack at any moment, I refused to fall out any gun's crews or control parties.

At the same time I made another signal to the C-in-C reporting that "Calcutta" had sunk. Just four and a half minutes elapsed between the moment "Calcutta" was hit and she sank.

There was not even a breath of wind, the sea was flat calm, a perfect summer day in the Eastern Med. On the surface of the sea was a circle of black oil, now nearly half a mile in diameter. How to approach to pick up survivors? I had vivid memories of being told of a destroyer in the First War, who, anxious to get amongst a crowd of survivors as quickly as possible, went in too fast and had to go violently astern on her engines to avoid overshooting. The result was that she chewed up a lot of men in her propellors. I was determined not to make that mistake. In the event I was too cautious. We turned through about 360 degrees and approached on roughly our original course, and stopped the ship with her fo'c'sle just in the circle of oil. The survivors swam towards us, many giving a cheer and shouting "Good old Coventry" as they came. "Calcutta" was our chummy ship, and every man had one or more friends in her.

Arrived alongside they were exhausted with their swim in the oil, and could not climb the flotta nets to the height to the fo'c'sle. Men got half-way up and hung exhausted. Further the flare of the fo'c'sle added to their difficulties. I had to move the ship ahead. Impossible to make men who were already grasping the flotta nets and ropes under the fo'c'sle to let go. I had to tow them with us, giving just a touch ahead on the screws and immediately stopping again, so that the ship just moved ahead.

All the time the radar was reporting aircraft, I was terrified we were going to be attacked while we were stopped, with the upper deck littered with survivors, many in not too good a shape gasping out oil fuel and water.

In the water all the heads looked exactly alike, smeared as they were with oil fuel. From the upper deck came shouts of pleasure as individuals were recognised as they were hauled in over the berthing rails. I kept trying to pick out Bunny Lees, and leaning over the bridge, I shouted to an officer on the fo'c'sle to look for him and bring him to me. Nothing happened. I kept shouting for Captain Lees. Then a quiet voice behind me said "It's alright William, I am here". Turning round I saw a bedraggled figure sitting on the step up from the bridge to the compass platform. Without his cap, and much smeared with oil fuel, no one had recognised him. He was very calm, sad and resigned. I asked him to go down to my cabin and ask my steward to give him some clean clothes. But he said "No, no don't worry about me, you are doing a magnificent job, get on with it". Realising that I could best comfort him by rescuing as many as possible of his ship's company, I turned back to considering the next move.

The "Calcutta" before she sank had managed to launch two or three flotta nets on which they had placed some of their more seriously injured men. These were being brought towards us by some of the stronger swimmers. We endeavoured to ease the ship towards them, and prepared with heaving lines to haul them the last few yards alongside the waist, where we could best hoist inboard the injured men. At the same time we realised there were some men on the far side of the pool of oil, who were going to take a long time to reach us if they ever got to us at all. I called away a whaler, she had to be manned by a scratch crew, as all the seaman ratings were closed up at the guns. I sent away in her a sub-lieutenant whose name I cannot remember. He had only joined us a few days before, had not been properly worked into the organisation, and was therefore more or less a spare number.

As a boat was being lowered I hailed him, and told him that if I was attacked I should immediately get underway. He was to remain in the same area, and I would come back and pick him up after dark. I didn't add "If I am afloat", although that thought was very much at the back of my mind. But in fact he picked up the half dozen survivors who were making heavy weather of their swim to the ship, had a look around for any others, and came back just as we hoisted the last swimmer aboard.

We hooked on the boat full speed, and I directed every man on the upper deck to man the falls, ship's company and any survivors who could stand, and as the boat left the water I put both telegraphs to full speed ahead.

"Coventry" seemed to almost leap out of the water as she got going, I think she was as nervous as I was to get away. We had been stopped for exactly twenty five minutes, the longest twenty five minutes through which I have ever lived.

With our patched bow, our speed had been limited to 22 knots. But the sea was a flat calm, I felt that if our bow was safe at 22 knots zig-zagging in a bit of a seaway, it was safe to go a little faster in such calm conditions. So we whacked her up to revs for 29 knots, which was about all her ancient engines would do. I felt that the spot where such great disaster had come upon us was a place of ill omen, and the sooner we got away the better. And the "Coventry" thought so too, she went like a bird.

Then it was time to sum up the situation. We found that we had onboard 255 of the "Calcutta's" crew, which included 32 more or less seriously injured men. I think it shows what a high standard of discipline there must have been in the "Calcutta", that, in the four and a half minutes between the time she was first hit and the moment when she finally disappeared, that they had got 32 injured men on to rolled up flotta nets and organised gangs of swimmers to swim the nets to the "Coventry". But it meant that about a hundred men were missing, I can't remember now whether we were exactly a 100 short, and one or two more subsequently died in hospital, or whether the deaths in hospital brought the number up to a hundred.

We were back in Alexandria in the early afternoon, with orders to go alongside in the dockyard and land our survivors. We had to go to the far side of the main jetty into a space between "Resource" and a covey of trawlers and drifters. Kerrush sketched out the track we must follow on the large scale chart, pointing out to me that having made our big swing around the end of the jetty, we must them immediately reverse the swing on the ship to get into the only small space vacant, and then quickly take the swing off the ship again before we hit the wall broadside on. Easy to explain on the chart what was required, but when I saw the small space into which I had to fit the "Coventry", it looked almost impossible that I could get her in.

But it was no use hesitating, the sooner I got those injured men into hospital the better. I had asked for the assistance of a tug, but had been told that none would be available for at least an hour. It was early afternoon, so the sea breeze had hardly started to blow which helped. Kerrush encouraged me to use plenty of power on the engines, and the "Coventry", always a perfect lady, did exactly as I told her, so that as I finally reversed engines and rudder we arrived in our berth alongside the wall, and I don't think we should have cracked an egg, had anyone been foolish enough to hang one over the side.

The Captain of the Fleet, and one or two officers from C-in-C's office, were on the wall to welcome us, together with several ambulances and a mobile canteen run by the Alexandria ladies. Several people congratulated me on the way I had brought the "Coventry" alongside, but I felt such a load of gloom on my shoulders that I could not appreciate their remarks.

My cabin was of course a first aid station and full of injured men, so I walked out on the jetty where everyone I met told me of disasters to the Med. Fleet, and it was clear that poor old "Coventry" with her damaged bow was one of the few units which was still a going concern.

We got the injured men away in the ambulances as soon as possible, then divided the survivors up into groups, while they were fed on tea and buns by the ladies, ready to be put into transport as soon as it arrived to take them to temporary accommodation. Then I collected Captain Lees, and persuaded him to accept the loan of one of my suitcases filled with a few clothes. He was loathe to take them, but I knew it would take him several days to collect together an outfit from the much depleted shops of Alexandria. So eventually he took the suitcase, extracting a promise from my steward that he would come and collect it from the place Captain Lees was going to be accommodated.

Then the officer who was carrying out the duty of Harbourmaster, came and asked me to take the "Coventry" back to her usual berth on the detached breakwater, as he wanted our berth alongside again immediately. He apologised for not having a tug available to help, but remarked that after the way he had seen me bring the ship alongside, he didn't think I should have any difficulty.

So I took the "Coventry" back to the detached breakwater, and so ended my first ten days in the ship. It can be given to few officers to take their first command into action quite as often in their first ten days of command. On the other hand there can be few officer's who have had the good fortune to take over such an experienced set of officers and ship's company, who in such a remarkable degree combined their major virtues of loyalty, efficiency, and courage combined with the minor virtue, if it is indeed a minor virtue, of cheerfulness. From their pirate of a First Lieutenant, to the junior rating, they were the most cheerful ship's company I have ever known, and I suppose that is what stood us in such good stead, not only in the Ten Days of Crete, but also in the months to follow.

CHAPTER SEVENTEEN

TROUBLE IN SYRIA

Back from the unlucky sortie with "Calcutta", that had marked the close of the Crete evacuation, there were some days in harbour. Whilst we followed normal harbour routine, it was only too evident that the state of the Fleet was abnormal. So many of the ships had a bad list, many were damaged around gun turrets and upper works, the usually immaculate grey paint blackened by explosive flame or fuel oil fires. Many of them would have to leave the Mediterranean for extensive refit, and quite a few would be in the hands of the local ship repairers for several weeks. During the night of June 4th, a large force of enemy aircraft arrived to lay mines. The depleted Fleet nevertheless met them with a barrage that seemed as heavy as ever.

Next day at dusk, the cable party was piped, and it was not long before we were on the open sea. We speculated on what employment we should have, now that there were no more convoys to Greece or Crete. "Coventry" ploughed on under the stormy sky, with no sound other than the swish of the waves, or the discordant song of engine room ventilator fans. Early next morning the horizon suggested the faintest smudge of land, and in due course we approached a not unfamiliar coast. Ultimately we entered harbour at Port Said, and shortly after arrival, went alongside a tanker to refuel. All that day we waited in harbour at Port Said, stirred by various rumours. At dusk we raised anchor and started another night's cruise. There was a "buzz" that we were accompanying "Glengyle", which carried commandos, who were going to land in Syria.

At dawn we were off the Syrian coast, bouncing on a choppy sea. The Eleventh Australian Brigade was advancing north along the Syrian coast. General Wavell had scraped the Syria force together with difficulty, provided with the minimum of armoured vehicles. General Dentz of Vichy, his opponent, had forty five thousand troops, 90 tanks, and ample aircraft for resistance, and his resistance was proving stubborn. The Australians were nearing the estuary of the Litani river, and on the day previous, had been shelled by Vichy destroyers. So "Glengyle" was to land No. 11 Commando, mainly Black Watch, with Colonel Pedder in command, with the object of seizing the bridge over the Litani, ready for the advancing Australians. But on our arrival, the seas were too steep for the landing craft. This forced a hurried decision to make the landing on the next night; so while "Glengyle" retired, "Coventry" proceeded south to patrol off Tyre, that fabulous city of the ancients. Here we saw destroyers bombarding the coast in support of the Australians; and along the coastal valleys the projectiles were evidently doing considerable damage. During the day there were frequent reports of Vichy fighters, but Royal Air Force and Fleet Air Arm cover drove them off. Meanwhile, the sea was subsiding, and at night we returned to the Litani estuary with "Glengyle".

In darkness we approached the shore, wondering what would be the reception for the commandos, but there was a silent and swift landing, after which we left the coast, escorting "Glengyle" out to sea. At dawn we were called to Action Stations. In the chill silence, the growing light revealed "Glengyle". The coast came in sight and "Glengyle" came near; but we saw little activity. Within two hours we were heading with "Glengyle" for Tyre. Gradually, pieces of news leaked out concerning the commando operation.

The surprise which the commandos counted on had not been achieved, and the bridge had been destroyed by Vichy troops before the landing was made. The landing too had gone awry, as many of the commandos had been landed on the wrong side of the river mouth. Thus the operation had been disastrous, resulting in the death of the Commanding Officer and all other officers, with three quarters of the commandos. A sad ending to our expedition. However, the resourceful Australians were able to cross the Litani that day, using a pontoon bridge.

Having escorted "Glengyle" clear of the hostile coast, we joined the fifteenth cruiser squadron of Vice Admiral King, which comprised the cruisers "Phoebe", "Ajax", and "Coventry", supported by eight destroyers. Admiral Cunningham, aware of the vital need to keep a destroyer force in being, required air cover for them during operations, and insisted that where there was no air cover, destroyers should only be risked to gain principal objectives.

Late in the afternoon, we, with "Phoebe" and "Ajax", turned towards Haifa. Afterwards we heard that once the cruisers had left the patrol area, Vichy destroyers, "Valmy" and "Guepard", had appeared off Sidon, and opened fire on our destroyer "Janus". Three hits were made on the bridge of "Janus", stopping her. Then two more shells hit "Janus". Fortunately destroyers "Hotspur", "Jackal", and "Isis", appeared on the scene bringing the Vichy ships in range, at which they swiftly made off.

During the next days patrol there were several reports of enemy aircraft, but the fighters kept them clear of us. Returning to Haifa we anchored, soon to be bathed in bright moonlight. Almost at once the alarm rattlers sounded for an R.D.F. report of enemy aircraft.

Quickly we brought our guns to the ready, urged on by the drone of aircraft engines, and the realisation that our ship was virtually floodlit. There was no supporting barrage of the Fleet, as at Alexandria, and this harbour was much smaller. Also, instead of laying mines, the enemy's object was to carry out a bombing raid, the principal target being the oil pipeline. The aircraft used for this operation were Junkers 88's. Several bombs exploded near the oil installation, then we fired three salvoes on R.D.F. bearing. Soon after this came the scream of bombs, and a succession of explosions announced a stick of bombs on the port side. Thereafter we had relative quietness, but dawn had extinguished the stars before we left action stations.

That morning we lay off the Palestine coast, but after midday, resumed patrol off Tyre. Before long, a Vichy fighter dropped out of the sun, and with a staccato rattle, a stream of bullets swept the upper deck. One bullet fanned the nose of Able Seaman Abrahams, whose only comment was "Ee! that were pretty close."

With the R.A.F. fighters, that challenged the numerous Vichy bombers and fighters, were Fleet Air Arm Fulmars from Palestine. Sea borne aircraft were necessarily of inferior performance to their land based counterparts, and we had on one occasion the disheartening spectacle of a Fulmar shot down by a Vichy fighter.

After 48 hours patrol, we returned to Haifa, anchoring in the harbour at night. As before, an air raid quickly brought us to action stations. We fired one or two salvos by R.D.F., and a stick of bombs exploded near us without doing damage. We finally crawled away to our hammocks, ruefully reflecting on yet another missing nights sleep.

On the 14th. June we returned to coast patrol, and used our guns on several occasions to drive off Vichy aircraft. These were very active today, as Sidon was being attacked by the Australians, supported by bombarding destroyers.

Late on that day, two Vichy destroyers were sighted. We started in chase and opened fire at once, but our projectiles fell short. The Vichy ships kept out of range, and once in sight of Beirut Harbour made for it. Here were shore batteries of 9.2" guns which effectively deterred us, and "Coventry" kept a respectful distance.

On the way back we were attacked by a group of German bombers. They attacked from high level, and although some bombs exploded close, none did any damage. We were not long clear of them before a second group came in, and half an hour later, the third and last wave of them came. All these aircraft were based on Crete. The Germans persisted in their attacks all next day whilst we were on coast patrol, but these were repelled without damage. Towards evening, however, a group of nine Junkers 88's were sighted, which split up to make simultaneous attacks on "Coventry" and our accompanying destroyers "Isis", and "Ilex". Both destroyers were hit, but were able to keep steaming. Subsequently we all retired to Haifa, where the destroyers entered harbour, whilst we continued south. At 20.00, on June 16th. we entered harbour at Port Said.

Here we spent three days, but left harbour at midday on the 19th. Next morning, about breakfast time, we entered Haifa harbour. By now the army in Syria was making rapid progress. It had been possible to add reinforcements of troops formerly employed in putting down the Iraq rebellion. Soon after this, Sidon and Damascus were captured by our troops.

Our stay in Haifa lasted a week. During this time there was a night air raid during which several bombs exploded near the oil installations, and consequently, near us. But Haifa gave us some very pleasant runs ashore. The town was modern, and more European in character than any other we had hitherto visited. Several of the ship's company were hospitably entertained by the residents. The latter were largely Jewish immigrants from every corner of Europe, and several of them spoke English. A favourite excursion was to enjoy the view of the town whilst walking on Mount Karmel.

During this time came the news, that Hitler had let loose the Wehrmacht on the Soviet. Generally it was appreciated that this must mean some relief for those at home, maybe even for ourselves. No one seemed to recall, that our war had started soon after Molotov had made a non-aggression pact with Ribbentrop. Rather there was hope that the German forces could be beaten. But the opinions of the best informed persons at that time were mostly in agreement with the forecast of Hitler, who was confident of taking Moscow before winter came.

We left Haifa early on the morning of Saturday, the 26th. June, heading for Alexandria. During the morning, there was an alarm on radar, reporting approaching aircraft. When they came in sight we met them with the usual barrage. They did not manoeuvre to attack, but deviated from their course and flew on, leaving us with an uncomfortable feeling that they might have been our own aircraft.

On Sunday morning, arriving in Alexandria Harbour, we saw the Fleet, to all outward appearances recovered from the strain of Crete. During our absence, the army had attacked Rommel, using the tanks brought by convoy "Tiger". The object of the attack was to relieve Tobruk, and this would have released the navy from costly convoy operations along the "Stuka Coast". But operation "Battleaxe" had failed, according to informed comment of after years, because there was not enough air support, and also, because the training of the tank crews had not been completed.

Now the Luftwaffe from Crete joined the Axis efforts to make Alexandria Harbour untenable. There were constant night raids, regularly met by the Fleet barrage. Many bombs, however, exploded in and near the dockyard, resulting in a wholesale exodus of the population. The majority had little enough possessions. A mule cart could carry all the family, with the cooking utensils and half a dozen cushions. The Commander in Chief was concerned because the entire dock labour force disappeared, and catastrophe seemed to loom. But to his relief, the men returned once their families had been taken to safety. The Egyptian Government arranged for trains to carry all who wished from the town at night, and to bring them back in the morning. Many of the Arab lads would be seen in the morning, running races on the roofs of the incoming trains.

Soon after our arrival, "Warspite" left for refit and repair, to be followed by "Orion". Mines were now dropped not only in the approaches to the harbour, but among the anchored ships. On the morning of the 10th. July, one of these exploded close to "Coventry's bows. To the sound of a tremendous explosion, and overwhelmed by spray, the ship reared so sharply that most of us were sure that our time had come. Down she plunged, with an alarming roll, but eventually settled on an even keel undamaged.

After a fortnight in harbour, we began to wonder if there was some special reason for our not having operational sea duties. This led to hopeful speculation that we might follow "Warspite" and "Orion". Would it be U.S.A., U.K. or even South Africa?

The time in harbour stretched to the unprecedented length of three weeks, but on the 16th. July we left harbour, and the "buzz" was Port Said. We must be going for refit! Where would it be? But off Port Said we met a slow convoy for Beirut. The cruise to Beirut was uneventful. By now Syria was completely under Allied control.

Arriving on the afternoon of the 18th. July, the first ship we noticed was H.M.S. "Carlisle". At dusk she left, and "Coventry" took on her duties as guardship and general H.Q. for the area. The next daily orders to appear, made it clear that a recreational period was beginning. Subsequently, daily orders were concerned solely with sporting activities, interspersed with the practice of "Evolutions" and "Exercise action stations".

A water polo championship was organised, and there were ample opportunities for bathing. Ashore we found a land of plenty, and notably a wonderful variety of delicious fresh fruit. The bars and cabarets were luxurious, but here the atmosphere was now and then uncomfortable, when an establishment used by one of the French factions was entered by a party of the opposite side. The ships company were invited to use the sports facilities of the American University. Very popular was the swimming pool, also the tennis courts. A ships tournament was arranged. Another popular diversion was sailing in the ship's whalers. Marksmen were not forgotten, and a small bore rifle range was soon constructed.

Everywhere the Australians hailed us as friends and brothers. Frequently they had army trucks at their disposal, and invited us to come and see the world with them. Nearby, in the wonderfully fertile valley behind the mountains, was the ruined Roman city of Baalbec with its towering colonnades of marble and richly carved walls. Further north was Byblos, with its historic link with the Crusaders, who paused here, and built a forbidding fortress overlooking the sea. Thus, most of us were able to visit villages in the mountains of Lebanon, and few made the trip without abiding memories of the mountain roads. There was always a long journey over winding roads punctuated by hairpin bends; and here on the sharp curves, there was usually very little road to spare, and a sickening drop to enjoin caution. More than one "Coventry" group made the trip with the Australians, who drove their trucks to the limit of speed with safety, seemingly oblivious to mountain perils. Occasionally, there would be stops at the first class refreshment hostels on the way, before arriving at a village. Here would occur a most friendly reception by the villagers, followed by a meal, sightseeing, and generous rounds of drinks.

Towards evening the party would pile into the trucks for home, then the "Coventry" men would realise that they were on the mountain roads, and the truck driver somewhat exhilarated. Much more terrifying than the heaviest air attack, were some of those return journeys; but the drivers never exceeded their capabilities, or failed to bring us safely back to town, when they asked, with a grin if we had enjoyed the ride.

On the 6th. August, three Vichy liners arrived, to collect the troops and officials who had opted for return to Vichy territory. Of the 38,000 French nationals, 32,000 returned to Vichy. The 6,000 Gaullists had undoubtedly been most effective, and had the support of the Syrians.

Now the Commander-in-Chiefs, wished to withdraw their forces from Syria to more threatened areas, and on August 13th, with considerable regret, we left the pleasant harbour of Beirut.

In the forenoon of the next day we sighted Alexandria, and once in harbour proceeded to a tanker for fuel, afterwards taking on stores. We left harbour that evening, arriving at Port Said in the forenoon. There we saw the ill fated "Barham", emerging from the canal approach, having returned from a refit at Durban. Our duty was to escort "Barham" to Alexandria, where we arrived during the forenoon of Saturday, the 16th. August. We little realised that she was heading to a savage and fearsome end.

CHAPTER EIGHTEEN

A NEW SUPPLY LINE

Alexandria was no longer the starting point for convoys to Malta. The Fleet was considerably reduced, and still without air support. With the Afrika Korps at Alamein, the Luftwaffe based along the Cyrenaica coast, (combined with their fellow airmen in Crete) controlled a bomb alley that threatened almost certain destruction to ships venturing there without air cover. "Tiger" had been the last convoy of Middle East reinforcements coming through the Mediterranean.

Now it was possible to supply Malta, only by convoys from Gibraltar. In July, convoys "Substance", and "Style", had been fought through from the west, and in September, convoy "Halberd".

Middle East reinforcements were possible only via the Cape route, and in the Red Sea these convoys were joined by American ships with 'lease lend' war materials, now arriving in increasing quantities through the good offices of President Roosevelt.

The enemy, now that all Italian forces on the Red Sea coast had been eliminated, tried to stop this traffic by using his air arm based in Crete. The Luftwaffe, in addition to mining the Suez Canal, sent Focke-Wulf Kondors down the Red Sea to prey on the north bound ships. But his most promising method of attack, was to bomb the ships at Tewfik while they were being unloaded. On the 14th. July a hit had been scored with phosphorous bombs on the trooper "Georgic", which had been beached, and was now a gutted wreck. The Red Sea R.A.F. could provide more effective protection with Radar direction, and H.A. guns were necessary at Tewfik. These considerations would dictate "Coventry's" next operation.

Having refuelled and replenished stores, we spent three quiet days in Alexandria, though on the third day, high flying Axis reconnaissance aircraft paid a visit. On the evening of that day, we left harbour, and on the next, we entered the canal. We arrived at Port Tewfik after dark on Wednesday, the 20th. August. By morning light, the wreck of the "Georgic" came into prominence, something of an object lesson. It was difficult to reconcile the rusting hulk with the splendid liner we had once known. Just before noon we left harbour, heading South through the Gulf of Suez. Cruising without alarm during the afternoon, we anchored towards evening. At the anchorage, which was in sight of Mount Sinai, were the troopers, "Ile de France", "Orion", and "Nieuw Amsterdam". During the night there was no disturbance, and at 05.00 the cable party was piped. With the troopers we headed for Tewfik at 20 knots, arriving at mid-afternoon. Quickly the soldiers were landed, then the empty troopers sailed south with "Coventry" as escort.

For a week we escorted different troopers from the anchorage in and out of Tewfik. On several occasions the Luftwaffe attacked as soon as we arrived at Tewfik. We never failed to keep them at high level, and not one of their bombs was effective. At the end of August, "Carlisle" arrived to relieve us. We did not leave, however, until the evening of "Carlisle's" day of arrival. So when the Luftwaffe attacked at dinner time, they were met by double the usual barrage, much to their discomfiture. Precipitately, they jettisoned rather than aimed their bombs, and cleared off.

Our evening departure from Tewfik was on a southerly course. An exceptional quantity of stores had been taken aboard, and the combination of these events greatly cheered the few who wishfully thought on the lines of a refit. They were somewhat disappointed when the cable party was piped just after dawn, and we moored at what was clearly another anchorage. A few merchantmen were there, and we were close to the shore, but the scenery was no more than endless barren sand hills. This was "F Anchorage", and it's function was a night staging point for supply ships. In daylight, these ships, with R.A.F. cover, would make for Tewfik. Daylight for us brought scorching rays from a blazing sun, boredom, and discomfort. A popular diversion was to shoot at the sharks with a ·303 rifle, or fish for them with a grapnel. Lieutenant McKean won the competition for landing the biggest shark.

On our second night here, action stations sounded, as the result of an R.D.F. report. After some time of anticipation in the darkness, came the faint drone of engines, and soon afterwards the guns, trained on R.D.F. bearing, loosed two salvos. Some time afterwards, came the scream of descending bombs, and the sound of several explosions, but no damage was done.

At the same time, twenty-four hours later, R.D.F. reported aircraft again, and action gun's crews stared into the blackness and strained their ears. By the time half an hour had passed without event, tension had been replaced by that disgruntled feeling, and on "Fall out action stations", we returned speedily to our hammocks. There followed a routine day of defence stations, and shark fishing, with a night undisturbed. On the morning of the 7th. September, we raised anchor to steam south. Soon, we were informed that we were on our way to an island fifty miles away, to pick up survivors from the United States freighter "Steel Seafarer" of New York. This ship had been sunk by a Condor, on the night we had manned action stations for an enemy that passed us by.

Back at the anchorage we spent another day, but on the morning after, we were glad to weigh anchor and head for Tewfik. This hitherto despised harbour had now been promoted in status in our eyes, and was a welcome sight on arrival in the afternoon.

Next day, the Captain and Officers of the "Steel Seafarer", gave a dinner at the Hotel Bel Air to their "Coventry" counterparts. The Luftwaffe were still making constant bombing attacks on Tewfik. A very heavy raid occurred on our third day there. Oil storage tanks ashore were hit, and belched black smoke over the town for hours.

On the 16th. September, we again sailed for"F" Anchorage, arriving late in the afternoon. An hour after anchoring, the R.D.F. broke down, and the consequence was a return to Tewfik. Here, the R.D.F. staff worked tirelessly to find and correct the fault. The first day brought no result, and on the second, work went on after dark and through the night. On the following day, R.D.F. recovered it's protecting power.

We left Tewfik for "F" anchorage, in the early morning of Monday the 29th. September, arriving there about tea time. After four days of familiar monotony, the troopers "Orangitiki", and "Napier" arrived. Next day we accompanied them to Suez, arriving during mid-afternoon, without incident.

Very early next morning we entered the Suez canal, for the fourth time since leaving home. This time we were forcibly reminded that the enemy was active and ubiquitous. At mid-morning, a tremendous explosion roared astern of us. The oil tanker behind us had triggered off an acoustic mine, and we looked back to see her wreathed in black smoke and sinking rapidly. With mixed feelings of regret for the merchantmen, and gratitude for our own good fortune, we went steadily on, arriving at Port Said just after dinner. At dusk we left the harbour, and were soon cruising at speed. Half way through the middle watch we were nearing Alexandria, when R.D.F. reported the approach of a large group of enemy aircraft. Roused by the rattlers, we hurriedly manned the guns, and soon heard the drone of aircraft motors. We trained on the R.D.F. bearing, and loaded and loosed several salvos in the teeth of this group of Luftwaffe returning from a raid on Suez.

Subsequently, we were gratified to learn that our slumbers had not been needlessly broken. A Focke-Wulfe, which came down in the sea off Crete, was reckoned to have done so following damage inflicted by "Coventry's" guns.

Anchoring in Alexandria Harbour at mid-morning, we were able to enjoy a run ashore that evening. Next day mail arrived, and was duly appreciated. It brought contentment more than ever this time, as an exceptionally strong "buzz" about a refit was going the rounds. On the morrow, in the late afternoon, we left harbour. Arriving at Port Said next morning, we entered the canal once more. Little heed was given to the canal banks, or the wrecks in the lakes. There were high hopes that we should not be coming back this way. Once in the Gulf of Suez, the Captain cleared lower deck to tell us that we were going to Bombay for a two month refit. Not the U.K., S.A. or U.S.A. after all, but it would be a welcome change. We joined a nine knot south bound convoy, and by Saturday, the 11th. October, we were close to Aden. In early afternoon, we left the convoy, and hurried into Aden to refuel. By next day we were clear of the Red Sea. In the Indian Ocean the temperature was exceptional, and three stokers became unconscious through heat stroke.

It was not, however, full speed to Bombay. Towards evening, we sighted the Norwegian tanker which we had been ordered to escort back to Aden. The next day was hot, but uneventful, and on Monday, the 14th. September, we, with the tanker, entered harbour at Aden.

Here we spent two days. All-night leave was given, and the repose and luxury offered ashore were freely indulged in.

On Wednesday, the 15th October, we left Aden, accompanied by a Greek destroyer which had been with the convoy from Suez. Next day we cruised in the Indian Ocean, and the Mediterranean, with it's constant alarms, seemed an age away. We arrived off Bombay on the 18th. October in early morning, eagerly scanning the prospect of the port, and each fancifully searching individual imagination as we read the inscription on the massive archway,–"The Gateway to the East".

CHAPTER NINETEEN

BOMBAY REFIT

Now the fabulous East was in sight, and few, even among the regular sailors knew much of it. But the first pleasure we experienced, was just a simple change of routine. At sundown there was no pipe of "Darken Ship, close all scuttles and deadlights". Ventilation was now unrestricted, electric lamps glittered on deck, and on shore, a host of lights winked a welcome.

All-night leave was piped, and many of us celebrated this first run ashore, with walks among well lit thorough-fares like Hollamby Road, and a meal at Chinese, or other attractive restaurants.

Next day, "Coventry" moved into the dockyard, where routine was to work aboard in the forenoon only. In the afternoon we either used the sports facilities of the Willingdon Sports Club, and the former "Japanese Gymkhana", or went bathing at Beach Kandy. In town, there were excellent air-conditioned cinemas, and one of the programmes featured the popular Salvation Army film—"Major Barbara". As in every port, there was ample provision for the traditional returned sailor, and suitable establishments existed opposite the dockyard gate.

It was intended that each watch in turn, should spend three weeks at a recreation camp in the hills of Deolalli, some 120 miles distant. While this was being organised, an invitation came from the Nizam of Hyderabad, for a party of sixty to visit the province as his guests for a fortnight. The party was chosen by lot, from those who had served in "Coventry" from the time of Narvik.

Right from the start every opportunity for shore leave was well used, and the only case of abuse was that of Jock, who had joined the ship at Alexandria. Jock was a dun coloured dog who had arrived in a returning liberty boat, found a billet on board, and following exemplary behaviour, been rated as an A.B. and duly victualled. Whenever enemy aircraft were sighted, he was one of the first at action stations, growling defiance at them. If shore leave were piped, it was only a matter of minutes before, handsomely groomed and wearing a clean and beautifully pressed collar, he waited the call "Liberty men fall in". On arrival at Bombay, he stepped eagerly ashore with the very first party.

But as the refit period lengthened from weeks to months, his behaviour became erratic. First he tried to join another cruiser, to be sent back under escort with an explanatory note for the Officer of the Watch. And following this escapade, he failed to return to the ship. There was general regret at this lapse, and all men going ashore kept a lookout for him, in the belief that some friendly advice might bring him back to the straight and narrow path. Eventually, however, it was accepted that he never would return. Some of us believed that he had succumbed to the charms of the local females: others that he had been snared by the official dog catcher. But in view of the subsequent history of "Coventry", there is room for the theory that some mysterious animal instinct prompted him to make a change of residence.

First to leave the port area was the party for Deolalli, who departed from Bombay by train at midday. They were soon aware of the differences from the familiar working procedure of railways at home. There was a slow journey to the foothills behind a steam engine; then an electric locomotive replaced it, to haul them up the slope. Finally a steam engine took them to their destination. They revelled in the sight of mountain scenery, green trees and green grass. On arrival at the camp, they were shown their billets, with mosquito net protected "Charpoys" for sleeping. Until it was time to turn in, they refreshed themselves with beer.

On the morning they were somewhat taken aback, when servants known as "boys", brought tea to their bedside. Even more so, when barbers arrived to shave them before rising from their beds. Their only obligation was to amuse themselves. The diversions laid on were, the Garrison Cinema, a tea and sandwich canteen organised by the local ladies, and strolling through the bazaar in the village. Everybody was pleased by the semi-official rumour that "Coventry's" stay at Bombay might last six months.

On November 5th. a grand celebration was organised. A huge bonfire was lit on a hill top, and a first class firework display took place. Later on, several men of the party, hired bicycles for local touring. They found it warm work. A ship's football team was formed, which in the evenings played frequent and exciting matches. Another evening entertainment was ballroom dancing, but the scarcity of ladies somewhat reduced its appeal.

There was considerable satisfaction at the announcement, that the three week stay would be extended to five weeks, but eventually came the return to Bombay.

The duty watch was meanwhile living at Calabar Reinforcement Camp, working ship in the forenoon only.

Concurrently with this recreational leave, the Hyderabad party was also enjoying Indian hospitality. On the 16th November, this party left Victoria Station, Bombay, for Hyderabad, their journey lasting two days. On arrival they were greeted by the Palace Supervisor, who took them to the Nizam's summer residence for an elaborate meal.

Having spent the night in comfortable quarters, the day began with breakfast at 8 a.m. On this first day, the entertainment programme did not start until tea, at 4.30 p.m. After tea, the Nizam's guests took a drive around the Gumpat. At 6.40 they went to a cinema show, and after 9 p.m. dinner, retired.

On the second day, following breakfast, there was a visit to the museum and mint. Lunch was taken at 1 p.m., then an afternoon siesta. After tea the party drove around the city of Hyderabad, arriving at the Nizam's palace at 6 o'clock to be entertained by fakirs, who achieved some amazing illusions. Dinner was at 9 p.m. followed by a ball, well supported by the local ladies.

On subsequent days the programme was equally crowded, including swimming pool sessions, football matches, and dances. There was wonderful hospitality from both British and Indian citizens.

Very much enjoyed, was an afternoon with the R.A.F. at the local airport. We took joy rides in the aircraft, and revelled in bombing the installations with flour bags. Our fortnight was nearly ended, when a signal from Bombay gave us a further week's leave. During this time, we gave a ball, inviting everyone who had entertained us, and the occasion was a great success. There was a natural reluctance to leave this happy haven, but at the same time a sense of relief. The hospitality had been overwhelming, and left us well nigh exhausted.

Now it was back to Calabar camp, and for some, a move shortly after to the Apollo Hotel. The most notable thing about the Apollo, was the size and number of the bed bugs.

The afternoons at Bombay were memorable for such pastimes as bathing at Beach Kandy, tennis at the Japanese Gymkana, and for a few, golf at the Willingdon Sports Club.

In addition, several members of the Bombay Yacht Club made their vessels available to the ship's company, who sailed them under the genial supervision of Capt. Peyton Jones, R.M.

A patrol was established, and the personnel were billeted at Neville House. Members of the patrol were amazed at the large force of servants employed there.

On the 2nd. December came the incredible tale of Pearl Harbour, to be followed by the bitter news that "Repulse", and "Prince of Wales", had been sunk. Thereupon Bombay began a moderate black-out, and "Coventry" mounted R.D.F. watches. A quarter of the guns were manned throughout the night, and all special parties, such as the patrol, returned to the quarters at Calabar Camp, whence they could at very short notice be carried by lorry to the ship.

Then came another Christmas in exotic surroundings. Most of us watched cricket at the Brabourne Stadium, where there was covered accommodation. In progress was a tournament known as the "Pentangular", in which the competing teams were Hindus, Parsees, Moslems, Europeans, and "The Rest". The tournament was won by the Hindu team.

Leave was granted to anyone able to use it for visiting friends, or organising his own tour. Several of the ship's company took advantage of it, and those able to visit British residents, gained some idea of what it was like to live like a lord.

In Bombay, many prominent members of the Indian community invited fortunate individuals to dinner. Those so invited were surprised, that the way of life in these houses so closely resembled their own home customs.

1942 wore on to May, and it was plain that "Coventry" would soon be leaving. A mild epidemic of German Measles occurred among the ship's company. This was the second visitation of this unusual infection since 1939. However, the infectious period being over, they were able to join the ship just before we left the dockyard. As is usual in such circumstances, there were many heavy hearts.

Whilst lying off the "Gateway to India", we stored ship, and took on ammunition. Expecting departure at any time, we were not surprised when the anchor was raised after dark. But instead of putting to sea, we went alongside at Bombay Fort, near Ballards Pier. Here, in conditions of great security, several heavy metal bound boxes were brought aboard and taken to the Captain's day cabin. Thereupon a heavy Royal Marine Guard was mounted.

Next day, with overhauled engines, and structurally sound, we pushed a white bow wave toward Aden.

Four days cruising brought us to that by now familiar port. There was time for shore leave, and a renewed acquaintance with old haunts; but next day we left harbour on a northerly course. The Red Sea heat was still uncomfortable, and the routine monotonous; but interest was awakened when we came abreast of Port Sudan, and turned eastward. In the silence of early morning, we approached close to the Arabian coast and dropped anchor. We were close to Jiddah, the port for Moslems on pilgrimage to Mecca.

Soon after our arrival, a graceful sailing craft, an Arab dhow, was seen coming from the shore. Closer it came, and we saw, seated astern under a decorated awning, a man who was being treated with considerable deference. He was in fact a Sheikh of great influence.

Furling its sail, the Dhow came quietly alongside. A Marine guard of honour was mounted, and the Captain welcomed the Sheikh aboard with marked pomp and circumstance. Thereafter they proceeded to the Captain's day cabin. Shortly afterwards the principals re-appeared, followed by Royal Marines bearing the metal bound boxes. These were duly loaded aboard the dhow. The Sheikh took solemn leave of the Captain, to be once again ceremoniously installed on the throne beneath the awning. Then the sail of the dhow swelled slightly, and it gathered way toward the shore. After a considerable interval, we raised anchor and headed for Suez. In due course we learned, that we had witnessed the payment by the British Government of £250,000 in gold to Arab Rulers, for their good offices in this part of the world.

Our next stop was Suez, and shore leave was given. Some of the ship's company received invitations to a dance organised by the W.R.N.S. During the evening, we were surprised to learn that the Wrens knew a good deal of "Coventry's" past, and that she had arrived from Bombay. Even more astonishing, the Wrens prophesied that the ship would soon take part in an operation to Tobruk. While making the canal transit, those to whom the future had been revealed, pondered the truth of the forecast, and when it would take place.

Arriving at Alexandria, we saw the familiar landmarks, but were well aware that considerable changes had taken place, as regards the war situation, during our absence.

Gale in the Mediterranean

Fraternising in Athens
A.B. Skelly. A.B. Delmar and A.B. Miles

Naval Tourists at the Base of the Temple of Winged Victory
A.B. Temple. A.B. Boon. A.B. Forrest. A.B. Durno.

Athens

Overhauling the Pom Pom

Attack on the Convoy Leaving Piraeus

Plate Eighteen

"DIDO"

"ABA"

Rescue of the Hospital Ship "ABA"
"COVENTRY"

From a Painting by Charles Pears

H.M.S. "COVENTRY" in Suda Bay

C.P.O. Davenport
Deccan Hyderabad

Bathing Party in Bombay
"Nobby" Clarke.   Jack Spencer.   "Johnnie" Kirk.
"Slinger" Woods.   "Punchy" Griffiths.

"COVENTRY" Hit and on Fire

H.M.S. "BEAUFORT" to the Rescue

The Last Survivor

Abandon Ship

Plate Twenty One

Captain R.J.R. Dendy. The Provost of the Cathedral (Very Reverend Williams)
Vice Admiral H.R. Law. Captain W.P. Carne, and Captain D. Gilmour.

The Memorial in the Navy Room
Vice Admiral H.R. Law. The Provost of the Cathedral (Very Reverend Williams) Reverend Reade

Plate Twenty Three

Vice Admiral Law Inspects the Guard of Honour

Presentation by Frank Risdon and Eric Skelly of Painting of H.M.S. "Coventry" to the Coventry Sea Cadets

Plate Twenty Four

CHAPTER TWENTY

TURNED BACK FROM MALTA

Whilst we had been in Bombay, the British fortunes in the Mediterranean had continued to decline. "Barham" had been sunk by a "U" boat in November, 1941 **with** disastrous loss of life, and the following month, "Queen Elizabeth", and "Valiant", had been holed by the mines of Italian frogmen, causing these ships to sit useless on the bottom of Alexandria Harbour for months.

General Rommel, whose Afrika Corps had made a practically unhindered sea crossing to North Africa while Admiral Cunningham was occupied in Greece and Crete, had been attacked in autumn 1941 with the object of relieving Tobruk. But Operation "Battleaxe" failed.

During the winter of 1941, a second attack called "Crusader" had succeeded, so that British troops occupied Benghazi on Christmas Day 1941. But once beyond Tobruk, it had not been possible to send sufficient supplies to the British Army.

Consequently the Afrika Corps turned, and when we retreated back to Alexandria, both armies were facing each other at Gazala, in the Gulf of Sirte.

The Eastern Mediterranean C-in-C was now Admiral Harwood, of "Graf Spee" fame, who with a smaller Fleet, faced an even more formidable situation than had his predecessor. The only improvement was an increase in R.A.F. strength, that kept the Luftwaffe off the Egyptian coast as far as Tobruk.

Aboard "Coventry", Captain Carne had been replaced by Captain Dendy, and shortly after reaching Alexandria, "Coventry" was fitted with Oerlikon guns. The ship that had tested these guns when war was practically unthinkable, must have been one of the last pre-1939 ships to be armed with them.

After this, we had many days of gunnery practice and Fleet manoeuvres. For not only were we rusty after refit, but many veterans had been replaced by new drafts.

To informed observers it was clear, that if the tide of British fortune continued to ebb, we should be ousted from the Mediterranean. Malta was the outpost that enabled us to maintain a tenuous grip; and the months of inability to reach that island with effective relief, were straining the population and garrison close to breaking point.

The war cabinet pondered the chances of sending supplies to this outpost, on which the whole outcome of the war might depend. Also of returning to the 1,700 mile United Kingdom-Egypt supply line. The 12,000 mile Cape route was eating too deeply into shipping resources.

The Axis threat in the Mediterranean was formidable. 600 bombing and torpedo aircraft were strategically based along the North African coast, from Tripoli to Gazala, and on the islands of Sardinia, Pantellaria, Sicily, Crete, and Rhodes.

A convoy from Alexandria to Malta would have no capital ships to protect it, and the Italian Fleet might consequently be expected to intervene.

But the situation was so desperate, that it was considered just worthwhile to attempt simultaneous convoys to Malta from Gibraltar and Alexandria, such as had succeeded before the advent of the Luftwaffe. Six fast merchantmen would leave Gibraltar, to reach Malta at the same time as eleven ships arriving from the Eastern Mediterranean. As the westbound fleet had no capital ship cover, an attempt would be made to lure the Italian Fleet to the anticipated attack point, well before the convoy reached it. If this could be done, the prey would slip past while the Italians were running home for oil. But even as it proceeded to the attack point, the Italian Fleet would be attacked by our aircraft and submarines. Success of these attacks might even turn the Italians from their objective before they were near enough to attack the convoy.

The eastbound convoy was called "Harpoon" and the westbound one "Vigorous". The ships had no sooner been put in motion, than the Afrika Korps defeated the British armour at Gazala, and started to advance towards Alexandria.

"Harpoon" comprised six merchantmen which, with escort, left Gibraltar on the 11th. June. On the 14th. June, Axis aircraft from Sardinia sunk one of the merchantmen, and so damaged the cruiser "Liverpool", that she had to return to Gibraltar. On reaching the Sicilian Narrows, a force of Italian cruisers beset the convoy. H.M.S. "Cairo" and six destroyers held them off. During this action, the destroyer "Bedouin" was so badly damaged, that she had to be sunk by our own forces. This action also delayed the convoy, so that arrangements for air cover from Malta were upset. This enabled a large number of JU.88's to attack the ships, and they sank three merchantmen out of five. "Cairo" and the destroyers reached Valetta with "Troilus", and "Orare", two out of the six ships that had started from Gibraltar.

Our convoy "Vigorous" consisted of eleven ships, which were loaded at various eastern Mediterranean ports so that convoy preparations were not obvious. "Coventry", with six of the ships, would start thirty six hours ahead of the rest, go to a point on the longitude of Tobruk, then double back to the main convoy. The early starters, it was hoped, would stampede the Italian Fleet, so that, even if not deterred by our submarines and aircraft, the Italian Fleet would arrive too soon for the rape, and run short of oil whilst waiting.

On the 11th. June we took on extra ammunition and 200 bags of mail. One of the mail bags burst, and men gathering up letters, soon noticed that they all bore Malta addresses. The ship's company were thus informed early of the impending operation. The veterans hoped that the Oerlikons would make a big difference. At dusk we left harbour, and next morning came into Port Said. By evening we were again at sea with three merchantmen on the starboard beam, and three destroyers busily patrolling. Next day was sunny and pleasant, all the more so because we were covered by two R.A.F. fighters. Towards evening, however, R.D.F. reported enemy aircraft, and the rattlers brought us to action stations. Now came a change from the old routine of waiting for the enemy to attack, and all guns following director when he appeared. Our two fighters went at once to seek the enemy. Minutes later, high in the sky, and far off, we saw the tracer streams from a fighter. Then a ball of fire dropped into the sea.

But simultaneously R.D.F. reported more closing aircraft, though spotters scanned the skies in vain. The scream of wind through dive bomber rigging, and the shriek of falling bombs, announced an attack. We were in the act of turning to port when three J.U.88's placed a stick of bombs on either side of us. Running into a welter of spray and steel splinters, we were lucky in having no casualties. Then we noticed something wrong with " City of Calcutta". A bomb hit had so damaged her that she had to run to Tobruk. During the night, we reached the longitude of Torbuk, and doubled back for the main convoy.

The afternoon of the 13th. July, in the longitude of Alexandria, we sighted the main convoy and it's escort. Soon after this meeting, a Norwegian merchantman, unable to keep the convoy speed, was sent back. The Malta convoy had been reduced to nine merchantmen. Patrolling fighters were covering us again, and the convoy escort included several motor torpedo boats. That night we heard the engines of the Luftwaffe. Shortly after, we saw their flares dropping to illuminate the sea over which we had passed, less than half an hour before. We did not oblige by opening fire.

Next morning the seas were rising, and we were hoping that a storm would develop. Unfortunately, the only result of this weather change, was that our escorting motor torpedo craft were sent home.

That afternoon two corvettes turned back with engine trouble. Later, it was found that the Dutch ship "Aagtekirk" could not keep up, so she turned back in the direction of Tobruk. Later we heard that having arrived within twelve miles of that port, a group of forty JU.87's and 88's sunk her. We had so far experienced little trouble from enemy aircraft on this day, due to the work of some of our fighter planes that had been detached from the work of army support. But from tea time onwards we met seven attacks from large groups of JU.87's and JU.88's. We had never known such continuous shooting. Now and then a stick of bombs fell close from a direct attack, but the Luftwaffe concentrated on the merchantmen, and at 6 p.m. "Bhutan" was sunk. "Potaro", damaged shortly afterwards, was able to keep up with us. We saw two corvettes hastening to pick up "Bhutan" survivors.

Just before sunset there was an order for redoubled vigilance from anti-submarine look outs. The destroyer "Packenham" had just avoided a torpedo. A broadcast made a few minutes later informed us that a group of six enemy motor torpedo craft, escorted by fighter planes, had been reported. Darkness was indeed welcome, though the Luftwaffe again made an unsuccessful search with flares.

It would not have been reassuring, on this day of constant action, to have known of the signal received by Admiral Harwood in Alexandria. It said that Admiral Iachino, who had evidently not been taken in by the early start ruse, had that afternoon left Taranto, with battleships "Littorio" and "Vittorio Veneto", 8" cruisers, "Gorizia" and "Trento", 6" cruisers "Garibaldi" and "Duca d'Aosta", and twelve destroyers. He intended to meet our convoy at 9 a.m. next morning.

In consequence, Admiral Vian, commanding our convoy, was ordered to keep going until 2 a.m. next morning, then double back. At the point of turn, some fifty miles of sea would separate us from the heavy Italian guns.

Cruising through the night we relaxed from the day's alarms, and the turning back was noticed by very few of the ship's company. But just afterwards, the gun's crews on watch heard a muffled explosion. Our cruiser "Newcastle", had been torpedoed by an enemy motor craft. Fortunately the damage could be made good, and "Newcastle" stayed with the convoy. Before the end of the middle watch came another violent shock through the water, accompanied by a louder explosion. A torpedo boat had sunk the destroyer "Hardy".

Grey dawn broke the night sky, and the light grew stronger. Near breakfast time the convoy made a reverse turn. Admiral Vian was renewing the attempt to reach Malta.

Soon the R.D.F. began its reports of enemy aircraft. The Luftwaffe made constant attacks on all classes of ships in the convoy and escort. Where to store the empty brass propellant cases was becoming a problem.

Meanwhile, eight Liberator bombers had attacked Admiral Iachino's battleships, and claimed hits on both of them. But this did not daunt them and they kept on course. Earlier that day, the Italians had been obliged to leave behind them the cruiser "Trento", which had been hit by a torpedo from a Wellington aircraft at 6 a.m. At 10 a.m., our submarine P.35, having sighted "Trento" which had stopped, torpedoed and sunk her.

Aboard "Coventry" we noticed another change of course at mid-morning. Once again we had turned east, as Admiral Vian saw no prospect of getting his convoy past the oncoming Italians. If the morning air attacks had been persistent, those in the afternoon threatened to be overwhelming. Convoy and escort were constantly taking avoiding action as bomb loads dropped toward them, and all the time, at least one of the escort was shooting. At half past three, we saw the destroyer "Airedale" hit by an avalanche of bombs which sank her. Near what should have been tea time, Admiral Vian received a signal from the Commander-in-Chief advising him to make for Malta, if the principal ships had enough fuel left to reach the island.

Meanwhile, action raged, and at 6 p.m. the destroyer "Nestor" was hit. It was two hours after the C.-in-C.'s signal, before Admiral Vian had received from all ships their fuel and ammunition reports. Most of them had expended 70% of their ammunition, and were still using it fast. This gave no hope of bringing the remaining seven merchantmen to Malta. Whilst we continued back to Alexandria, air attacks were unrelenting. There was one moment of satisfaction, when an approaching torpedo bomber was suddenly converted to a harmless cloud of smoke.

Dusk was welcome, and darkness doubly so. Darkness brought defence stations and recuperation after the day's alarms. We had survived the worst period of constant bombing to date, but it was a new and depressing experience to be turned back by the enemy.

Halfway through the middle watch, two explosions announced further disaster. U.205 had torpedoed cruiser "Hermione", which sank in twenty minutes. Only 88 survivors were picked up.

By morning light we were almost within R.A.F. protection. There was the melancholy necessity of scuttling the badly damaged Australian destroyer "Nestor". Soon we had R.A.F. cover, and reached Alexandria Harbour by evening. It was the 16th. June. Out of the 17 ships leaving Gibraltar and Alexandria with stores for Malta, only two had reached the Island.

On top of this came news that the Afrika Korps had beaten the Desert Army, and even taken Tobruk. At this critical period "Coventry" was ordered to Port Said, and through the canal.

After a short stop at Tewfik for fuel, we headed south through the Gulf of Suez; There were no complaints about the climate, and even the anchorage where we were stationed to give anti aircraft protection seemed pleasant enough. The place was called Abu Zenima, and boasted about three houses and a manganese mine. Nearby was an emergency landing field for the R.A.F. But these features were almost lost in a waste of sand hills.

Our function was to repel night air attacks, but there were only three minor attacks during the month we were there. To this end we manned action stations all night, and relaxed through the heat of the day. Leave was given for two hours every evening, during which swimming was possible.

We did on two occasions leave the anchorage. Once to return to Tewfik, whence we came south again escorting the "Queen Elizabeth"; and on another occasion we escorted two fast merchantmen, with a load of tanks, in the opposite direction.

After this we returned to Port Said. Here we stayed a few days, and were subsequently delighted to leave harbour, headed for Beirut. Once more we savoured wonderful fresh fruit and vegetables, and there was opportunity for touring excursions. We made trips to places like Baalbek again, and enjoyed the mountain scenery, with frequent stops at most delectable refreshment stations.

Now it was August, 1942. The Afrika Korps had been stopped at Alamein, and the main concern of the news service, was the German advance in the Caucasus. Our week in Beirut passed quickly, and we were sorry to leave harbour. Our next port of call was Haifa.

At 1600 on the day of arrival, a large party of liberty men, exceptionally well turned out, waited the order to fall in; meanwhile, they reflected on the splendid places they would revisit.

Just then, pandemonium was let loose, as shore batteries opened fire on a seaward target. The alarm rattlers sped us to action stations. Soon the reason for the shooting was broadcast. A patrolling anti-submarine trawler had depth charged on Asdic indication, and promptly an Italian submarine had broken surface. It was immediately bombarded by the shore batteries and in minutes the submarine rolled over and sank. As it turned, a number of "Chariots", used by frogmen for sinking ships in harbour, were seen to be secured to the submarine. The wide awake trawler had certainly preserved several ships then berthed at Haifa.

Early next morning "Coventry" left Haifa, with two large merchantmen. At noon we joined the Fleet, which had a considerable convoy. Next day we were steaming west and pondered our chances of reaching Malta. R.D.F. indicated enemy aircraft, but none of them approached to attack. Presumably they were spotters. Steaming westward into the night, we speculated on what the Luftwaffe had in store for us at morning light. But while it was still dark we doubled back, and at evening next day entered harbour at Port Said once again. Later it was explained that the operation had been a ruse to occupy the attention of as much of the enemy Mediterranean strength as possible, while convoy "Pedestal" proceeded from Gibraltar to Malta. Despite this action, the "Pedestal" convoy was costly enough. Of the fourteen merchant-men leaving Gibraltar, only five reached Malta, and during the operation, our sister ship "Cairo" was torpedoed and sunk, in addition to "Eagle", "Foresight", and "Manchester".

From Port Said we returned through the canal to Tewfik, then to Abu Zenima for another three weeks as guard ship. The shipping traffic was exceptionally dense, but the Luftwaffe failed to put in an appearance. With the spell as guard ship completed, we returned through the Canal to Port Said. During a stay of several days, our liberty men found the Fleet Club the most congenial rendezvous. Most of the ship's company acquired there, a taste for Australian beer, and there were memorable evening parties, where many tables joined end to end, were occupied solidly by "Coventry" ratings.

No sooner had this Levantine Valhalla started to grow, than it was blighted by startling rumours. It was alleged that many of the ship's records had been sent ashore for storage. Then an R.A.F. Officer was instal-led in quarters aboard. He was in frequent conference with the Captain, but the only hint of his reason for being there were the words "Fighter Direction", overheard by one of the Marines. But what really startled several of the seaman, was when the Arab dhobymen brought back their beautifully washed and ironed number six suits, a day before they had promised. When questioned about this departure from custom the Arabs answered, "Your officers luggage carried to Fleet Club—you go to Tobruk". On that same day of Saturday, the 12th. September, some of the regular service veterans received their U.K. draft,—C.P.O. Tollerfield, in charge of stores, blithely waved goodbye to his messmates. C.P.O. Davenport, range taker, and senior rating in the director, also the "Chief Buffer", shook hands all round the mess, and as a parting jest said, "Well, I've kept you out of trouble for three years. Now you must look after yourselves".

Long overdue to start a Warrant Officer's course, C.P.O. Davenport had remained in "Coventry" for the "EXIGENCIES OF THE SERVICE". His Warrant Officer's Course would in due course be further post-poned by a U boat commander operating off Cape Town, but this was behind the veil of the future.

CHAPTER TWENTY ONE

FINAL DUEL OF A FIGHTER DIRECTOR

After dark, on that 12th. day of September, 1942, we put to sea from Port Said, and the words of the dhoby-men, with rumours that ships records had been stored ashore, raised an atmosphere of unusual excitement. The superstitious recalled the torpedo off Bardia, just two years ago, and looked to the future with foreboding. As we now know what was then known only to a few staff-officers, let us start with an outline of the operation that was in motion.

At this time of crisis in the Mediterranean theatre of war, Colonel Heselden, of the Long Range Desert Group, had suggested that he could destroy the Axis bomb proof fuel tanks at Tobruk, with the object of slowing, and maybe halting, enemy armour. Ensuing intelligence reports on Tobruk suggested that the only defenders of that disputed outpost were "German technicians, and low grade Italian troops". At once, a most daring plan of seaborne invasion took shape, whose success would depend on the continuance of these conditions:— faultless execution, exceptionally good weather, and, above all, surprise. By the time preparations had been completed, a new C. in C., General Montgomery had assumed command of the Desert Army. He was told nothing of the impending Tobruk raid.

The plan decided on, was that the Long Range Desert Group of Commandos, in addition to entering Tobruk for the purpose of destroying the fuel tanks, would smuggle into Tobruk another force of Commandos, eighty-three strong, which after entry would divide. Under cover of a heavy air raid, the first party would seize coastal guns at Mersa-Sciause Bay, just east of the harbour boom defence nets; whilst the second, would secure a beach head on a tongue of land three quarters of a mile north of the harbour. Both groups, if successful, would radio Alexandria H.Q. If the success signals were received in Alexandria before 0.200, the code word "Nigger" would be transmitted thence, to destroyers "Sikh, and "Zulu". From these ships, a force of three hundred and fifty Royal Marines would proceed in landing craft to the "North of Harbour" beach. At the same time, one hundred soldiers waiting in motor launches off Mersa-Sciause Bay, would be landed there. The Marines would be guided in by signalmen, landed in a rubber dinghy from the submarine "Taku", and the soldiers, by aldis lamp signal from a Commando Officer. Once ashore, the invaders with beach head parties would converge on the harbour, taking and using coastal guns en route. The motor launches would enter harbour to destroy shipping, after which "Sikh", and "Zulu", would come in to land demolition parties. The invaders would range through the town, driving out the garrison and time the operation to end at 14.00 on the 14th. September. At this time, the Royal Marines and soldiers would re-embark for Alexandria, whilst the Commandos, in captured transport, would carry on along the coast to effect further destruction.

Vaguely aware that an unusually hazardous operation might be our lot, we peered into the gathering darkness, and saw what seemed to be destroyer silhouettes. They were in fact 'Hunt' class destroyers "Croome", "Dulverton", "Hursley", and "Belvoir". On a choppy sea, we pushed on through the night, with an occasional disturbing thought about, what morning might bring.

The light came, with a brisk wind and rising seas, stimulating everyones observation. Breakfast was enjoyed with very near the traditional Sabbath calm, and there was no excitement until an hour later, when we descried ships ahead. On coming close, we identified "Sikh", "Zulu", "Hurworth", "Beaufort", "Exmoor", and "Aldenham". Signal lamps in all directions were flashing for such long periods, that we were confirmed in our suspicions of a very special operation. Then, numbers of men in khaki were seen aboard the destroyers, and a landing was at once surmised. The constant movement of the radar aerials was also remarked on.

The morning wore on to 10.15, when radar reported aircraft to the bridge. The R.A.F. Control Officer held the opinion that they were our own, but Captain Dendy at once altered course north, as if making for Crete, or Rhodes. From Alexandria one hour later, came a signal that an intercepted Axis radio report was known to be giving our position. Thereafter, came no disturbing observations or signals, and late in the afternoon, having no more time left for misleading possible Axis observers, the Captain altered course, and turned south-west. With dusk, relaxation began, and by the time darkness had cloaked our grim group of ships, almost complete calm reigned. During this Sunday the 13th., there had been no greater alarm than a radar report. At 21.00, speculation began when the ship turned. Some of the signalmen realised that we were headed for Alexandria with the eight 'Hunt' destroyers, while "Sikh" and "Zulu", with their soldiers, carried on westward. A few stars winked benevolently out of the sable sky, as we rolled and plunged in steep seas; the superstitious checked the clock and wished the 13th gone, but most of the ships company were easy in their minds. During the night, men on watch glimpsed fires and gun flashes indicating fighting ashore, but there were no alarms for us.

Dawn flushed the sky, and the prophets of gloom were jocularly reminded that the thirteenth was behind us. When two Beaufighters arrived to patrol above us, there was even more reassurance, but at 06.00 the broadcast system crackled, while the ship slowed in a reverse turn. It was announced that "Sikh" had been sunk at Tobruk, and that we were turning to meet fleeing "Zulu". Six of the destroyers came with us, but "Aldenham" and "Belvoir" carried on towards Alexandria for refuelling.

Captain Dendy anticipated meeting "Zulu" at 13.00 but even now, racing home at 30 knots, she was constantly attacked by groups of eight or nine dive bombers. These were met by the guns until bomb release; after which avoiding action was taken.

For a time we sped over the swell in brilliant sunshine, with nothing to think about but increasing speed; but at 08.30, radar reported several unidentified aircraft at eighty miles. There was light cloud at 4,000 feet, and the Fighter Direction Officer wanted the Beaufighters to investigate. Communication proved a long and difficult business, in which it was necessary to use radio, but the subsequent reconnaissance produced an "All clear" report. Shortly afterwards, a signal was received from Alexandria, warning "Coventry" to move out from the coast. Then radar reported three groups of enemy aircraft shadowing. The Beaufighters, directed to seek out the shadowers, made sweeps in different directions, but sighted no enemy.

Near eleven o'clock, the Captain broadcast to the ships company the current intelligence on operation "Agreement", which was substantially what follows, but without some of the detail now known.

At dusk, on the 13th September, the Long Range Desert Group, with the additional eighty three Commandos in the guise of prisoners of war under guard in three German lorries, arrived at Tobruk. There were tense moments as the "Officers in Charge" were questioned by the German Military Police, but soon the group exulted in having achieved it's first object,—getting into Tobruk unknown to the enemy.

By midnight, the Mersa-Sciause group had signalled success, but one hour later, Alexandria H.Q. were still anxiously waiting to hear from the North of Harbour party. The clock told 02.00 in Alexandria, and the Staff both in H.Q. and in the waiting ships, expected the operation to be cancelled. But at the very last moment the success signal arrived, and the "Go ahead" was transmitted to "Sikh" "Zulu", and the motor launches.

Rough seas had mauled the launches, so that they arrived late. Unable to identify their landfall, they waited in vain for the Aldis lamp signal from the beach, because the responsible commando officer had lost the lamp in somewhat mysterious circumstances. He substituted a pocket torch, and thanks to this, one launch was able to land five men with a machine gun. This was the only reinforcement which reached the Mersa-Sciause party.

The North of Harbour party were even worse off, because owing to rough seas, the submarine "Taku" could not land the signalmen who were to mark the beach for them.

The "Sikh" and "Zulu" party of Marines, had at 03.48, embarked in their landing craft. These were clumsy wooden dumb lighters without engines, dubbed "boot boxes" by the Marines. The "boot boxes" had capacity for only half the landing force, so that the first party ashore would have to wait while the "boot boxes" went back for the other half. All the manned "boot boxes" were towed by a single launch.

At 04.30, "Sikh" and "Zulu", realising that the landing craft were overdue for collecting the second party of Marines, moved carefully inshore to look for them. Quite soon they found the towing launch drifting—it's engine had failed very soon after setting out. All the tow ropes had soon broken, due to the swell, and the landing craft were scattered and lost in the darkness. In fact, two landing craft were thrown on to a reef at Menga el Auda, two miles from the designated beach head, and many of the Marines crushed or drowned. The survivors had advanced on to the Harbour objective, but had been quickly overwhelmed.

The destroyers continued to close the coast, but at 05.15 a battery of shore searchlights instantly floodlit "Sikh", and salvos from shore guns quickly disabled her. "Zulu" passed a towing hawser, which had hardly taken the strain, when it was shot away. The attempt was renewed, watched by the crews and soldiers of some of the motor launches, also the helpless men in the drifting landing craft. There was no success with the second tow, and at 06.30 a signal from Alexandria ordered all craft out of Tobruk.

By now the L.R.D.G., having achieved its object, was breaking out; Col. Heselden, with the Mersa-Sciause party, had been killed, and the party was completely surrounded by a strong German force. Nothing was heard of the North of Harbour party. While the guns of stranded "Sikh" kept firing, and watched by the hapless men in the drifting landing craft, "Zulu" cleared the harbour exit, and by 07.08, was speeding home on the open sea.

The news sobered us all, and we at once wondered why "Coventry", near enough to the enemy coast and Tobruk, had not been sought out for attack. How fortunate that the Beaufighters flew steadily overhead.

The sunshine was brilliant now, and last night's choppy sea subsiding. Most of us though shocked by the disaster at Tobruk, overestimated our own security, and were looking forward to dinner. To improve contentment, came the pipe for collecting the grog issue, and cheerful individuals carrying their own, and "on watch mess mates" mugs, made for the distribution point on the upper deck. Under the strict eye of the Gunner, the solemn ceremony of grog issue proceeded, with now and then a friendly wink or smile on what was a recognised social occasion.

But the usual gaiety was absent, and there were conversations in low tones about the Captain's broadcast. Many doubted if "Zulu" would still be floating when we reached the rendezvous.

Meanwhile, defence stations gun's crews had been alerted, on a radar report that enemy aircraft were in the vicinity. The guns were following director, which had a distant snooper as target. A.B. Foster, noticing this, anticipated "Action Stations" and went to the mess deck for the lifebelt, which by standing orders he should have been wearing all the time at sea. Many of the ship's company were, however, unaware of the gunnery preparations.

On the bridge, the Fighter Direction Officer was intent on a Beaufighter that had just broken below cloud, and was signalling.

Even as he yelled "Enemy aircraft astern", fifteen JU87's were plummeting on "Coventry". The scream of rigging and the shriek of falling bombs, accompanied by the roar of engines, galvanised the sailors, who started for action stations, spurred on by the crackle of the Oerlikons. Quickly one Oerlikon was silenced, when Spike Sullivan, scalped by cannon fire from a Stuka, slumped to the deck.

Exploding bombs made the sea boil under the ship, as on many previous occasions. A searing flash and sickening jolt shocked us. Next came a vast out pouring of black smoke. Four times in quick succession the ship shuddered,—in a way never before felt by those who had the time to fall flat on the deck.

A.B. Foster got to his feet, groping his way through the smoke, from the galley flat to the upper deck. His action station was at one of the Oerlikons. As he went forward, the smoke began to clear, and he made out twisted and shattered wreckage. He guessed that there must be several men killed.

Once outside, he saw chaos. Twisted girders, broken electric cable, and bent steelplates, showed through the drifting clouds of steam and smoke. Here and there, fires were blazing, and somewhere, ignited small arms ammunition was exploding. One bomb had hit the fo'c'sle square in front of No. 1 gun. From the waterline, all that remained was twisted metal licked by roaring fire. There had been another eruption by the base of the tripod main mast, breaking two of the struts and tearing platforms and ladders. Finding a remaining iron ladder to the gun deck, he made towards it, and in the process noticed 'Sticks' Hancock, the seaman bugler, lying quite unconcerned on the deck. The man that had called us to action stations for our very first shooting in the 1939 war, would never sound another note. Foster found his Oerlikon undamaged and loaded it. L/S Eric Skelly, off duty, and walking cheerfully from astern to collect the grog ration, was galvanised into action by the screaming Stukas and the shriek of bombs. He noticed a line of small, evenly spaced water columns, rapidly extending towards him, and leapt through a bulkhead door for cover. The deck reared up beneath him, and colliding with a heavy object, he was flung helpless across the deck space, conscious only of an Oerlikon firing over the increasing roar of aircraft engines.

Once recovered, he was aware of the First Lieutenant calmly saying, "Away you go to action stations", L.S. Skelly hurried to the after director, and with the trainer, started the usual drill. In seconds, they realised that the apparatus was shaken out of alignment, and quite useless for lack of electric power. While they busied themselves with the procedure, laid down for such moments of catastrophe, the word was passed "Abandon Ship".

Leading Seaman Carter's action station was below decks. His duty was to maintain the electric power supply to the gunnery plotting room, where calculating machines converted enemy range, speed, and course, with correction factors to bearing, elevation, and fuse setting for the guns. Quite remarkably, he found that here the electric power supply was 100% sound. Proceeding forward to assist in damage control, he came on a sort of crater blasted through several decks. Sunlight filtered through the weaving smoke columns, and fell on a bare torso, burned by flash, and hurled against a stanchion. He could make out the sky, where a steel deck had once supported the radar cabin. Three minutes ago twenty men had been active in a variety of ways. Now there was only silence, and a cloud of steam.

"Coventry", the intelligence centre, and succour for the raiding ships in case of need, had been completely eliminated. The fighting ship of three minutes ago was now a drifting burning wreck.

The Stukas had attacked in pairs, diving so low, that one collided with a radar aerial, and went with it into the sea. Spike Sullivan's Oerlikon, which destroyed one Stuka, was the only retaliatory action from the ship, but the Beaufighters shot down five of the Stukas. The earliest bombs missed, but the cannon fire was lethal. Then four bombs hit along the centre line in quick succession, destroying the fo'c'sle as far as No. 1 gun, the lower steering platform, and associated main mast structures, the radar transmitter cabin, and the boiler room beneath it.

Captain Dendy flooded the foremost magazine. All fire pumps were useless, and the conflagration spread unchecked. The engine room was undamaged, and the ship could move slowly astern on one engine. The hull was evidently still intact, and "Coventry" stayed on an even keel. C.P.O. Foster's faith in the "Blucher" design had been justified.

But the ship was utterly defenceless, and almost incapable of movement. Communications were non-existent, fire was spreading, and sixty-three men had been killed. The Captain decided that he must abandon and sink his first command. A bitter draught for an officer steeped in tarpaulin tradition. Within minutes came the C-in-C's own order from Alexandria, that this must be done.

Fortunately for the survivors, there was no leakage of oil fuel. Descent from the damaged main mast and blazing bridge was a hazardous undertaking. But fire, and the complete failure of communications, made "Abandon ship" a ragged affair. The destroyer, "Beaufort", came bows on to the stern of "Coventry", where a large group was gathered on the quarter deck. These men scrambled aboard quickly, the last to do so being Captain Dendy, who was carrying the ship's papers and confidential books.

Simultaneously, a group of men on what remained of the fo'c'sle, were tending three comrades grievously wounded and laid on stretchers. Captain Peyton Jones R.M. appeared, and assisted the party to take to the sea. Already he had told survivors to throw overboard all life rafts and floats. Most of the ship's boats had been stove in by blast and steel splinters. The Captain of Marines organised search parties to comb every accessible corner of the ship, and bring out trapped and wounded men.

The men from the fo'c'sle were in the sea for half-an-hour, before a whaler from "Dulverton" picked them up. The rescue of survivors during an air attack was always a hazardous business, as the rescuing ships could not weaken preparedness for action, until there was evidence of a lull in the battle. In Crete this was frequently impossible until after dark.

There were, of course, a large number of men able, and prepared, to swim towards one of the accompanying destroyers, and Eric Skelly was among them. The nearest destroyer seemed well within his swimming powers, and it was high time to leave the burning hulk. By the deck rail he noticed several rows of boots and shoes, some kicked off, some carefully placed, by those that had gone before him.

Once in the sea he was astonished at the height of the waves, and daunted by the depth and long duration of the troughs. What had seemed an attractive refuge from burning "Coventry", now proved to be a formidable situation. The destroyer seemed much further away. Having swum steadily for several yards he realised that his overalls were a hindrance. The trousers had been tucked into his socks as an anti-flash precaution. Shedding the overalls, clad in nether garments but still armed with the "pussers dirk" on a lanyard round his neck, he pushed on.

At length he reached his objective, with enough strength remaining, to hold on to one of the scrambling nets that had been lowered over the ship's side. Within minutes he was strong enough to climb the net. His feet found the iron deck, and at once he realised that it was blistering hot. Quickly he hopped to a more comfortable position. Someone came forward to help him. Promptly he was taken to the Coxwain, who after noting name, rating, and official number, motioned a waiting sailor to take him below for a double tot of rum and dry clothing.

An hour had gone since "Coventry" had been blasted into impotence, and she was a sad spectacle, motionless on the sea, billowing clouds of black smoke. Many of her uninjured survivors, now safe aboard "Beaufort" or "Dulverton", gazed with varying degrees of regret at the deserted ship. Some had lost close friends, even the most fortunate would lose some treasured possessions. Among the injured, were some in whom the flame of life would soon be extinguished, some who would realise with horror, what their injuries would take from life.

For Captain Dendy it was a bitter occasion. Naval tradition was strong in praise of Captains who had fought their ships to the last gun; but here it was imperative to withdraw from a hopeless encounter, with the smallest possible loss in life and material. It was some comfort that the Commander in Chief had independently ordered the sinking of "Coventry". A torpedo would speedily accomplish the distasteful duty, and he prepared to frame the signal to the executioner. Then, he recalled that only two of his destroyers had been armed with torpedoes, the two that had been ordered to Alexandria for refuelling. Nothing for it, but to order the six remaining destroyers to sink Coventry by gunfire. Thereupon a tornado of shells rocked "Coventry", but as the minutes went by, she remained obstinately afloat, as had old "Blucher" on which she was modelled. Now came the irony of silencing the guns, and signalling constantly bombed "Zulu" to put down the ship that had started out to the rescue.

Time dragged as we circled the blazing and battered, but still upright, "Coventry". There was a shout as "Zulu" came in sight, with half a dozen Stukas screaming down at her. The bombs raised close packed waterspouts that hid her completely from view, but eventually she came steadily on, while the aircraft sped home to re-arm.

At 15.05, so near to us that we gave a cheer of welcome, she slowed to end the career of abandoned "Coventry". Two torpedoes sprang from "Zulu" and raced to the kill. Within seconds the "Old Lady" was settling gracefully in the blue water that mercifully engulfed her.

Launched too late for her 6" guns to shell the Kaiser's ships, she had nevertheless given a good account of herself in many a hectic gun battle with the deadly bomber of modern maritime warfare, the scourge of convoys and warships alike. It was ironic that after a successful defence with her own gunnery system for three years, she should fall victim on the first occasion she placed reliance on the new technique of fighter cover. So ended an epoch.

CHAPTER TWENTY TWO

THE LAST SIX MONTHS
THE RECOLLECTIONS OF CAPTAIN DENDY R.N.

I relieved Captain Carne some time in late March 1942.

About early April 1942, the new bow was complete and the refit ended. So after trials we left Bombay, to rejoin the Mediterranean Fleet at Alexandria. An uneventful trip, and we finally arrived in May to find the "Cleopatra", "Dido" and "Euryalus", under Admiral Vian there, as well as a flotilla of "Hunt" class destroyers. The submarines had moved to Beirut since their depot ship "Medway" had been sunk. Other than some exercises to get all back into form again, and me in particular, to learn the wiles of an A.A. Cruiser, the only incident I remember is, of one night, when we were berthed at the detached mole astern of one of the Vichy French ships, of an unsuccessful human torpedo attack, combined with an air raid. Here I recall a low flying aircraft coming in, calling out on R/T, "Friendly, Friendly", and then dropping his stick of bombs across the Frenchman without hitting it.

Then in early June, we had the big Malta convoy, when we were reinforced from the Eastern Fleet. Known as operation "Vigorous", the overall plan was, that at the same time as our convoy sailed from Alexandria, another one equally strong and reinforced, would leave Gibraltar. It must be remembered that the holding of Malta was the key to our North African campaign, as well as far wider issues.

All was comparatively peaceful the first day, but on the second and third, there seemed to be endless air attacks, so much so, that I remember ordering to cut down our rate of fire in "Barrage", as our ammunition was getting uncomfortably low. I think it was during these days that "Hermione" and some of the convoy were sunk.

This was my first experience of being on deck during air attacks, for in "Repulse"—my immediate previous ship to "Coventry",—I was in her lower conning tower with damage control to supervise. I think my personal reaction to this "christening" was the overall gunnery efficiency of the ship. With targets changing rapidly, somehow part, if not all, of our armament seemed to get on to them with hardly any directive from me.

Any idea of the ship being hit, or a personal wound, never entered my head, as far as I can remember. I suppose there was too much going on all round, including the handling of the ship itself to maintain our "A" arcs of fire, and/or to avoid collisions, during these attacks.

Amongst the convoy was the old battleship "Centurion", put there to offer a more tempting target than the merchant ships. This was highly successful, for she always seemed to be surrounded by near misses. For some reason unknown to me, she had been fitted with scuttling charges, and some of these detonated as a result of the near misses, so she started to draw very much more than her original draught,—a factor which influenced me, when I received this information from her Captain when we arrived back in Alexandria, to unprime our own charges which had been fitted at some earlier date.

One problem which was always a worry to me was when to revert from action to cruising stations, for I detested keeping everyone closed up unnecessarily. But whenever I wanted to revert, radar always seemed to come up with a contact which might be a "hostile group". I knew too well that one can keep everybody closed up all day with action-station meals, etc., but there is a physical limit beyond which we all just can't take, especially those for the night watches, after all-day action stations.

I think it was at the end of the third day, that Admiral Vian decided, or may have been ordered, to try no longer to force our way through, as we were all getting low in ammunition. Also some of the Italian Fleet were reported ahead of us, blocking our direct route to Malta, and so we were in a poor state to engage them.

So we turned back, and to our surprise, the expected M.T.B. attacks that night, never materialized. A few minor raids the next day, and so back to Alexandria, only to hear of the fall of Tobruk and the falling back of the Army. A very gloomy overall picture as we heard of the losses in the western convoy from Gibraltar, including the "Eagle", and also of the arrival of the tanker "Ohio" in Malta.

But the fact remained, the enemy front line was now only 50 miles away from us, and obviously there would be an all out effort by them to get to Cairo and the Canal. Alexandria was hardly a good base to operate from, and so most major units went further east to ports such as Haifa, Beirut, or Port Said. "Coventry" went to the Canal Area, and linked up every day with the local "Filter Room" to join in with the A.A. defence organisation.

Except for a short visit to Beirut, we stayed in the Canal area until September, working between Port Said, Tewfik, and Suez, often transitting the Canal twice a week. So it was obvious to me, that an enormous quantify of supplies and reinforcements were being poured in to Egypt, which must mean not only a stubborn defence, but also an impending counter attack, and advance back again along the Western Desert and Libya. I remember one of the Canal Pilots came on board us so often, he used to either go to my sea cabin, or a deck chair at the back of the bridge, so that the Navigation Officer and I could get on with it.

So to the last operation,—called "Agreement", which has been well detailed in Gordon Landsborough's book "Tobruk Commando". Although I didn't know it at the time, it seems to have been a model of complete insecurity for an operation, as any native boatman in Beirut, Port Said, or Alexandria, could have told units where they were going that night.

Anyway, if I can summarise what did happen, I hope I may be excused for any inaccuracies for something that happened nearly 30 years ago, to what was then a twenty five year old light cruiser, built in the days when ships were made by craftsmen and workers who knew their jobs, and not just bolted together like some prefabricated structures.

I believe the original plan for the operation started, when a unit of the L.R.D.G. wanted to raid the enemy transport lines around Tobruk with a force of two or three trucks, but like Topsy it "growed". The idea fitted in with the overall plan of the major impending offensive, but the initial idea of the raid became enlarged to such an extent, that it involved landings by R.M. Commandos on the north shore of Tobruk for one diversion; a landing on the south shore from motor launches and motor torpedo boats to create a second diversion for that on the north side; a sea bombardment further east to draw attention away from Tobruk and, of course, an air raid on Tobruk just to help everything.

So on Friday, the 13th September, we left Port Said with four "Hunt" destroyers, and rendezvoued with "Sikh" and "Zulu", who had the Commandos on board with another three or four "Hunts" all sailing from Beirut. I had an R.A.F. squadron leader as liaison officer on board, and shortly after rendezvous with "Sikh" and "Zulu", we had a long range radar contact of some unidentified aircraft. My R.A.F. Liaison Officer reckoned it was a P.R.U. aircraft he didn't know of. But I was not quite sure, so I held on to a N.N.W. course for some time, hoping to mislead it. Actually, it seemed to have been an enemy reconnaissance plane who reported our whole force, and in consequence Rhodes was put on an alert basis for a landing that night.

But if "Sikh" and "Zulu" were to get to the release point on time, where they would have to separate from us, I couldn't hold onto this course for long, so about midday I turned to the west. A quiet day—no contacts on our radar screen, except obvious ones over the coast at very long range.

At about 22.30 we got to release point, and "Sikh" and "Zulu" went off, whilst we and the "Hunts" reduced to 12 from 20 knots. If all went well, I expected to intercept "Sikh's" "success" signal that her landings were complete, by about midnight, but it was not until nearly 01.30 I received it, when I turned all our force—"Coventry" and the eight "Hunts",—back to the east, and increased to 20 knots, our full speed.

During the night, we heard of "Sikh" being sunk, and then the whole force withdrawing, followed by a signal from "Zulu" that she too had been attacked on withdrawing, but was able to maintain speed, although hit.

Eventually it seemed to me that "Zulu" was now withdrawing at about 28/30 knots, so I turned our force to the west once more with the idea of rendezvous with her at about 13.30. But as we had all been steaming at nearly full speed for 48 hours, I was uncertain of the fuel situation in the "Hunts", especially those who had left Beirut. So, on getting in the reports, it became clear that they had little or nothing in hand, for any diversions or extraneous measures for the return to Alexandria. So I sent the two worst off into Alexandria, to refuel and then to return to rendezvous with me.

At this time we had our fighter cover overhead but R/T with him was very poor. Nothing on our radar screen, and the fighter had nothing to report. Cloud base started to become rather low, so I brought the fighter down to just under cloud base, and still a blank screen and nil reports. "Zulu" seemed to be coming along all right and for the moment affairs were peaceful. Also the R/T with our fighter was much better now.

But about 11.40, a yell from our fighter cover, "look out—a hell of a mob coming at you".

The first attack of J.U. 87's who came out of the cloud got one hit on our bows and blew that off, starting a fire, followed by another direct hit somewhere near the engine room and boiler room. The next wave got us right under the bridge, knocking out the Radar and W/T Offices and all around them. By some miracle the compass platform was not damaged. I think there were about three hits around the bridge and foremost funnel area.

I ordered "A" magazine to be flooded to avoid further damage to our bows, and managed to get details of what else was damaged. I don't remember if there were any more attacks,—there may have been, but no more hits, only near misses.

So now the position was we had no bows, a fire near a magazine which might blow up at any moment: no W/T, or radar. Damage,—a fire in the engine room and a boiler room, and steering engine out of action. By going stern first with hand steering, and possibly being towed as well, we would probably get back unless attacked further.

But to get back to Alexandria, we had to pass within 80 miles of at least two enemy air fields. Even if we got in, the chances were that two or more of the "Hunts" would be damaged in the inevitable attacks, and we would incur more casualties ourselves. The result would be that the C-in-C would be landed with an immobile twenty five year old light cruiser with a very doubtful gun potential; no W/T or radar; having lost two or more "Hunts" in the process.

As I knew that there was obviously an impending major offensive, from my personal observation when we were in the Canal area, when every small ship of every kind would be needed. I decided to abandon ship and get the "Hunts" to torpedo and sink her.

They closed in and picked up our survivors, "Beaufort" coming alongside our port quarter. I, after throwing over board such cyphers, etc, that were in my cabin, and ensuring that, as far as I could see, everybody aboard was out, stepped out over her anchor. It was then I discovered that the only torpedo carrying "Hunts" were those I'd sent in to Alexandria to refuel.

They all tried firing 4" shell at her, but her old armour belt stood up to that. In any case they were getting low in ammunition, and couldn't afford heavy expenditure. Learning from the "Centurion's" experience in "Vigorous", I had had our scuttling charges unprimed, for I had seen no reason for "Coventry" to be put out of action by near misses setting them off. Further, it was too late, if not impossible, to get back on board again to reprime and set them.

So I signalled "Zulu" to torpedo and sink "Coventry" as she passed in about an hours time. About this time I think C.-in-C must have ordered the "Hunts" to return to Alexandria. Also he must have signalled me to sink and abandon "Coventry". I never saw this signal until after we got in about 20.30 when I landed at Ras-El-Tin.

I've little recollection of our passage back. I know I saw "Beauforts" Medical Officer and Sick Bay Staff looking after our casualties, as I made my way up to the bridge, to signal over to the Senior Officer of the "Hunts". I expect "Beauforts" Captain got me to go down to their Wardroom or his cabin. Probably he realised that I was a bit "Bomb Happy" for the hits under the bridge must have had some effect on personnel up there, even if they weren't wounded. So I suspect I "passed out" for in addition I'd had no sleep for about 40 hours.

There Admiral Creswell met me and ordered me to bed, as the C-in-C had 'phoned that I was not to come and see him that night, but next morning. So the mental agony of having to sink and leave "Coventry" was then relieved by seeing the C-in-C's signal to me, timed about 12.30, for the first time, assisted by "Zulu's" signal that she had sunk "Coventry", so I hadn't left a burning floating wreck at sea.

About the time I was turning in, we heard of "Zulu's" fate, but little or no news of the M.L. and M.T.B. force—so rounding off a melancholy day. "Agreement", rashly conceived in a desperate hour had exacted it's last ounce of flesh.

APPENDIX

PETTY OFFICER A. E. SEPHTON
A SHORT BIOGRAPHY

Born at Warrington, on April 11th, Alfred Edward Sephton was the first son of ex Sergeant Major Sephton, Royal Field Artillery. His mother's proudest boast was, that her grandfather had been a ship's Captain. Next year the family moved to Wolverhampton, where another boy and girl were born.

The children duly attended Dudley Road School, and went to the nearby church. The youngsters were supervised by Eva, their eldest sister, who recalls Alfred's abiding interest in the canal boats, and the skiffs on the pond at West Park. He was never unruly, but inclined to stray. One evening, his scared parents spent several hours in search, before finding him sleeping peacefully on the Church steps. Thereafter, his clothing carried name and address tags. His first suit was the "sailor suit" then fashionable for little boys, and gave him great pleasure.

As a schoolboy he sang in the church choir, and excelled at boxing and swimming, leaving school when he was fifteen. Then he tried two or three of the hum drum jobs open to Wolverhampton school leavers, including hotel work. But none of them satisfied him, and his sister Eva sympathised with his longing for a wider horizon.

So, on his sixteenth birthday, she gave moral and vocal support when he went to his parents to ask if he could join the Royal Navy. His father, as a boy, had gone to sea but left his ship after witnessing the brutal treatment of one of his companions; subsequently to enlist at Woolwich in Queen Victoria's Army. Parental consent was slow in coming.

When it came, Alfred declared that he would take care to be a credit to his parents, and would be wearing a collar and tie before his Navy service ended.

His Royal Navy service began in the training ship "Ganges", and when rated "Ordinary Seaman", he joined H.M.S. "Barham". Specialising in gunnery control, he also volunteered for training as a diver. During the years of peace, the most exciting event occurred whilst he was serving in H.M.S. "Ajax". An earthquake had devastated villages in the Gulf of Ierissos, and "Ajax" ships company landed to organise feeding and shelter of the children, and construction of temporary homes for the villagers.

During the latter years of peace, the voice of Hitler woke Westminster. The reserve Fleet was hastily refurbished, and six of the old ships re-armed solely with anti-aircraft guns; with the intention that they should protect convoys from enemy aircraft.

Acting Petty-Officer Sephton, now Director Gunlayer, was drafted to H.M.S. "Coventry" in 1939, then an experimental ship for anti-aircraft weapons. In August of that year, all except the key gunnery personnel of the ship were replaced by reservists. With his companion professional sailors, "John" Sephton with considerable tolerance and understanding helped to train gunners for the war that would begin early next month. In that testing year, he was rated Petty Officer, and made good his promise to be wearing a collar and tie before his naval service ended.

Near Crete, on May 18th, 1941, he was directing four of "Coventry's" guns in a fight against a squadron of Stukas sent to sink the Hospital Ship "Aba". Early in this concentrated attack, he was severely wounded by an air-cannon bullet.

At Buckingham Palace, six months later, King George VI presented the V.C. posthumously awarded to P.O. Sephton, to his parents.

Mr. Sephton still carried himself like a Warrant Officer, though the light in his eyes was gone; and his wife bore her grief in silence. The Stuka's bullet had killed more than one. Soon after the destruction of her home in an air raid, Mrs. Sephton was disabled by a stroke. Her husband, in steadily declining health, died three years later. The price of Admiralty had been collected by instalments.